James. E. McKen.
2006

THE RIFLES
ARE THERE

THE RIFLES
ARE THERE

The Story of the 1st and 2nd Battalions
The Royal Ulster Rifles
1939–1945

by

DAVID R. ORR

and

DAVID TRUESDALE

Pen & Sword
MILITARY

First published in Great Britain in 2005 by
Pen & Sword Military
an imprint of
Pen & Sword Books Ltd
47 Church Street
Barnsley
South Yorkshire
S70 2AS

ISBN 1 84415 3495

A CIP catalogue record for this book is
available from the British Library.

Typeset in Sabon by Phoenix Typesetting, Auldgirth, Dumfriesshire
Printed and bound in England by
CPI UK

Pen & Sword Books Ltd incorporates the imprints of Pen & Sword Aviation,
Pen & Sword Maritime, Pen & Sword Military, Wharncliffe Local History, Pen
and Sword Select, Pen and Sword Military Classics and Leo Cooper.

For a complete list of Pen & Sword titles please contact
PEN & SWORD BOOKS LIMITED
47 Church Street, Barnsley, South Yorkshire, S70 2AS, England
E-mail: enquiries@pen-and-sword.co.uk
Website: www.pen-and-sword.co.uk

CONTENTS

Foreword   vi

Preface   viii

Acknowledgements   x

Introduction   1

PART ONE

2nd Battalion, The Royal Ulster Rifles   9

PART TWO

1st (Airborne) Battalion, The Royal Ulster Rifles   111

Roll of Honour   181

Glossary   258

Bibliography   264

Index   267

Foreword

by Major General Corran Purdon CBE, MC, CPM

The 1st and 2nd Battalions of the Royal Ulster Rifles landed in Normandy on D-Day – the 1st in the 6th Airborne Division, by glider at Ranville, and the 2nd in the 3rd Division, by landing craft across the beach slightly west of Ouistreham. No other regiment in the British Army had both its regular battalions in Normandy on D-Day. Field Marshal Montgomery, himself an Ulsterman, was particularly fond of the Rifles. The 2nd Battalion had served under his command in the 8th Division in Palestine from 1937 to 1939, when they had been awarded five MCs, four MMs and eighty-seven Mentions in Despatches. One of these MCs was awarded to Major Charles Sweeny, who became his ADC, and later, in North-West Europe, one of his liaison officers.

When Major General Montgomery, as he then was, took command of the 3rd Division, he specially asked for our 2nd Battalion. At the time of Dunkirk, when the Germans were attacking in great strength and Louvain was under great pressure, Monty is reported to have said, 'It's all right, the Rifles are there', hence the title of this book. David Truesdale and David Orr are to be congratulated on having 'caught the flavour' of this unique Regiment which captivated all who served in it.

Recruited from all over Ireland, it also welcomed English, Scots, Welsh and Canadians into its wartime ranks, all of whom, in addition to contributing their splendid national qualities, tended, if not to become more Irish than the Irish, at least to grow utterly devoted to the Regiment, and to their fellow Riflemen of all ranks. The Rifles are such a family Regiment, and the Riflemen are an honour and a joy to serve with. Tough, hardy and loyal, brave and uncomplaining, keen and confident, they have a terrific and very special sense of humour. The authors tell an easily read, lively story of the peerless men who made my Regiment – Riflemen, NCOs, officers, brothers-in-arms, filled with pride and affection for each other as they fought their war from Normandy to the Baltic, in our splendid 1st and 2nd Battalions. When we talk of 'our war', we are proud to say 'The Rifles were there' and we thank David Truesdale and David Orr for bringing these achievements to light and to life in such an easy and enjoyable read. Quis Separabit.

Preface

In this the year in which the nation has commemorated the 60th anniversary of the end of the War in Europe and the Far East, attention has rightly focused on those who lived through it all, and in particular the men and women who served in all branches of the Armed Forces. In close parallel with the broad examinations of the events of the Second World War, there have been intense efforts to listen, witness and record the memories of those who took part in the momentous events of those turbulent years. This ranges from small projects in towns and village communities, involving individuals and local museums, to the huge People's War project by BBC local radio. The work done throughout the UK recognizes not only the significance of such memories as history, but also the need to preserve them before they are lost in the passage of time.

It is therefore fitting that two historians with a passionate interest in the military history of Ireland have compiled this history of the Royal Ulster Rifles. It does not cover the Regiment as a whole, but concentrates on the two principal units which served during the War, the 1st and 2nd Regular Battalions. David Orr and David Truesdale have compiled a fascinating account which successfully combines the official record of the two battalions with the characters and stories of those who served in them. As a result it has provided a broader and more personal aspect to this history of the Regiment, which chronicles the outstanding service of both battalions during the War, at the same time reminding us all that regiments and their battalions are not nondescript, faceless organizations, but bodies of soldiers bound by and fiercely proud of serving under a particular cap badge. In addition, the history describes the various theatres of war that the Regiment served in and shows how the battalions coped with different situations and circumstances. Moreover, the 1st Battalion, in its air-landing role in 6th Airborne Division, clearly demonstrated the ability of a county infantry regiment to change and adapt to whatever new task the Army might require of it.

Stuart Eastwood
Curator
Border Regiment & King's Own Royal Border Regiment Museum,
Carlisle Castle

Acknowledgements

Alan Brown, Curator Airborne Forces Museum, Aldershot

Major J.M. Campbell, D Company, 2nd Battalion, who showed us hospitality and kindness on a warm summer afternoon in June 2003

Colonel Robin Charley, a former Rifleman and a font of knowledge on the Regiment

Paul Clark, UTV

Richard Doherty, for assistance with research in the National Archive, Kew

Stuart Eastwood, Curator, Border Regiment and King's Own Royal Border Regiment Museum, Carlisle

Captain John England, D Company, 1st (A) Battalion

Lieutenant Colonel Rex Fendick

Cllr. Ronnie Ferguson, who made this book possible. Ronnie and David Truesdale have several things in common, including an interest in military history, and both being ex-Regular Army and ex-lance corporals in the Ulster Defence Force. Their paths parted for a time when David Truesdale joined the RUC and Ronnie became one of the 'political parasites', but that does not make him a bad person. The authors and the Museum of the Royal Ulster Rifles owe Ronnie a great deal.

Bob Gerritsen, of Holland

Margaret Graham, of Newtownards, Co. Down

Bob Hilton, ex 2 Para

Colonel Ian Hogg, Curator, King's Own Scottish Borderers Museum

Captain Jaki Knox, RUR Museum, Belfast

Lieutenant Alan Malcolm, D Company, 1st (A) Battalion

Ian Martin, King's Own Scottish Borderers Museum

John McCabe, Co. Antrim

Kenneth McClurgan

Gary McCrea, son of Rifleman Charles McCrea, 1st (A) Battalion

Roy McCullough for his help with the maps

Vera McCutcheon, widow of CSM William McCutcheon, 1st (A) Battalion

Molly Pollock McFarland

Craig McGuicken, Somme Heritage Centre, Newtownards, Co. Down

Dougie McGurk, for assistance with the photographs

Amanda Moreno, Curator, Royal Irish Fusiliers Museum, County Armagh

Terence Nelson, RUR Museum, Belfast

Colonel Terence Otway, 9th Parachute Battalion

Mr Harry Pegg, 1st (A) Battalion

Major Cyril Rand, C Company 2nd Battalion

Jim Ryan, son of Sergeant John Ryan, County Armagh

Carl Rymen, of Belgium

Rifleman Bobby Smyth, 2nd Battalion

Major Roy Walker, RUR Museum, Belfast

Les Waring, of Uruguay

Eugene Wijnhoud, of Holland

Molly Wilson, for her knowledge of the men of the 1st (A) Battalion

Chris Wise, for his valuable time working on our behalf in the National Archive, Kew

George Wylie

Tom Wylie, whose good humour and encouragement has, as always, kept us going

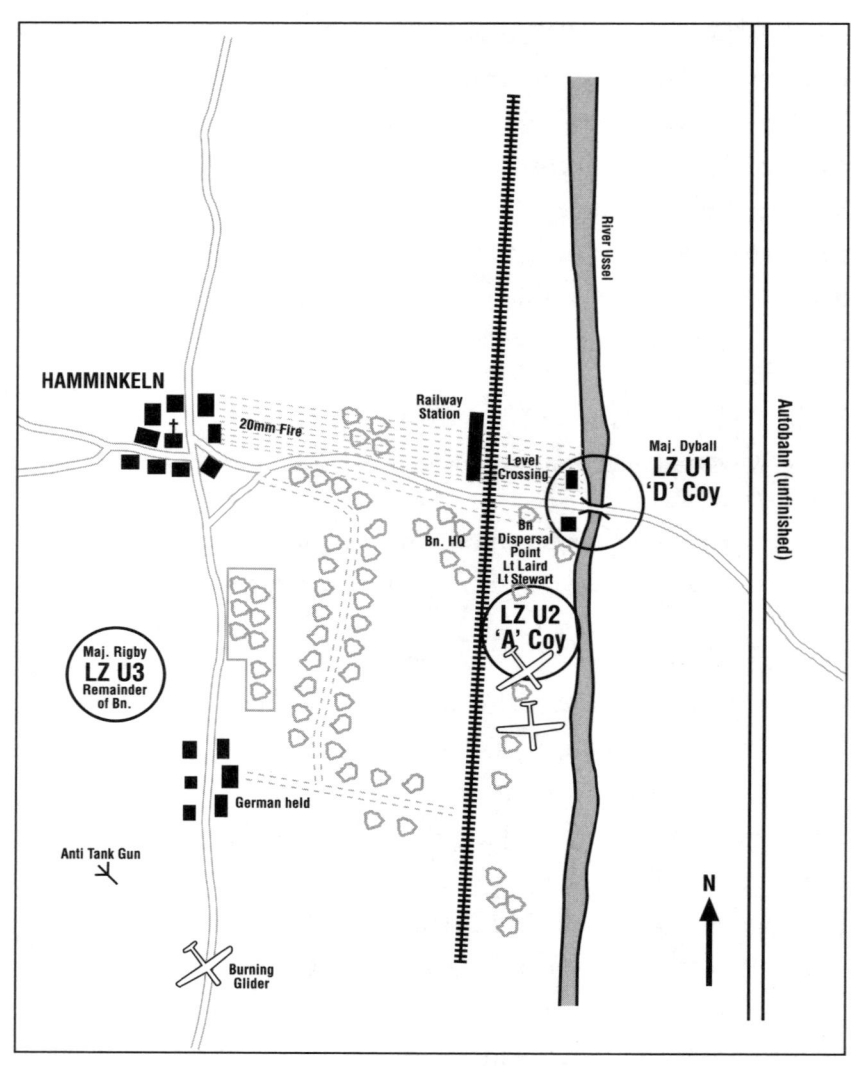

Operation Varsity, 24 March 1945

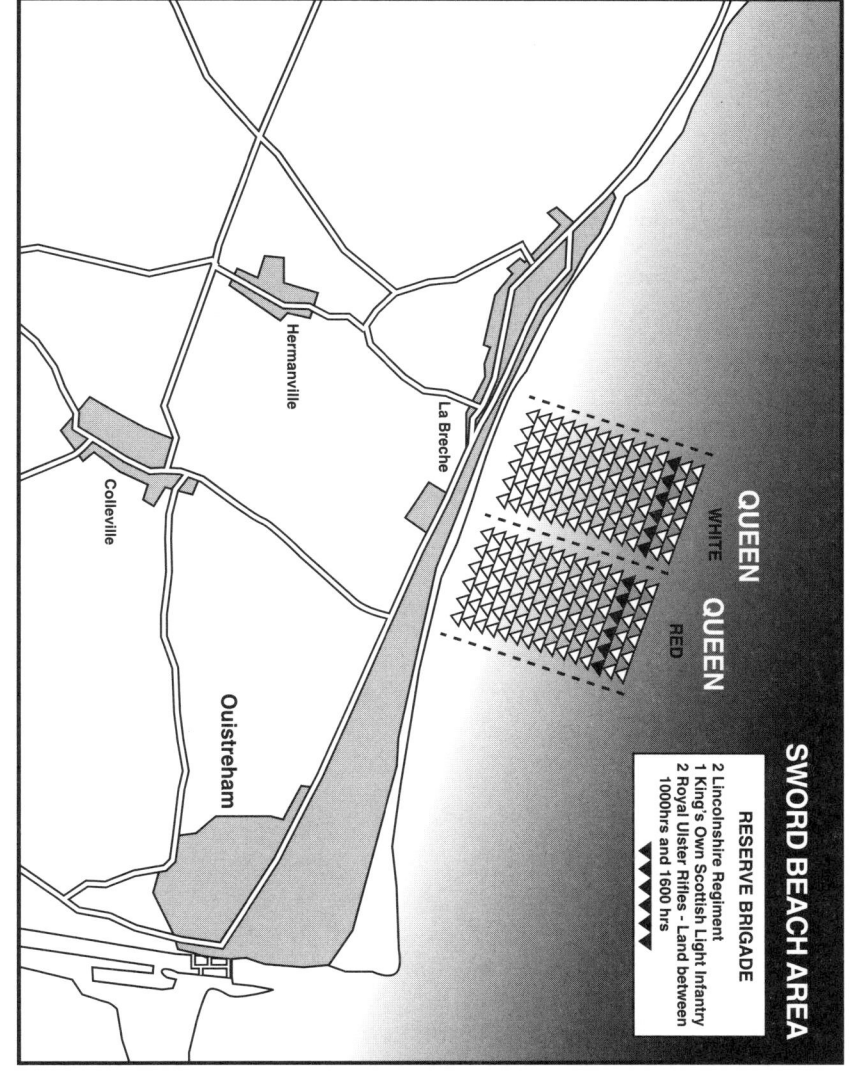

D-Day, 6 June 1944

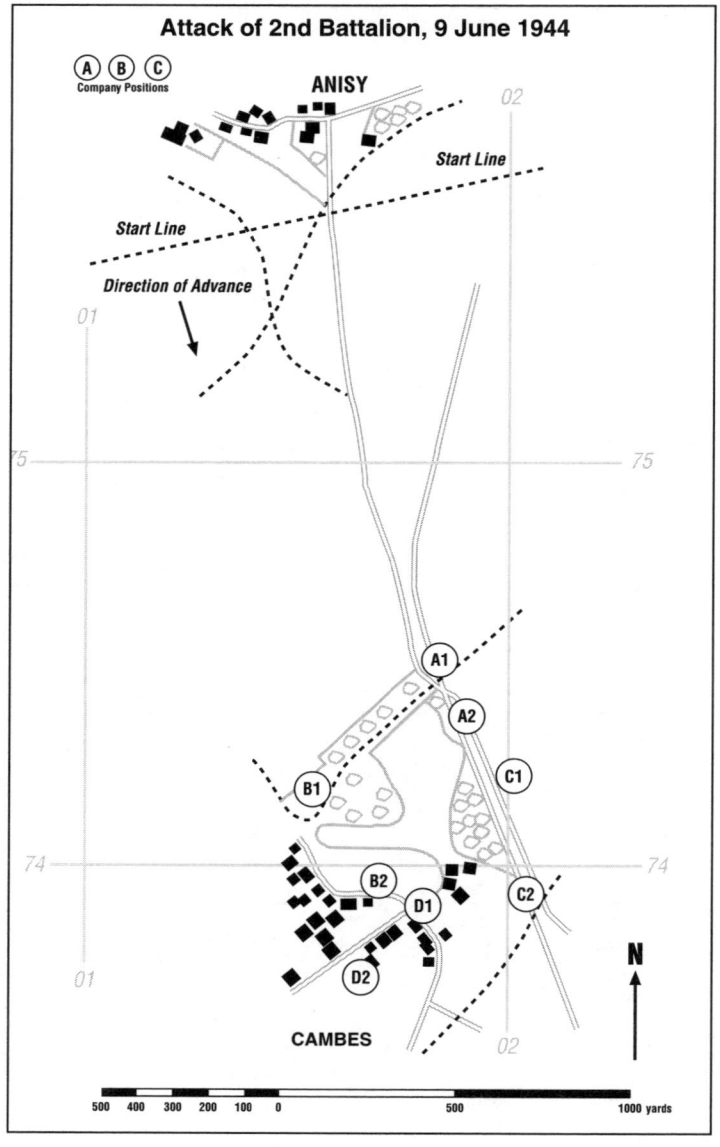

Attack of 2nd Battalion, 9 June 1944

(A) (B) (C) Company Positions

ANISY

02

Start Line

Start Line

Direction of Advance

01

75   75

A1

A2

C1

B1

74   74

B2

D1   C2

01

D2

CAMBES   02

N

500 400 300 200 100 0   500   1000 yards

(A1) = first objective of A Company
(B1) = first objective of B Company
(C1) = first objective of C Company
(D1) = first objective of D Company

Introduction

In the period before the invasion of Iraq by American and British forces in 2003, much was made of the logistical effort required to put those forces in place and to sustain them in battle. Coalition triumph was attributed as much to those supporting the front-line troops as to the front-line troops themselves. Much the same has been said of the first Gulf War in 1991, for modern logistics had played a vital part in the success of that operation.

Many of those making those comments were probably blissfully unaware that, almost fifty years before the first Gulf War and almost sixty years before the second, those efforts had been dwarfed by an invasion that did not have the assistance of computers, microwave communications and satellite reconnaissance. Furthermore, it was made against a defended coastline in the face of what was regarded as the most professional army in the world and one well versed in fighting a defensive battle. That operation had been based on paper and the brainpower of hundreds of officers and men of the British and American armies and remains to this day the greatest military operation in history. Indeed it is unlikely ever to be surpassed. That operation was the invasion of France on 6 June 1944, the first step in the liberation of occupied Western Europe from Nazi tyranny. Officially it was known as Operation Overlord, but it is remembered popularly as D-Day.

For any regiment that took part in the invasion of France on D-Day, the date became an important one in regimental history and tradition. This was especially true for the Royal Ulster Rifles who can lay claim to being the only British regiment to be represented on D-Day by its two regular battalions – both the 1st and 2nd landed on Norman soil on 6 June. Not only that but the regiment was represented in other elements of the invasion, many riflemen served in the 9th Parachute Battalion, responsible for the destruction of the Merville Battery, and commanded by Lieutenant Colonel Terence Otway, a Rifles officer.

The soldiers who were to do the fighting on the ground arrived in Normandy either from the sea or from the air. Airborne divisions from both British and American formations were dropped on both flanks of the invasion area to protect against German counterattacks and to secure certain river and canal crossings. These troops arrived either by parachute or flimsy wooden glider. The Royal Ulster Rifles arrived in Normandy from both the sea and the air. The 2nd Battalion came ashore on Sword Beach brought from ship to sand in landing craft as part of the 3rd British Division. The 1st Battalion came by glider and arrived in the early evening of D-Day, landing on the left flank of the 3rd Division as part of the 6th Airborne Division.

Both battalions had relatively unscathed arrivals. First to land in France were the men of the 2nd Battalion who came ashore in the late morning and afternoon of D-Day. As one of the three battalions of 9 Brigade, the last element of 3rd Division to land, the horrors of the initial assault across the beaches were spared them. That evening as they awaited the call to action they could see the aerial armada that was carrying the 6th Airlanding Brigade fly over towards the landing zones. One Rifleman is reported to have quipped: 'I suppose that's what the ruddy 1st Battalion call a ruddy route march.' His language may have been a little more colourful.

Although they had expected to suffer casualties from enemy antiaircraft fire over the beaches and in the glider landings, the 1st Battalion lost only one man, a casualty from German mortar fire shortly after landing. This was quite a relief; one officer described the gliders as being so lightly constructed that 'you could read the cricket scores' on the recycled newspaper from which they were alleged to have been constructed.

The airborne troops had the task of ensuring that 3rd Division was not attacked from the flank as it came ashore as well as eliminating German shore batteries that might take a dreadful toll of the landing craft. They were successful in this task and ensured that the men of the Division were not subjected to heavy shelling as they made their landing. When the 1st Battalion arrived they were assigned the task of capturing enemy strong points that would enable the airborne bridgehead to be further consolidated and expanded. By their very nature airborne forces are not designed to carry out lengthy operations against a well dug-in enemy with the advantage of artillery and armoured support, but the Rifles, with their comrades, were destined for just such a fight. Not until the battle for Normandy was over, in late August 1944, were they withdrawn from active operations and returned to the United Kingdom to rest, reform and prepare for future operations. They would return to Europe in December 1944 to play their part in what became known as the Battle of the Bulge, where they endured one of the coldest winters in memory. In March 1945 they took part in Operation Varsity and from there continued on fighting through Germany until VE-day.

On Sword Beach, the British 3rd Division landed on a much narrower front than on the other British/Canadian beaches. Only one brigade made the initial assault and the intention was that elements of the Division would pass through the initial units to race for the city of Caen which, with Bayeux, was to be taken by British Second Army on D-Day itself. The 50th (Northumbrian) Division captured Bayeux on 7 June, while Caen defied the Allies for a month before it finally fell. During that period a number of attempts were made to break through to and capture the city. These did not achieve their objective and General Montgomery excused his strategic failure by claiming that his plan was to draw the bulk of the German armour on to the Allied left flank, the British and Canadian forces. This would allow the Americans to break out to the west and then begin a swing towards the River Seine. During that month, 2nd Battalion Royal Ulster Rifles were involved in heavy fighting and suffered many losses, as well as gaining many decorations. When Caen finally fell, the Rifles had the distinction of being the first British battalion to enter the city, by then a mass of churned rubble. They would continue to fight from Normandy to the Baltic.

In 1940, during the retreat from Belgium towards the beaches at Dunkirk, when asked if a certain part of his defence line could be held, Montgomery replied reassuringly, 'It's all right, the Rifles are there.'

This then is the story of these two battalions of riflemen, told mostly from the men themselves, with further information from war diaries and personal journals. It is not concerned so much with the grand strategy of generals, but with the day-to-day events that made up the rifleman's life during the Second World War.

Form, form, Riflemen, form!

Colonel William Fitch raised the 83rd Regiment of Foot in Dublin in 1793, the third regiment to bear this number. They first saw action in the West Indies during the Maroon War of 1795, while part of the Regiment was engaged at St Domingo. The Regiment remained as garrison troops for the following seven years. During this time they, in common with all other regiments in such service, lost more men to diseases such as yellow fever than to enemy action. The Regiment returned to Ireland after the peace of Amiens and here raised a second battalion to meet the expansion of the army as a result of the Napoleonic Wars. In 1805 the 1st Battalion landed at Cape Town in South Africa and quickly subdued the small Dutch garrison. The Battalion remained in South Africa until 1818.

In 1809, the 2nd Battalion became part of Wellington's Peninsula Expeditionary Army in Portugal. For the following five years they marched and countermarched the length and breadth of Spain and Portugal, until finally crossing into France. In that time they gained twelve battle honours. Of these two deserve particular mention. In the action at Talavera fought on 28 July 1809, the Battalion suffered over 50 per cent casualties including their commanding officer, Colonel Alexander Gordon. Wounded early on by a French musket ball, the Colonel was being carried from the field on a blanket by four of his men when the party was hit by a howitzer shell and blown to pieces.

Such were the officer casualties in the Battalion that Sergeant Major Joseph Swinburne was granted an Ensigncy for his distinguished service and was appointed Adjutant. Joseph Swinburne was one of the few men in Wellington's army to rise from the rank of Private to Brevet Lieutenant Colonel, receiving the Peninsula War medal with ten clasps and serving for forty-four years as an officer before retiring in 1853 with a Major's full pay.

At Badajoz on 25 March 1812, Wellington ordered an assault against Fort Picurina, part of the defences of the town. A 'forlorn hope' of 500 men included 2 officers and 50 men from the Battalion. A hero of the assault was Sergeant Thomas Hazlehurst, responsible for saving the life of Captain Powys who fell wounded in the breech and would have been bayoneted to death but for the actions of the determined Sergeant.

The 86th Regiment of Foot was raised in Shropshire by General Cornelius Cuyler and went by the name 'Cuyler's Shropshire Volunteers'. Recruiting initially proved difficult, with more men wanting to work on the land than take the King's shilling. The Regiment therefore moved to Ireland and was allotted the province of Leinster as a new recruiting area, the men becoming known as the 'Irish Giants'.

The 86th had their first taste of action while serving as marines and were engaged in several actions against the French. A detachment of six companies accompanied the expedition to Egypt in June 1801 and carried out an epic march of some 80 miles from Suez to Cairo, the whole time under a blazing sun. During this time there were no provisions and the column's water supply had become polluted with maggots. The men were dressed in the heavy scarlet coats of the time, but despite this only seventeen stragglers were reported, of whom eight died.

This campaign resulted in the end of Napoleon's dream of an Egyptian empire and by royal decree the emblem of the Sphinx, inscribed 'Egypt', was added to the regimental crest.

During the Indian Mutiny both the 83rd and 86th Regiments played their part and were involved in many of the actions, perhaps the most famous being the assault on Jhansi on 3 April 1858. The strength of the garrison of the city at the time of the assault was unknown, but was estimated at no less than 13,000 men, supported by some forty pieces of artillery crewed by well-trained gunners. The assault was both fierce and bloody but the storming party surmounted the walls despite a terrible fire from enemy musketry and cannon. There was bitter hand-to-hand fighting and many casualties were sustained, but eventually resistance was crushed and victory went to the British.

Three Victoria Crosses were awarded to the 86th. These were Lieutenant H.E. Jerome, and Privates Byrne and Pearson. Jerome had been born 'in the regiment' and would later be promoted to Brevet Major; his brother also served with the 86th and was later its commanding officer. James Byrne came from County Wicklow, survived to old age and died in Dublin in 1872. James Pearson, from Queen's County (Leix), died in India in 1900.

In 1881 the 83rd and 86th Regiments amalgamated to form the Royal Irish Rifles, 1st and 2nd Battalions respectively. The Royal North Downshire Militia formed the 3rd Battalion, the Antrim Militia the 4th, the Royal South Down Light Infantry the 5th and the Louth Rifles Militia the 6th.

The 2nd Battalion was mobilized for duty in the South African War on 9 October 1899. Of the 704 men called to the colours only nine failed to appear. As none of these men were ever heard of again, evidence would point to the fact that they had died prior to the call-up. The Battalion left Victoria Barracks, Belfast on 25 October and travelled south by train to Queenstown. From here they embarked on the SS *Britannic* for South Africa, arriving in Cape Town on 13 November. Throughout the War the Battalion served at Cape Colony, Orange Free State, Belfast (SA), Ladysmith, Paardeberg, the Transvaal and Tugela Heights. They were also present at Stormberg, the anniversary of which is commemorated to this day at the City Hall in Belfast, Northern Ireland.

No Victoria Crosses were earned in the conflict, but three DSOs and ten DCMs reflected the service and valour of both officers and men.

In a brief introduction such as this there is little space to record the heroism and devotion displayed by the Rifles in the First World War. The 2nd Battalion formed part of the Expeditionary Force that fought at Mons during the Retreat, and subsequent battles of the Marne and the Aisne, prior to moving north into Flanders. In the ensuing trench warfare the 1st and 2nd Battalions served throughout the War, losing many times their number in casualties. The 6th Battalion served with 10th (Irish) Division at Gallipoli, in Macedonia and Palestine. A further fifteen battalions of the Rifles were formed, all but one of which served on the Western Front, mostly with 36th (Ulster) Division.

In 1921 came another change of title when, with the partition of Ireland, they changed to the Royal Ulster Rifles. (Actually as a result of a War Office decision to mark the province of Ulster with a regiment, Leinster, Connaught and Munster already having regiments.)

With partition the British Army lost the services of the Royal Irish Regiment, Connaught Rangers, the Leinster Regiment, the Munster Regiment, Royal Dublin Fusiliers and the South Irish Horse.

In 1937, the London Irish Rifles joined the Regiment as a Territorial Army battalion. The LIR had been formed in 1859 as a 'Corps of Irish Gentlemen at Arms', subsequently becoming a Volunteer Corps. They had served in the South African War and in the First World War as part of the London Regiment; they would see further service in the Second World War in the Middle East, Sicily and Italy.

At the beginning of 1939, both Battalions of the Royal Ulster Rifles were serving abroad. The 2nd Battalion was in Palestine and by the time it left to return to the United Kingdom a total of 5 MCs, 4 MMs and 87 Mentions in Despatches had been awarded.

PART ONE

2nd Battalion
The Royal Ulster Rifles

France, September 1939 to June 1940

The 2nd Battalion Royal Ulster Rifles received its orders to mobilize on 1 September 1939. Three days later a party of 208 reservists under the command of Lieutenant E.D.D. Wilson had arrived from the depot at Gough Barracks in County Armagh to bring the Rifles up to war strength. For the remainder of the month 'old' and 'new' soldiers trained together to form a battalion fit enough to take the field.

The Rifles on parade numbered 23 officers, 20 Warrant Officers and 674 other ranks. Like their predecessors of 1914–18, they wore khaki and carried the Lee Enfield .303 rifle as standard issue; the equipment had changed since the First World War, as had the design of the uniform. The Battalion was organized into a headquarters and five rifle companies, A, B, C, D and a Support Company. These were in turn organized into three platoons, each platoon having a headquarters and three sections commanded by either a corporal or lance corporal, with ten men armed with nine rifles and a Bren gun. Within the platoon headquarters of an officer and six men were an anti-tank rifle and a 2-inch mortar. An issue of the Boyes anti-tank rifle was made prior to embarkation for France, but few men had the opportunity to fire it before crossing the Channel. As the Riflemen assembled they began to form a cohesive unit from the mixture of 'old soldiers' from Palestine, many of whom were not so old, and the new recruits, recently enlisted.

Although this was the Royal Ulster Rifles the men who filled the ranks from 1939 to 1945 came from many places within the United Kingdom – there were 'loyal' Ulstermen, 'neutrals' from Eire, cockneys from the East End of London and men from the Home Counties. Both Protestants and Catholics were present in large numbers, plus enough men of the Jewish faith, to warrant a church parade on a Saturday. From the old sweats of Palestine to the new recruits, all trained together for the coming conflict.

Among the officers was Lieutenant Corran Purdon. Deemed too young to accompany the battalion to France, he applied for the Commandos and took part in the raid on St Nazaire on 28 March 1942, leading a demolition party with great success despite being wounded. Subsequently taken prisoner, he was awarded the Military Cross for his actions during the raid.

Charlie Alexander who came from County Antrim was reading medicine at Queen's University, Belfast but he interrupted his studies to take a commission in 1940. 'Billy' Baudains, who had enlisted at the age of thirteen years as a band boy, had previously served in India and Palestine and was a first-class rifle shot. As a Sergeant he would be awarded the Military Medal for his actions at Louvain in 1940. He was later commissioned in the field in 1943 and would serve in Normandy as a Captain. Eric Boyd from County Tyrone had been educated at RBAI and was well known in amateur music circles in Belfast prior to his enlisting.

Not all riflemen would serve with the Regiment. John Ryan had been born in Dublin in 1909. On leaving school he went to Canada to seek his fortune only to find himself in the middle of a depression. One winter's day while standing in a soup kitchen queue he, along with several other men, were approached by some people who were handing out blankets and clothing to help keep out the bitter cold. A young girl draped an ex-army greatcoat around John Ryan's shoulders and wished him good luck. A few days later he boarded a ship and worked his passage to Belfast. On arriving in the city in September 1931, he made his way to the recruiting office at Clifton Street and asked to join the Regiment indicated by the buttons on his greatcoat. So John Ryan found himself in Palestine with the 2nd Battalion Royal Ulster Rifles. He was discharged to the Reserve on 18 September 1938 on completion of seven years service with the Colours, but John was recalled to the Colours on 14 December 1940 and was posted to the Maritime Artillery Regiment. He served on board various ships seeing action in the Atlantic, Mediterranean, Indian and Pacific Oceans. He eventually left the Army on 29 May 1950, one of the few riflemen to have earned the Pacific Star.

On 3 October 1939, the Rifles went to war under the command of an officer who had witnessed the horrors of 1914–18. Lieutenant Colonel Gerald Whitfeld had graduated from Sandhurst in April 1915 and was appointed as a Second Lieutenant in the 1st Battalion Royal Irish Rifles. For the following two years he experienced almost continuous severe fighting on the Western Front. During his time in the trenches he was wounded, awarded the Military Cross and received a Mention in Despatches, later being attached to the Royal Flying Corps as an observer.

Between the wars he saw the name of the regiment change and returned to Sandhurst as a member of Staff, he saw service in India before being posted to the regimental depot in Armagh. Promoted to Lieutenant Colonel in 1938, he led the 2nd Battalion to the Holy Land. Now he was returning to France, commanding a battalion that contained some men who were the sons of those he had served with over twenty years before.

The Rifles boarded their troop train at the market town of Sherborne in Dorset and travelled the 60 odd miles to Southampton. After a brisk march from the railway station to the harbour 717 officers and men crammed aboard the *Mona's Queen*, a small, elderly Isle of Man packet boat. It quickly became evident that the 'ship' was unsuitable for the job in hand, there was little room to stand much less sit down and any chance of a hot meal was totally out of the question. Nevertheless, the crossing to Cherbourg went ahead, and after an uneventful voyage the Rifles disembarked, cold, wet and hungry. From the seafront another march brought them to another railway station and as darkness fell the Rifles boarded their second train of the day. Shortly afterwards they left the port for the town of Silly-le-Guillaume, a journey that lasted throughout the night. From here it was again a matter of boots on pavé until they reached their final destination at Parennes where billets were found for the men which were described as comfortable, but somewhat scattered for a unit supposed to be on active service.

The Rifles' stay here was short lived and soon they were on the move again. Another train journey and they found themselves at Templemars, arriving on 12 October; two days later and it was on

11

to Lezennes, a suburb of Lille. On 4 November the Rifles experienced their first air-raid warning as the sirens wailed out over the town.

Armistice Day dawned dank and misty and the men were informed that all leave had been cancelled – it was to be a Christmas away from home.

During this time the Rifles received a number of high-ranking visitors, but in December a very special one arrived – 6 December was the birthday of His Majesty King George VI and he elected to spend some of it with the officers and men of the Royal Ulster Rifles. While carrying out his inspection the King again met Second Lieutenant Charles Sweeny having previously done so when presenting him with the Military Cross in a muddy field in England. Charles Sweeny had been born in Limerick in 1917, was educated at Haileybury and attended Sandhurst. He was commissioned into the Regiment on 27 January 1938 and by the following May was involved in guerrilla warfare against the Arabs in Palestine. Here he first met Bernard Law Montgomery on whom he made quite an impression – Sweeny is probably the only man in the British Army to receive a congratulatory birthday telegram from the future Field Marshal. It was also in Palestine that Sweeny had earned the Military Cross, one of five awarded to the Rifles; to this must be added four awards of the Military Medal and eighty-seven Mentions in Despatches.

The following day brought home to the Riflemen just how cold this winter was to become. Overnight the temperature had dropped considerably and now the ground was frozen making digging difficult.

The Rifles celebrated Christmas in the usual manner and held a party for some 375 French schoolchildren. In the aftermath of this some men were heard to mutter that facing the Germans would be a piece of cake!

On 7 January the Rifles suffered their first officer casualty when Captain Philip Ashton from London was killed in a road accident, his car skidding on ice.

February and March were spent in Lezennes carrying out various exercises, including withdrawal from prepared positions and a course of night driving for the benefit of the drivers of twenty-five TCVs (Troop Carrying Vehicles), which arrived with the Rifles on

5 March. The course covered some 20 miles in darkness with only the leading vehicle using headlights, the rest following the dim red tail light of the lorry in front.

Lieutenant Colonel Whitfeld received word on 4 May that he had been appointed as AAG, GHQ and with a heavy heart he said goodbye to the riflemen, wishing them good luck for the forthcoming campaign, but assuring them they were to be left in good hands. Two days later Major Fergus 'Gandhi' Knox was promoted to Lieutenant Colonel and took command. Fergus Knox was another veteran of the First World War having served with the 2nd Battalion Royal Irish Rifles from 1916. He had quickly come to notice as an officer with a natural gift for leadership and promotion was assured. After the First World War he served in Egypt and had demonstrated his abilities while leading his platoon during the various bouts of street disturbances. He had spent some time with the 1st Battalion before accompanying the Rifles to France; now he was being given the chance of command.

The following three days were spent on long country route marches, which were to prove of great value sooner than anyone could expect.

On 9 May there was considerable enemy air activity and despite a prodigious expenditure of ammunition from British anti-aircraft guns, the Luftwaffe was able to inflict considerable damage on the local RAF and French airfields.

The next day the Duty Officer was approached by a number of the local French population who inquired if he had heard 'it' on the wireless. This 'it' was the official news broadcast at 0800hrs, local time, that Germany had invaded Belgium and Holland. At 0815hrs, the Rifles were put on four hours' notice to move. The phoney war was over and now the killing was to begin.

On 11 May, the Rifles crossed the frontier into Belgium at about midnight and were met by crowds of dejected civilian onlookers, doubtless remembering a similar incident some twenty-six years earlier.

This advance was made in conjunction with the remainder of 9 Brigade, which in turn was part of the British 3rd Division, commanded by Major General Bernard Law Montgomery. Each man wore on his sleeve the new divisional patch, three black triangles surrounding an inverted red triangle, signifying the three battalions making up the three brigades that made up the 3rd Division. 9 Brigade consisted of the 2nd Royal Ulster Rifles, 1st King's Own Scottish Borderers and 2nd Lincolns. Montgomery called it his 'International Brigade'.

The advance across Belgium took the riflemen through towns such as Roubaix, Oudenarde and Alost, names familiar to their fathers and those with a historical bent. The Rifles were positioned in the woods approximately 2 miles to the west of Louvain, while a reconnaissance was carried out of the defences to the east and west of the city.

That morning Louvain was dive-bombed by the Luftwaffe, a foretaste of things to come. At 1130hrs, Lieutenant Colonel Knox led Tactical HQ, A and D Companies into Louvain and occupied the prepared defence line along the main railway line on the eastern side of the city. A short time later Headquarters, B and C Companies moved into positions to the west of the city.

This was a time of rumour and counter rumour, of parachuting nuns, fifth columnists and strange signals that were supposed to be indicating British troop positions. Most of these were quickly laid to rest by responsible officers, but one rumour did affect the Rifles as they made their way into the city that day.

Gas! Its very mention brought back memories of the horrors of the First World War. As the Rifles approached their positions reports arrived from Corps HQ that the Germans were using chlorine gas and despite the best reassurances of some officers the majority of the Rifles arrived in the city wearing their respirators. Not only did this lower morale, there was the physical effort of carrying out a route march while wearing a respirator on men already suffering a degree of fatigue. The apparent source of the 'gas' was the smell of fumes from a local factory that made electric batteries and had been visited previously by the Luftwaffe!

The front covered by the Rifles at Louvain extended for some 2,200 yards. On their right were the 2nd Lincolns and on the left was 7 Guards Brigade. Lieutenant Garstin's platoon was selected to garrison the railway station. Patrick Bannister Garstin was the son of a Dublin family and a born soldier, as the coming battle would prove.

All bridges in Louvain were prepared for demolition, those to the

14

front of the Rifles being completed as a Belgian cycle unit arrived and dug in to the flank.

On 13 May it appeared that the entire Belgian Army was withdrawing through the city. The Rifles spent the day improving their defences, trenches were dug, landmines laid and fighting patrols sent out. RQMS Cadden and a party of men returned from leave in the UK, having been involved in what was described as a 'nasty' accident on the way. In England the blackout was in force and driving conditions during the hours of darkness extremely hazardous.

The Commanding Officer and his second in command, with memories of the First World War, knew what to expect within the next twenty-four hours, while the remainder of the Rifles sat tight, the majority allowing their imaginations to run wild.

During the following day Belgian units continued their withdrawal through Louvain. Accompanying them were some British reconnaissance units, including the armoured cars of the Inniskilling Dragoons, who were maintaining their tradition of 'first in and last out'.

Situated immediately on A Company's front was a small anti-tank minefield. A Belgian ammunition lorry, the driver doubtless exhausted by many hours on the move, left the road at this point and crashed through the fence surrounding the minefield. As the vehicle ploughed into the field the resulting explosion killed not only the driver of the truck, but also Corporal John Moore from Manchester, with five further riflemen being injured by flying shrapnel.

The blazing lorry with its intermittently exploding ammunition successfully blocked the road for the next two hours. A German fighter later strafed Battalion Headquarters and Rifleman Ritchie Matthews from Belfast was killed. By 1500hrs, all withdrawing Belgian and British troops had passed through the Rifles' position and the town was now deserted, the majority of the civilian population having also gone west. At 1600hrs two explosions signalled the destruction of the bridges across the River Dyle.

There now came the introduction to the German machine gun known as the MG34, which would become known to both British and American soldiers by the generic name, the Spandau. With its high rate of fire due to being belt fed as opposed to the Bren gun's thirty-round box magazine it was superior in firepower, if not accuracy, to anything the British had at the time.

The Germans also showed their prowess with the mortar, their counter-battery fire being both quick and accurate. Nevertheless, first blood went to the riflemen when a German motorcycle combination slowly nosed around a bend in the road and was quickly despatched by a burst from a Bren gun. Shortly after this came the mortar bombs and long bursts of fire from MG34s. The firing in both cases was extremely accurate and both the Rifles and the Belgian bicycle unit suffered casualties.

As darkness fell the Riflemen saw that the innocent bushes in front of their position had taken on a life of their own and shadows both real and imaginary began to cause some alarm. There was nothing imaginary about the withdrawal of the Belgian cycle unit at 2150hrs, which retired in good order, despite having at least twenty men killed. It is said you should not judge a man until you have walked a mile in his shoes, or in this case bicycle saddle. As nothing was known of the morale or training of the Belgian unit, perhaps they should not be judged too harshly.

One hour before midnight, C Company, under the command of Captain A.W. Ward, was ordered to move into Louvain to act as a reserve and be available for any required counter-attack. The following morning Lieutenant Arthur Davis and B Company were also moved up into reserve, while Lieutenant Colonel Knox established his Headquarters in Louvain Town Hall at 0530hrs.

With dawn came a strong German attack on the railway station preceded by a heavy bombardment from German artillery that fell all over the defence lines. Using machine pistol and hand grenade to good effect German infantry broke into the railway station positions, but a swift counter-attack drove them back out just as quickly.

The Rifles now came under very heavy German artillery fire which was countered by return fire from 7th Field Regiment, RA, equipped with 18- and 25-pdr guns, the duel lasting for some two hours. Fatal casualties to the Rifles included Riflemen Joseph Coyle, from County Armagh, Charles Doyle from Belfast and William Hamilton, also from Belfast.

Captain Ward was severely wounded in the late evening of 16 May and Lieutenant Garrett assumed command of C Company.

A communiqué issued by GHQ on 17 May 1940 can be viewed with a certain degree of understatement: 'The BEF are in contact with the enemy and fighting is in progress. Attacks on Louvain have been repulsed.' At 0800hrs General Montgomery paid a visit to the Rifles Headquarters and stated he was well pleased with the behaviour of the men and their defence of the town. That afternoon Fergus Knox attended an 'O' Group and was informed that the Brigade was to withdraw.

Orders were issued that evening for the Rifles to march out from its positions at Louvain and make their way to a rendezvous some 2 miles to the west of Brussels. This was to be a forced march of some 20 miles along paved roads – a 'piece of cake' to the Lincolns, 'wee buns' to the Rifles.

A withdrawal, or retreat, in the face of an enemy is one of the most difficult manoeuvres to accomplish successfully so it is to the credit of the Rifles and the Brigade as a whole that their movements from Louvain went undetected by the Germans. As far as the Rifles were concerned this was largely due to the efforts of Lieutenant de Longueuil and his Carrier Platoon who, with the able assistance of Sergeant McConville, undertook their role of acting as rearguard while the remainder of the Battalion marched away. Driving their carriers about the streets they used the engine noise to drown out the sound of steel-shod boots on Belgian pavé.

By 2230hrs, the last British troops were clear of the town with no sign of a follow-up by the enemy. Any man glancing backwards as the Rifles marched into the hills to the west saw nothing but darkened streets and the flash of an occasional exploding shell, although within the Battalion there was the feeling that their departure was premature. They had more than held their own against all that the Germans had thrown at them and were confident of taking much more.

As daylight broke over the eastern horizon at 0600hrs on 18 May, the Rifles were passing through Brussels. It had been a long march so far, with full kit and all weapons, including Boyes anti-tank rifles, cumbersome weapons over 5 feet long and weighing 36 pounds, a two-man load at the best of times. Despite the fact that some men fell asleep even as they marched, they were roused when necessary and a good impression was made on the local populace as they marched smartly through the city.

Montgomery's insistence earlier in the year that all battalions under his command practise long route marches was paying off. At 0900hrs, a halt was called and the men enjoyed a most welcome break of two to three hours. Tea was brewed and feet inspected, with treatment applied where necessary. Lorries arrived and the withdrawal west continued at a faster pace, the next destination being Leeuwergem, to the west of Brussels. Despite being only 9 miles distance, it was over six hours before they arrived thanks to sporadic enemy air attacks, other troops having priority at road junctions and the roads being choked with fleeing refugees. By 1830hrs the Rifles were now in position, more or less, close to the river.

At 0500hrs on 19 May, all the bridges were blown along the front and as always happens in these circumstances someone arrives just that little bit too late. In this case it was two British Mk VI light tanks crewed by six very aggrieved tank men. As this was a long time before the advent of the DD tank* there was nothing the crews could do but render their vehicles inoperable to the enemy by setting fire to them. The crewmen then swam across the river into the welcoming arms of the Rifles. Close to where the tank men elected to cross was a fish factory. As the crewmen waded ashore on the western bank, Captain E.D.D. 'Ted' Wilson was one of those who extended a helping hand, but his generosity resulted in him falling into the river and up to his armpits in a combination of rotting fish and accompanying slime. A fresh pair of trousers was found, but not a jacket. Although the Captain soon got used to the odour, unfortunately the remainder of the Rifles did not and he led a somewhat lonely existence for the remainder of the campaign.

At 0700hrs contact was made with German reconnaissance units in the shape of light tanks and motorcycle combinations in the area west of the River L'Escaut. The Rifles were beginning to feel the effects of little sleep and thankfully no attack was made that day. Nevertheless, there was a certain amount of shelling and A Company Headquarters was extremely lucky when an enemy shell

* The circumstances where a tank was fully waterproofed and had a canvas surround that raised the freeboard. DD stands for Duplex Drive, the means by which the tank was propelled in the water. They were successfully used on D-Day.

18

penetrated the roof of their building, passed through the floor and exploded in the cellar, which was thankfully unoccupied. No casualties were reported. The deteriorating situation elsewhere on the front was causing problems and again the CO was called to Brigade Headquarters for a briefing on further withdrawals.

Once again the Rifles packed up and prepared for a move of about 33 miles. As insufficient transport was available all non-essential stores were dumped and men crowded on to the various vehicles of the battalion. Prior to this move the Rifles had acquired quite a collection of local civilian vehicles, including motor cars, delivery vans and lorries, motor and pedal cycles, enough for all the Rifles to be 'mounted'. This withdrawal was to present difficulties not before experienced. The Rifles were not to leave their positions until 0800hrs, a time of day when it was fully light.

Those officers with First World War experience remembered such battles as Le Cateau and thought this was pushing their luck just a bit much. In the final hours of darkness a candlelit briefing took place at Battalion Headquarters and the officers then dispersed to brief their own sub-units.

Before dawn, Headquarters, A and D Companies quietly moved out towards the west, leaving in position B and C Companies of the Rifles, a company of the 2nd Lincolns, and the machine-gun platoon of the 2nd Middlesex Regiment, all under the command of Lieutenant Colonel Knox and his tactical headquarters.

In the quiet of the early morning the various platoons and companies retired across the open ground. At first all went well, but then about 0800hrs, shelling began and casualties were caused by shrapnel airbursts, one of those killed being Corporal William Nesbitt from County Armagh. This shelling prompted an increase in the momentum of the force, but cohesion was maintained and soon the RV point had been reached where a collection of vehicles had been left for their use, among which was a very large red lorry weighing almost 20 tons. It was to the relief of Lieutenant Davis, the elected driver, that the local roads were both long and straight. While the leading elements of the Rifles suffered the ever-present problem of refugee crowded roads, by the time Lieutenant Colonel Knox and his command took up the journey things were a lot quieter.

By 1200hrs the Rifles, once again a full battalion, were now at Tieghem, 6 miles south-west of Oudenarde. Few men had slept in the past seventy-two hours, but despite overwhelming tiredness, tea was brewed and the strength to carry on was found. As in times past a mug of 'char' was found to work wonders.

The hope of a night's sleep under cover proved to be forlorn. A briefing was held between Montgomery, Brigadier Robb and Lieutenant Colonel Knox at which it was made clear that no friendly troops were positioned between the Division and the advancing enemy so the Rifles were ordered to take up positions close to Bossuyt facing north east along the Courtrai–Bossuyt Canal and south-west along the River L'Escaut.

At 1830hrs the Rifles had halted and the exhausted men again dug in. Part of this defensive position lay in an open meadow and a hole in the ground was the only cover available.

As daylight broke across the eastern sky on 20 May, German troops could be seen in various places on the eastern side of the river. Despite the enemy presence it was a quiet day and between improving the defences and running communication lines most men got some sleep. More rumours circulated in the Rifles. This time German spies were reported attempting to infiltrate the lines dressed as refugees or British staff officers, a rumour that caused no loss to morale; in fact the opposite was achieved as everyone wanted to have a shot at a staff officer!

It was ten days since the German XIXth Panzer Corps, under the command of General Heinz Guderian, had crossed the French border, now they were on the French coast near St Valery. It would take two days for their infantry support to catch up, then they would turn towards Boulogne, Calais and Dunkirk. The net was closing in on the Rifles and those other units of the BEF.

21 May was a warm quiet day that was spent digging slit trenches and loopholing various buildings. There was the continuing sound of artillery to the north and south, but no enemy was seen. Enduring rumours warned of enemy troops dressed as refugees wearing black dresses with yellow belts in order to identify each other, with others dressed as British officers from various head-quarter staffs. The weather was sunny and within the ranks morale was high, despite the news, which was not good.

22 May was another warm, quiet day and although there were successful attacks against French positions, the Brigade was left alone. Time was taken to forage in the surrounding countryside and

a plentiful supply of eggs, butter and champagne was collected; unfortunately beer was in short supply. In the morning orders were issued for a further short withdrawal that night to Tourcoing. By now the well-rehearsed moves came as second nature to the riflemen and all went well. As dusk fell, advance parties under the command of Major Benson moved off to the new positions.

253 Field Company, Royal Engineers was responsible for marking the route to be used and worked throughout the night. The Anti-tank Platoon, along with a detachment of Sappers, was to defend the still intact bridges which were not to be blown before 0330hrs, unless threatened by an enemy advance. At 0100hrs the reserve companies and the Machine-Gun Platoon moved off, with the forward companies disengaging at 0230hrs, covered by the now experienced Carrier Platoon.

At the halfway point to Tourcoing the carrier platoons of the three battalions were brigaded together and went into a defensive position between the main Courtrai–Coyghem road between the latter place and Guezenhock.

Again the Germans failed to follow up this withdrawal and the new positions were soon occupied at Tourcoing, one mile west of the Belgian–French border, the troops moving in just before dawn. Not all the positions were ideal. B Company was placed in a large cotton warehouse where the risk of fire was considerable, added to which was the difficulty of sighting weapons from existing windows. Soon the sound of pickaxe and shovel was heard as loopholes were constructed where required. Roadblocks were put in place and patrols sent out to give warning of any German advance, but no contact was made.

On 24 May the Germans attacked the defences at Gravelines, 15 miles from Dunkirk. On the outskirts of Lille Padre Neill came upon an abandoned train filled with NAAFI supplies, loading up his transport he returned to the Rifles with the welcome refreshments. The same day Captain Nicholas Grimshaw returned to the Rifles having been left behind with a small rearguard on 10 May.

Casualties to date amounted to one officer and 10 other ranks killed, 34 wounded and 8 missing.

At 1030hrs on 25 May, the Secretary of State for War cabled General Gort predicting the 're-embarkation' of the British Expeditionary Force. Even in the midst of war there is time for ceremony. At 1200hrs, in the main square of Tourcoing, the Rifles paraded and General Montgomery decorated Lieutenant Colonel Knox with the DSO, Lieutenant Garstin with the Military Cross, Sergeants Henderson, Baudains, Kiley and Corporal Martin with the Military Medal.

Two days later, Lieutenant Anthony 'Buck' Ruxton arrived at the Rifles Headquarters with a warning order that another move was imminent, the destination Boesinghe, situated some 4 miles beyond Ypres, on the western bank of the Yser Canal, a total distance of 18 miles. With no fresh supplies having reached the Battalion the reserve rations were broken open.

Information on what was happening on the flanks varied from sparse to non-existent, so all weapons were carried in a state of readiness. These included the Boyes anti-tank rifles and arrangements were made to distribute them between men to ease the burden. At 2130hrs, in the midst of a bout of enemy shelling, the men moved out, less two vehicles lost to shellfire. Using secondary roads the column of vehicles, both military and commandeered civilian, snaked their way towards the west. Lieutenant Robert Gordon navigated the way through the darkened countryside with some skill and only rarely was a speedy reversal from a Belgian farmyard needed.

By dawn the destination had been reached and digging in started all over again. By midday the defences were complete and tired men waited for the enemy to appear. Lieutenant Bala Bredin's D Company was hit in the early afternoon. Humphrey Edgar Nicholson Bredin, the son of a colonel in the Indian Army, was born in Peshawar on the North-West Frontier of India on 28 March 1916. Educated at King's School, Canterbury, and Sandhurst he was commissioned into the Royal Ulster Rifles in 1936. By joining the Army he was continuing the family tradition of military service, for his forebears had fought on both sides at Agincourt in 1415, his father was in the Punjab Regiment and grandfather was in the Green Howards, and two of his uncles had served in the Royal Irish Regiment.

While at Sandhurst, Bredin acquired the nickname 'Bala', the name of the fort in Peshawar and his place of birth; it was also the name of a horse owned by the Aga Khan that had been racing with some success at the time. Remarkably, when posted with the

Ulster Rifles to Palestine, he found himself quartered in an Arab village called Bala. He was awarded the Military Cross soon after arrival for a successful patrol against superior numbers and was later chosen for special night work by Captain Orde Wingate, later to be the creator of the Long Range Penetration Groups (Chindits) in Burma, earning a Bar to his Military Cross.

Two separate probing attacks were made against D Company, both with the usual mortar and artillery support, but were beaten off with the able support of a section of Vickers machine guns of the 2nd Middlesex. Enemy casualties were reported to have been considerable. Throughout the action the Company stretcher-bearers, under the command of Bandsman Ellis, did commendable work in recovering the wounded, some of whom were lying in full view of the enemy and considerable risks were taken under mortar fire.

Later on the evening of 28 May, in the Company HQ area Corporal Jimmy Crowe, the company cook, received a flesh wound while preparing supper. His war would come to an end on 24 March 1945. Total casualties for the day were three riflemen killed and a dozen wounded.

That night it was discovered that there were no maps to cover the countryside between Boesinghe and the coast! There had been ample maps for the planned campaign, but this had not included a withdrawal of some 95 miles in a few days! A quarter-inch map was found from somewhere and Fergus Knox used this to plan the remainder of the journey, while the officers had to make do with hasty sketches and an air of resignation. As the riflemen left their positions and moved west a tremendous German artillery barrage fell on the empty slit trenches.

At 0430hrs on the morning of 29 May, the Rifles arrived at Woesten. Here in the darkness company positions were allocated and the men began the laborious process of digging in. Daylight revealed a nasty surprise. This was to be far from an ideal place to defend for the position occupied a forward slope and was bereft of any natural cover. There was nothing to act as a natural anti-tank ditch or other obstacle and slit trenches became just that little deeper!

Throughout the hours of daylight there was no sign of enemy infantry, but his artillery fire was plentiful and many casualties were caused. At 1100hrs, Battalion Headquarters received a direct hit and six men were killed, including Rifleman Leslie Thomas from Belfast and Lance Corporal Samuel Smith from County Armagh. Thankfully this was to be a short stop and shortly afterwards orders were received for a further move westwards, destination Bulscamp, some 3 miles to the south of Furnes.

For the remainder of the day all stores and equipment not immediately required were systematically destroyed. These included blankets, packs, greatcoats, groundsheets, officers' valises and the remaining rations. The Rifles' transport had been much reduced and room had to be made for the men on board the vehicles. As evening fell Fergus Knox began to thin out his forward companies, while maintaining the illusion that the line was still held.

As the Rifles prepared to move out, the Germans seemed to be preparing to attack. The weight of artillery falling on the battalion's positions increased and long-range machine-gun fire began to fall around the trenches making any movement above ground dangerous. At 2030hrs, enemy infantry rushed the Rifles' positions in a concentrated assault. In the forward trenches the fighting was at extremely close range and for a while it looked like hand-to-hand combat would develop. As the companies withdrew an under-strength platoon on the extreme right became cut off as enemy infantry streamed around both flanks. Just as they were about to be overrun, three Bren gun carriers from the 2nd Lincolns Carrier Platoon arrived. Deploying in line abreast they brought down a devastating fire from their Vickers machine guns on the enemy, under cover of which the surviving riflemen climbed aboard the carriers and all made a safe withdrawal.

A section of the Anti-tank Platoon was not so lucky. The two 2-pdr guns had been left in position as long as possible in the event of an attack by German armour, but in the confusion of the moment the crews were overrun, some being captured and others killed. As the remaining units of the battalion made their way to the rear, Stuart de Longueuil brought forward the Rifles' Carrier Platoon to take on the role of rearguard.

The Carrier Platoon rattled along the road, turning every now and again to check for pursuit, as the Rifles main body made heavy weather continuing on its way towards the sea. The road to the coast was congested by men and vehicles from what seemed every unit in the BEF, with some French troops thrown in for good measure. All the time the column was under fire from enemy guns, with shells of various calibres falling on a regular basis. It was close to midnight when the head of the Rifles column reached the bridge over the Yser Canal, only to find it had been destroyed, whether by enemy fire or prematurely by friendly forces was not known. A pontoon bridge erected by the Royal Engineers close to the site was on fire and the crossing point was under continuous shellfire. A careful study of the quarter-inch map showed a minor road that crossed the Canal some 3 miles distant. On arrival the bridge was found to be intact and the Battalion crossed with equal amounts of both haste and dignity.

For the remainder of the night it became a matter of inch forward, stop, forward, stop. Sometimes the halt lasted a few minutes, sometimes much longer and usually started again when the call of nature was in mid flow. On one occasion it was found that the driver of a vehicle had fallen asleep and on commencement of the convoy had not woken up, but Bulscamp was finally reached, 12 miles and six hours later. Not all of the Battalion arrived at once and throughout the day men and vehicles drifted in. One of the last to arrive was Captain Davis and his big red lorry. Having overshot the rendezvous point he had found himself at the coast where a beach master had directed him and his men towards a fleet of small boats that were ferrying men out to a waiting destroyer. Inquiring as to the whereabouts of the Battalion and not receiving a satisfactory answer he refused the offer, turned his lorry around and drove back inland until Headquarters was found.

By midmorning on 30 May the riflemen were once again digging in, no easy task for the ground about had been flooded and the water table was found about 2 feet down. B C and D Companies held the line, while A acted as reserve. Headquarters had been established in a farmhouse with a fine view from its roof of the surrounding countryside. While the farmer had decamped to safer parts, his cellar was crammed with refugees of various shapes and sizes. As dinner time approached so did Captain Henniker, his truck arriving at Headquarters as empty as a politician's promise. This was the first time in the campaign that the Captain had failed to provide for the men, but given the circumstances it was understandable.

Nevertheless, dinner was required and soon foraging parties from the companies went out and about, milking cows, gathering eggs and slaughtering anything that was moving and edible. Despite near constant shelling throughout the day there was only one fatal casualty, Lance Corporal Edward Devine from Belfast. The King's Own Scottish Borderers on the Rifles' right flank had quite a fierce battle to contend with during the afternoon, but no serious attempt was made against any of the Rifles companies.

In the early hours of the morning a Brigade conference was held and orders were issued for the final withdrawal from French soil. An operational order sent out by Lieutenant Colonel Knox was recalled by one of the company officers: 'A Rifleman arrived with a very dirty white envelope. On it scribbled in pencil was the following, "Dear Nick, the KOSBs have taken a kick in the pants. The Bosche is across the canal on your right. Be prepared to counter-attack, and Christ help you. Fergus." '

It was not the most uplifting experience. After just three weeks of fighting the British Army was being driven from the field, despite several local successes, notably by the 1st Army Tank Brigade near Arras on 21 May, an event described by the future Field Marshal Erwin Rommel, then commanding 7th Panzer Division, as 'an extremely tight spot'.

An attempt was to be made to embark both the 3rd and 4th Divisions that night. The present positions were to be held until 0230hrs on 1 June, when the men would begin moving towards the beach. When they reached La Panne guides from the Division Control Staff would put them into groups of 200 and lead them down onto the beach, a journey to be made on foot. All vehicles were to be rendered immobile by draining the engine oil and running the engines until they seized. The breech blocks were removed from anti-tank guns and buried, while mortar tubes were flattened with sledgehammers. The infantry were ordered to carry rifles, Bren guns and Boyes anti-tank rifles along with 100 rounds of ammunition. Those riflemen who were walking wounded would be brought along; the others were to be left in the care of the medics. Embarkation at La Panne would stop at 0400hrs and any troops remaining were then to proceed to Bray-Dunes. On returning to his battalion Fergus Knox briefed his officers on the withdrawal and the following timetable.

2110hrs:	*QM and Padre, key NCOs and men under the command of Major Ryland*
2115hrs:	*Battalion HQ (less Tac HQ) and HQ Company*
2130hrs:	*A Company*
0130hrs:	*Company HQs and reserve platoons of B C and D Companies. Battalion Tac HQ*
0145hrs:	*Thin out forward platoons*
1230hrs:	*Rear party under command of Captain R.R.B. Dickinson.*

As a plan it was fine, but the enemy was intent on making it as difficult as possible to implement. During the afternoon and early part of the evening of the 31st, the enemy made it clear that there was to be no peaceful withdrawal. The King's Own Scottish Borderers were particularly hard pressed and at one stage the Rifles' A Company had to be brought into position to repel an expected breakthrough. German artillery continued to fall, becoming heavier as the day progressed. Added to this was the now almost constant rattle of machine-gun fire as enemy infantry closed in on the defences.

By 0230hrs on 1 June, the last riflemen had left their slit trenches and the supporting guns of 7th Field Regiment fired off the remainder of their ammunition. Moving towards the beach, both Headquarters and HQ Company under the command of Major Ryland and Captain Allman were constantly shelled, especially in the area around the Addenkirk Bridge. Nevertheless, the bridge remained intact and both transport and personnel crossed without incident.

La Panne was a seething mass of chaos, the darkness lit by the flames of blazing houses and the white flash of exploding shells. The control staff could not be found nor was there any sign of reception camps. It quickly became obvious that to remain within the town was not a good idea and Lieutenant Colonel Knox gave the order to proceed to the beach where cover could be sought in the sand dunes, but unfortunately the withdrawal plan had not allowed for this and no battalion rendezvous point had been allocated on the beach. In the darkness and confusion there was no hope of keeping the men together and responsibility devolved to individual officers, NCOs and in some cases riflemen.

When dawn broke the scene revealed various groups of men waiting on the beach and in the sea, standing up to their waists in the cold water. As riflemen wandered about the beach C and D Companies met up. Each consisted of approximately fifty men, so they joined forces and proceeded to equip themselves with abandoned weapons. Men exchanged rifles for Bren guns and anti-tank rifles, prepared to fight on if necessary. It was a time of confusion with units and sub-units being separated. Lieutenant Robert Gordon was alone on the beach and wandered about until taken aboard a minesweeper. Patrick Garstin found himself aboard a ship. Being sent below deck he had just stripped off his wet clothing when the ship was bombed and began to sink rapidly. The only way out was through a porthole and it was only by being undressed that he was able to slip out just as the ship went under.

Bala Bredin and the remnants of D Company found themselves on an Isle of Man steamer. As the men clambered aboard the Captain of the ship looked with alarm as more and more men climbed onto the deck. His ship had previously suffered in an air attack and all around shells were exploding, but a decision to leave behind some of the Company was overturned through the persuasion of Bredin. While the steamer made her way out to the open sea more shells fell close by and German aircraft circled looking for an opening through the ack-ack barrage being put up by the waiting warships. As he lay on his back looking at the shrapnel-riddled funnel Bredin was approached by a steward replete in white jacket with silver tray and napkin. In answer to the offer of a drink Bredin asked for a glass of beer – the reply was that alcohol could not be served until the vessel was outside the 3-mile limit, but would Sir like a cup of tea! Bredin left the Rifles in early 1944 to take command of the 6th Battalion Royal Inniskilling Fusiliers in Italy.

Those who had not managed to get away during the hours of darkness made their way to Bray-Dunes, where an improvised pier made from lorries driven into the sea reached out towards the waiting ships. Here the remains of the battalion waited in vain for a ship. All around enemy aircraft swarmed and made strafing runs along the beach. Due to a combination of soft sand and the efforts of both British and French anti-aircraft gunners these attacks caused the riflemen few casualties. Those aircraft of the RAF that were available also did their bit.*

When it was obvious that no embarkation would take place from the lorry pier the men continued their march towards Dunkirk, which was now visible, as was the thick pall of black smoke rising above it. By 1100hrs the riflemen were on the West Mole. The first few in line were taken aboard HMS *Esk*, a waiting destroyer, but this was suddenly stopped as the warship was called away to an emergency in mid channel. At approximately midday those riflemen below decks on the *Esk* heard a scraping along the side of the ship and assumed they had landed in Dover, but when the riflemen went up on deck they found that the destroyer was close against a ship that was in the process of both burning and sinking by the stern. This was the SS *Scotia*, a railway steamer, laden with some 2,000 French troops. The Captain of the *Esk*, Commander Couch, placed the bow of his ship against the forecastle head allowing many men to cross onto the destroyer. All the time German aircraft made strafing runs and dropped bombs on both ships. French soldiers were thrown into the water and riflemen assisted the crew in pulling them aboard the British ship. As the destroyer's guns continued to fire at the attacking aircraft the remainder of the crew and soldiers were removed from the sinking steamer, the Captain being the last to leave. Thirty crewmen of the *Scotia* were lost along with an estimated 200–300 French soldiers. Were it not for the actions of those aboard the *Esk* this loss of life would have been much greater.

Back on the West Mole the remainder of the Rifles waited their turn. At 1700hrs Major Charles Durtnell of the 7th Battalion Cheshire Regiment arrived on the beach at Dunkirk along with a small party of soldiers. As he organized his men into a queue he noticed that the adjoining queue consisted of men from the Rifles. Both a destroyer and a minesweeper were lying offshore to evacuate the men, but there was no means of reaching the ships. Three large rowing boats were observed floating some distance from the shore; one was only 300 yards away, while the others were nearly

* Air Historical Branch Narrative (Appendix M) reveals that during the nine-day battle the home-based RAF lost a total of 145 aircraft, not including losses to aircraft borrowed from the Fleet Air Arm.

half a mile distant. A staff officer from 5th Division HQ requested the Cheshire officer to organize the recovery of the boats to facilitate the removal of men from shore to ship, and then produced a small canvas punt with two paddles. The Major called for volunteers and the first to answer was a Rifleman. Leaving their weapons, equipment and outer clothing in the care of a second Rifleman, they began to row out to the drifting boats. The first boat was reached without much difficulty and was found to contain two oars. Transferring into it, the canvas punt was tied behind and the pair set off in pursuit of the other two boats. By now they had drifted a considerable distance and it took over an hour to reach boat number two. After a short rest it was off again for number three. This was another long row, but eventually all three boats were under control and preparations were made for the return journey. This was the most difficult part of the exercise and it was a long time before the shore was reached. On returning to their point of departure they found it deserted, the queue having moved some distance to the south. With little hope of recovering either clothes or possessions the two searched around the beach. There he was! Sitting on the equipment, fast asleep, rifle across his lap, the Ulster Rifleman had kept everything intact. He had remained for four hours alone on a near-deserted beach, possibly giving up a chance to be evacuated – when stirred he remarked, 'I thought you were never coming back!' While the names of the riflemen are not recorded, both they and Major Durtnell did return safely to England.

Fate plays a hand in wartime, often in ways that seem strange. Rifleman 'Punter' McCartney, a veteran of eight years' service, was waiting on the beach. A few yards away, but unknown to him stood the boyfriend of his former girlfriend. 'Punter' had been writing to the girl on a regular basis since arriving in France, but had never received a reply, the reason being that the girlfriend's mother did not think 'Punter' was good enough for her daughter and was burning his letters as soon as they arrived. As she was not hearing from him the daughter had assumed 'Punter' was no longer interested and had got a new boyfriend. He in turn had been shipped to France, but as he fitted in with the mother's idea of a future son-in-law, his letters were passed on to her daughter. As things turned out a German shell changed things forever and when the smoke had cleared 'Punter' McCartney staggered to his feet and walked towards the waiting ship. On his return to Belfast 'Punter' married his former girlfriend, once she had got over her mourning.

At Dunkirk the majority of the remaining Rifles were eventually picked up and crossed to England aboard the destroyer HMS *Icarus*. Not all Riflemen got away on 1 June – two days later Rifleman Matt Taylor was killed while fighting alongside other troops who had failed to be evacuated.

It took a full seven days for the survivors of the Battalion to return. In a camp in Somerset the roll was called and revealed that the campaign in France and Belgium had cost the Rifles 34 killed, 70 wounded and a further 70 missing and believed prisoners. The casualties were described as 'light', small comfort to the thirty-four families who would or had received telegrams from the War Office.

Combined Operations Training

The Combined Operations Training Centre at Inverary, Scotland, a place once visited was rarely forgotten. In the summer of 1942, the 2nd Battalion Royal Ulster Rifles would, along with many other units of the British Army, have good reason to remember it. For ship-to-shore transfer initial training was carried out using primitive craft constructed of canvas and plywood, but each successive tour of duty at Inverary saw vast improvements in both the equipment and competence of the men.

Then there was the question of the bicycles, nicknamed 'iron horses' by the riflemen. Montgomery decided that some of those men selected to make the dash for Caen on D-Day should do so on bicycles. These were of a folding type and if great care was not taken in securing the central wing nut they had a habit of jack-knifing while going around corners and depositing the rider on the ground. Some men in the Rifles had never ridden a bicycle and much practice was devoted to making them proficient. CSM Samuel Fleming often led these exercises and on one occasion he reported to Major John Hyde, 'One hundred crutch weary warriors ready for dismissal, Sir.' Less one Bren gunner who had to be taken to hospital!

Weapon training was an important part of the daily grind. One cold winter's morning Rifleman Bobby Smyth was one of a party being schooled in the art of hand grenade throwing. The first thing to do was arm the grenade. Unscrewing the base plug a fuse was inserted and the plug replaced. The plug was then tightened and with the pin already in place it was ready for throwing. A simple procedure, but in the hands of a new recruit it was easy for something to go wrong. Bobby watched as one man successfully carried out the arming procedure and then prepared to throw the grenade from a shallow depression in the ground surrounded by a sandbag wall. As the recruit drew back his arm the grenade fell from his grasp and rolled about the bottom of the pit. The Sergeant in charge immediately picked up the grenade and threw it clear, but it exploded instantly and cost the Sergeant his hand.

There could also be problems with the 2-inch mortar. On one occasion Bobby Smyth was training on the range with his opposite number. First Bobby acted as loader or 'number two', dropping the bombs down the barrel and then moving clear while the 'number one' pulled the firing lever to detonate the propellant. After a number of shots the positions were reversed and Bobby lay behind the mortar while his soon-to-be ex-mate acted as loader. On loading the third bomb the firing lever was pulled with no result. On calling the officer in charge he told Bobby to have another go, but again the lever was pulled with no effect. There was nothing for it but to upend the mortar and gently drop out the offending bomb. As the bomb fell from the tube it was discovered that it had been put in the wrong way round – there was even a small dimple in the nose cone caused by the firing mechanism! It had almost been the end of the War for two riflemen and it was certainly the end of a partnership, for no one needs a dyslexic number two on a mortar crew.

Practising disembarkation drills was carried out from HMS *Campbeltown*. Each company spent a week aboard the ship and made many trips up and down the scramble nets attached to the side of the ship. Attempts by the crew to instruct the riflemen in the art of slinging a hammock and staying inside it met with failure and most men used it as a pillow and slept on the deck.

On 13 August 1943, Major I.C. Harris arrived in the 2nd Battalion to assume command. He was officially appointed on 23 August and granted the rank of Acting Lieutenant Colonel. Harris was the son of a County Tipperary horse breeder and had been educated at Portora Royal School, Enniskillen, before going to Sandhurst. He joined the Rifles in 1930 and soon acquired the nickname 'Tommy', due to his habit of addressing the riflemen as such, much to their indignation. During the first three years of the War he had held a number of staff appointments, but was now as well 'combined trained' as the remainder of the Battalion.

D-Day, 6 June 1944 –

'Faugh-a-Ballagh on Queen Red!'*

The 2nd Battalion of the Royal Ulster Rifles landed on Queen Red Beach, a sub-sector of Sword Beach, on the afternoon of D-Day, their exit from the beach being courtesy of a man from Waterford. This pathway from sand to soil had been cleared that morning by the armoured vehicles from 79 Assault Squadron, 79th Armoured Division. Major Redmond Cunningham commanded No. 1 Troop and had lost his tank early on to shellfire. Nevertheless, he went on to clear all the anti-tank obstacles from his sector of the beach and was subsequently awarded the Military Cross. He would be awarded a Bar for his actions at Nijmegen the following September.

For the second time in four years the Ironsides were going to War, returning to France to even the score for Dunkirk. Once again the 'International Brigade' was going into action – Rifles, Borderers and Lincolns – although no one battalion could claim a 100 per cent nationality! The Division would be known as the 3rd (British) Infantry Division, to differentiate from the 3rd Canadian Division, which would land on their right flank in Normandy.

On D-2 the Division embarked on their relevant vessels for the crossing to Normandy, in the case of the Rifles this was Landing Craft Infantry (Large) No. 973. The men settled down for the long wait, passing the time in the usual manner of soldiers, playing

* 'Faugh-a-Ballagh' is Irish gaelic for 'Clear the Way!' Originally the motto of the Royal Irish Fusiliers, on the amalgamation of the Royal Inniskilling Fusiliers, the Royal Ulster Rifles and the Royal Irish Fusiliers on 1 July 1968 to form the Royal Irish Rangers, it was adopted as the motto, and continues to be the motto for the present Royal Irish Regiment.

cards, sleeping and eating. The on-board catering was most satisfactory, with fresh bread and vegetables adding some variety to the more mundane compo rations. In the wardroom the company commanders were briefed on their various targets and objectives. The crossing was calm, with a thousand grey ships on a grey sea, then some two hours before their allotted landing time a swell began to run and seasickness made an unwelcome appearance in some of the men. While there had been an issue of tablets to try and combat this, they did not work for everyone and the sight of one's near neighbour throwing up his breakfast did little to comfort those unaffected.

As the LCI buffeted its way through the swell the men in the hold began to put the final touches to their equipment. John Hyde gave the order for B Company to arm grenades, the process where the bottom of the grenade is unscrewed, the fuse inserted and then reassembled. A short time later there was a hollow boom from the hold and Major Hyde descended the companionway three steps at a time to see several of his men lying dazed and covered in blood. As the cry for stretcher-bearers was about to be raised the awful truth dawned.

Throughout the generations, soldiers have suffered from fright, doubt or even downright panic, but none can be accused of lacking curiosity. There had been an issue of self-heating soup as part of the rations and disregarding the maxim, 'When in doubt read the instructions', the fuse had been lit without first puncturing the top of the tin. The riflemen had then sat around watching the tin swell with pressure until the inescapable detonation. The 'blood' was the contents of a tin of tomato soup.

As the Rifles waited to land some shells from German batteries at Villerville, Beneville and Houlgate fell in and around the invading vessels. Prompt return fire was delivered from the battleships *Warspite* and *Ramillies*.

At 1300hrs, as the Rifles' LCI approached the beach, the Battalion Intelligence Officer, Lieutenant Gordon Flack, observed one of the riflemen lying on the deck communicating with his 'Bag, Vomit'. On inquiring after his well-being he received the reply, 'It's in the bag, Sir.' The initial reaction to seeing the coastline was one of familiarity, before realizing that this was the 'wave top' views the men had spent such a long time studying and memorizing.

Despite the initial bombardment many of the houses on the sea front still remained standing, giving some men doubts about the effectiveness of the pre-landing bombardment. This was to be a wet landing, by now the tide had come in and with the LCIs unable to run up the beach, it meant a long deep wade to the sand.

With the occasional mortar bomb, shell and machine-gun bullet still falling on the beach CSM Walsh of A Company together with Rifleman Michael 'Sticky' Ryan MM of B Company were among the first ashore. Ryan had been awarded his MM for actions in the Dunkirk campaign and was regarded as an exceptional soldier in every way. They were able to run a lifeline from landing craft to beach, thereby enabling those men following to pull themselves onto dry land. Many of the riflemen were of small stature and a five-and-a-half-foot Rifleman does not do well in six feet of salt water! As a result of this the infamous folding bicycles had to be left on board the LCTs, those that were not tossed overboard, to be recovered later in the day when the tide had gone down. Rifleman Stanley Burrows was a Bren gunner in A Company, having joined the Rifles in 1940 as a young soldier. Prior to Normandy, Stanley had experienced two air raids on Belfast and twenty-five in England. He had originally served in the 1st Battalion, but a letter from his mother to his commanding officer informing him of Stanley's perforated eardrum had ensured a rapid transfer to the 2nd Battalion, and the mistaken belief that he would be somewhat safer on the ground. Now, as Stanley waited to go ashore, he had a folding bicycle over one shoulder and his Bren gun, named 'Betsy', over the other. With the remainder of his kit, weighing some 56 pounds, he reckoned he was almost twice his normal weight. There was nothing for it – the bicycle had to go.

Several men were wounded during the landing, none fatally. These included Lance Corporal Gooding of Support Company and Rifleman Troughton of Headquarters Company, both wounded by shrapnel in the head and neck, while Rifleman McGrath of A Company was shot in the thigh. B Company was led ashore by its commander Major John Hyde – it was his birthday and one he was unlikely to forget. Four years previously John Hyde had got another soaking from the sea when he was evacuated from Dunkirk as a platoon commander in D Company. Hyde was not the only Dunkirk veteran landing. The 50th Infantry Division was assigned to Gold Beach, with its Assault Brigade under the command of Fergus Knox DSO, who had commanded the Rifles in 1940.

Confusion reigns as to just what time the Rifles landed in Normandy. Volume III of the Regimental History states 1000hrs, the War Diary 1200hrs; the former may be the time Captain Ryan and his reconnaissance party landed. From various personal accounts it would appear that the landing took place from 1000hrs to at least late afternoon.

The last of the riflemen landed at approximately 1630hrs, these being the carriers of the Mortar Platoon. The unexpected high tides had a lot to do with the delay in unloading, with the beach supposed to be 30 yards wide being quickly reduced to 30 feet!

Moving inland the Rifles marched quickly towards the Brigade assembly area at Lion-sur-Mer, a small village approximately half a mile from the beach, where they rendezvoused with Captain Ryan and his party of guides who had landed earlier in the day. There was more shelling and the Brigade Commander, J.C. Cunningham MC was wounded, as a result of which Lieutenant Colonel Harris was ordered to take temporary command of the Brigade. This in turn delayed the advance as the Brigade waited for the arrival of Cunningham's replacement, which in turn delayed the Rifles' attack on Cambes, which would in turn cause many unnecessary casualties.

As the men milled about in the assembly area a random burst of fire from a German machine gun struck Captain Sellers of the Mortar Platoon in the legs, causing serious wounds that necessitated evacuation. Sergeant McCutcheon immediately took over the Platoon and would remain in command for some time.

Once organized the Rifles were ordered to occupy the high ground to the north-east of Periers-sur-le-Dan. On arrival on the ridge the riflemen dug in, something they would do a lot of in the coming months. Initially it was difficult to get those men who had not previously served in France to dig deep enough, but this would change rapidly. That evening Lieutenant Colonel Harris returned to the Rifles, a replacement commander having been found for the Brigade – Colonel A.D.G. Orr DSO.

On D+1, Lieutenant Colonel Harris received orders to capture Cambes, a village situated in a wooded area some 6 miles from the Normandy coast. Intelligence was of the opinion that the village was only lightly held by the enemy. Cambes was a typical Normandy community, the houses stoutly constructed of stone set in among the trees of the surrounding woods, which were in turn surrounded by a thick stone wall about 10 feet high.

What Intelligence did not know was that at 1615hrs, the 1st SS Panzer-Grenadier Battalion along with the 16th SS Pioneer Company and five Mk IV tanks of the 8th SS Panzer Company had begun to advance, their objective being the village of Anguerny. It was decided that the Rifles' attack on the village would be made in company strength with the remaining companies following close behind in reserve. D Company, led by Captain John Aldworth, a native of County Cork, would lead the attack. Despite suffering from a permanent limp from an earlier illness, he was a capable officer and well liked by his men. His second in command was Captain Jim Montgomery from Belfast, well known for his prowess on the cricket field. They would have the support of one squadron of Sherman tanks from the East Riding Yeomanry, who had previously assembled in the woods to the north-east of Le Mesnil. At 1700hrs, the Ford V8 engines roared up to their full 2,600 revs per minute and the Shermans clanked towards the village.

Crossing the flat open terrain the Yeomanry Shermans exchanged fire with the German Mk IVs coming from Anguerny. As the riflemen attempted to close with their dug-in opponents, the Yeomanry Shermans pumped shells at the German tanks and within a short time all five had either been destroyed or otherwise rendered immobile, without loss to the Shermans. This was probably caused by the lack of shooting skills on the part of the German tank crews for in April 1944, II SS Panzer Corps had allocated only five rounds per tank per month for target practice. Another advantage to the British was that one Sherman in four was armed with a 17-pounder gun as opposed to the more normal 75mm. These Shermans, known as Fireflys, were capable of taking on all German tanks including the dreaded Tigers.

The Yeomanry however did not get things all their own way, as tenacious German infantry worked their way in to close range and armed with Panzerfausts claimed three Shermans.

As D Company closed with the wood they had already lost several men to sniper fire. Now as German mortars and machine guns joined in there were more casualties.

Approaching the village John Aldworth took two platoons through the left side of the wood, while Jim Montgomery took the remaining platoon and Company Headquarters through the right side. As they entered the tree line they were met by interlocking fire from several machine guns and riflemen went down like nine pins, John Aldworth being one of the first to fall. As the riflemen attempted to return fire, Lieutenant Harry Green, a County Antrim man, was severely wounded while trying to rally his platoon, being hit in the chest and back by machine-gun bullets. The wood reverberated with the sound of machine guns, grenades and the cries for stretcher-bearers, in both English and German. All around the leaves and branches of the trees came down in a near constant shower, as shrapnel from mortar bombs exploded in the tops of the trees. Shells and mortar bombs that exploded in the trees did the most damage; even men in slit trenches had no protection from the shards of metal that flew down through the foliage. Those men treated for wounds to the back and buttocks did not have their backs to the enemy – they were lying down attempting to find whatever cover was available. For every man killed or wounded in Normandy by a bullet another ten suffered wounds caused by shrapnel.

With casualties mounting Captain Montgomery realized he had insufficient numbers to win this particular battle and ordered a withdrawal. The surviving Shermans, wary of German tank-hunting parties, stood off and gave what cover they could as the riflemen emerged from the wood. Sixteen men were wounded and fifteen were killed, including Rifleman James Hursey from Dublin, Lance Corporal Tom Kane from Belfast, Rifleman John Connolly from Glasgow and Corporal Albert Kohler from London.

Such was the weight of enemy fire that even during the withdrawal two stretcher-bearers were killed as they attempted to recover wounded men. Captain Montgomery led D Company back to Le Mesnil, their withdrawal covered by Allied artillery, including fire called in from naval forces lying off-shore. The death of Major Aldworth was a bitter blow to the Rifles – he was one of the many regulars of the Battalion lost that day. While reinforcements were available, it would take time to mould them into the Battalion, a job that would take much longer without so many of the old hands to show the way. It was decided that any further action by the Rifles would achieve nothing without more artillery support, so the Battalion retired and dug in on the right flank of the King's Own Scottish Borderers to await further developments.

It was not only D Company that lost men on 7 June. In Support Company Rifleman Ash received a gunshot wound to his leg, while in C Company Lance Corporal Brady had his wrist shattered by a piece of shrapnel. Headquarters Company came under fire and Rifleman Fairey was treated for shell shock. In the gun position of 33rd Field Regiment situated on the ridge above the village Lance Bombardier Falconer was brought into the Rifles aid post to have shrapnel removed from a lacerated thigh.

The following day the Rifles stayed in their positions taking what rest was available, a rest that was frequently interrupted by enemy shelling. In Support Company Lance Corporal Campbell and Lance Sergeant O'Callaghan were both admitted to the RAP suffering from shrapnel wounds, while Rifleman O'Halloran was brought in from C Company, again wounded by shrapnel. It was not only the riflemen who were suffering – from 101 Anti-tank Battery, Gunner Gates was logged in to the RAP log by CSM Drumgoole as having shrapnel wounds to his right leg.

In the meantime Lieutenant Colonel Harris and his company commanders carried out a detailed reconnaissance in preparation for another attack on Cambes, scheduled for the following day and to be carried out by the full battalion. The reconnaissance party included Lieutenant Colonel Hussey of the 33rd Field Regiment and Lieutenant Colonel Williamson of the East Riding Yeomanry. When the Rifles attacked again they would have close support from both these units. The reconnaissance was not entirely successful as the stone wall surrounding the woods and village made it imposs-ible to ascertain just how many defenders there were or where they were deployed.

Throughout the day the Rifles received occasional mortar fire and German machine guns made their presence known by the soon to be familiar high rate of fire, described by many as the sound of ripping cloth. The MG34 had been largely superseded by the MG42, a weapon capable of firing 1,200 rounds per minute, compared to the Bren gun's 500. The company commanders then carried out their individual reconnaissance patrols as well as could be expected owing to the openness of the terrain. As darkness fell several night patrols were sent out with the aim of keeping the enemy awake and hopefully instilling a degree of apprehension for the following day. One such patrol was selected and led by Lieutenant Cyril Rand. The patrol made ready their weapons and equipment. Rifle slings were removed to prevent them snagging on branches, all webbing save ammunition pouches and water bottles was discarded and faces blackened. A 2-inch mortar team was included in the patrol along with an extra Bren gun. Prior to setting out one of the patrol members came up to the Lieutenant and asked if Rifleman Moore could say a few words. Unsure what to expect the Lieutenant agreed. The following is taken from an article written in the regimental journal by Cyril Rand.

Then something happened that absolutely amazed me; they formed a half circle, and by the light of a torch concealed under a ground sheet Rifleman Moore produced a small book entitled 'The Daily Light on the Daily Path'. These books were often found enclosed with parcels of comforts kindly sent by various ladies' organizations, and until this moment I had no idea that anyone had actually bothered to read them. Moore quietly read a whole page of extracts taken from the New Testament, and when he had finished there were subdued murmurs of 'Thank you, John' as he replaced the book in his pocket. At first the episode struck me as being rather incongruous; these tough soldiers, some of whom had a reputation for hard drinking and pay-day brawling, and who had probably only seen the inside of a church on church parades, had obviously been quite moved. Were they searching for some kind of moral support? Was there some indefinable need to be sustained before setting out on what could be quite a hazardous expedition? Did they honestly believe their God would go with them, or were they clutching at straws? Then I remembered that the Commanders of this great undertaking were reported to have attended a vigil on the night before the invasion forces set off across the channel, and also that knights who accompanied William the Conqueror on his invasion in the opposite direction attended vigils in churches along this very coastline before setting out to do battle. I also said thank you to Rifleman Moore and like the members of my patrol, I meant it.

The line of men set out in single file making their way across the fields keeping to the shadows. Frequent stops were made to listen for sounds that were alien to nature, which for the 'townies' meant most of the sounds of the countryside. They reached a gravel track and here they were told to cross all at once as the sound would be less than each individual man crunching through the stones. On the far side the Lieutenant felt a tug on his sleeve and Corporal Baker pointed out the presence of a bicycle leaning against a nearby tree, strapped to the crossbar of which was the spare barrel of an MG42. To make matters worse the sound of voices could be heard coming from the undergrowth. This was obviously an advance listening post and one armed with a very good weapon. It was decided to bypass the post and if they were still present on the patrol's return an attempt would be made to take them prisoner.

In order to be sure that any other enemy in the area had not observed them, a short break was called and everyone settled down for a few minutes rest. The halt became a little longer than planned and this proved most fortuitous. As the patrol moved off Lieutenant Rand made towards a drainage ditch intending to use it as cover. Suddenly the night was split by the muzzle flash of a machine gun firing down the same ditch, a random burst fired on a fixed line, but one that could have caused injury and death to the patrol had they not dallied. For the next few hours the patrol moved about the countryside experiencing the bocage at first hand – with its high banks and thick hedgerows each field was potentially a self-contained fortress. Returning past the listening post it was discovered that the bicycle was still in place, but it was decided that as the patrol had been carried out without being detected it was best to leave it that way and the post was ignored. The only direct damage to the German Army by the patrol was one of the riflemen letting down the bicycle tyres!

During the day the Rifles had a further five men wounded while Support Company lost another man when Corporal Ernie Rogers from Essex was killed by shellfire. As darkness fell it began to rain. The enemy was also active in the hours of darkness and soon after the patrol's return a German fighting patrol of approximately 30 men launched an attack on C Company's position at Le Mesnil, but the attack was driven off after a brief exchange of fire. As the enemy withdrew a salvo of mortar bombs fell on Support Company and killed Rifleman Michaelides.

On 9 June, the fourth day of the invasion, the Rifles formed up at the village of Anisy, which was garrisoned by troops of the 3rd

Canadian Division. The riflemen lay on the warm wet ground waiting for zero hour, haversacks left in the care of the garrison – less weight to carry, more freedom of movement. A serge battledress was not the most comfortable uniform for a warm summer in France but a wet warm serge battledress smelling like a dead sheep was even less so.

At 1515hrs the riflemen left their start line and again set out for Cambes. The morning had been wet, persistent rain causing a fair degree of discomfort, a short dry spell just after midday having again given way to more heavy showers. From Anisy to Cambes the terrain was extremely open; for the first 400 yards towards the village the ground rose in a slight incline, the remaining 1,100 yards being flat and devoid of any cover whatsoever. Intelligence was now of the opinion that the enemy had reinforced their position as elements of both 21st Panzer and 12th SS Panzer Divisions had been identified as being present in the area. Major 'Digger' Tighe-Wood had found German dead in Cambes wearing the cuff title of the 12th SS Hitlerjugend Division and removed an officer's cap to show the Intelligence Section. Because of all this, support for the attack was considerable. Added to the guns of the Divisional Artillery, the 2nd Middlesex Regiment supplied two troops of 6-pdr anti-tank guns, a company of Vickers machine guns and a company of 4.2-inch mortars. There were also the Sherman tanks of A and B Squadrons, East Riding Yeomanry, five armoured vehicles of the Royal Engineers and offshore fire from the 6-inch guns of the cruiser HMS *Danae*. The Rifles were interested to know that Danae was the daughter of Acrisius and Eurydice and had spent some time in a wooden chest. Rifleman Bobby Smyth remembered that war was an education as well as an adventure.

While this seemed an awful lot of firepower for one attack, there were 1,500 yards of ground to cover, much of it waist-high corn, which would provide some cover from view but none at all from bullets or shrapnel. The enemy on the other hand had ample 'hard' cover with his artillery and tanks well dug in to the Normandy earth, so concentrated artillery fire would be required to help keep their heads down during the advance. From out of the clear evening air came the roar of guns as the supporting artillery fire arrived from the Royal Artillery, together with that from the offshore naval support which sounded like an express train passing overhead. The advance was to follow a 'rolling barrage' that would move ahead of the Rifles, while their own machine guns and mortars engaged any known or suspected enemy positions directly.

The companies advanced at zero hour. A and B Companies were to capture the edge of the village and act as flank guards, while C and D Companies advanced through to the other side, an action that would involve both street fighting and the clearance of the dense woods around the village.

In battle the time soldiers fear is not the combat, but the waiting – thoughts of what could happen, of failure, of letting the boys down, of home, of what's the bloody sense of it all anyway. All of these things went through the minds of riflemen waiting to begin what was for many of them their first experience of combat. Once battle is joined adrenaline takes over and with luck will last long enough to see men through the action.

The riflemen advanced at a rate of 100 yards every two minutes for that first 400 yards. Within a few seconds of the advance beginning the enemy opened fire with both machine guns and mortars. Added to this was the deadly flat crack of the German 88mm. Initially an anti-aircraft weapon, it was used by the Germans in a ground role both as an anti-tank gun and to deliver accurate high-explosive shells, which could be fused to explode above the heads of advancing troops.

The Middlesex were advancing in support, their 4.2-inch mortars having fired for twenty of the thirty-five minutes of the pre-attack barrage and were continuing to give support where possible. They were also suffering casualties both from the enemy guns and shells that were falling short from the rear. On reaching the crest the advance increased to 100 yards in one minute. As the riflemen walked through the almost waist-high corn it began to ripple and disintegrate as machine-gun bullets and shrapnel cut through the unripe crops. The initial sense of security soon vanished as men began to fall. In the ranks of A Company, Lieutenant John Cooper went down with shrapnel wounds to his head and leg. He would be found later in the day by the crew of a British self-propelled gun, but by then gangrene had set in. Nearby Rifleman Cope also went down with a wound from a machine gun bullet. As the advance continued the dead and wounded disappeared from view in the long corn, out of sight, out of mind, at least for the time being. For those who were entering their first battle and in the face of such opposition the urge to lie down and search for whatever shelter was available must have been strong. Nevertheless, within the ranks there were enough old hands to ensure that the lines kept moving.

Closing with the village the enemy fire intensified and A Company quickly lost more of its officers. During the initial stage of the attack Lieutenant Colonel Harris was positioned in the centre of the Battalion, where he was seen urging the men on with tremendous shouts of encouragement and brandishing his revolver about in such a manner as to bring fear to the most courageous enemy and not a little apprehension to those riflemen close by!

Supporting C Company were AVREs of the Royal Engineers and Sherman tanks of the East Riding Yeomanry. The AVREs were converted Churchill tanks designed to combat enemy strongpoints, being armed with a variety of weapons for that purpose. These particular tanks were fitted with Petard mortars, most suitable for destroying enemy bunkers. The tank commanders, an independent and fearless lot, did more than was asked of them and on one occasion took on and destroyed a German Mk IV tank. The Germans had their revenge when a well-placed 88 got the Churchills in its sights and within a matter of moments all but one were knocked out. As the riflemen went forward Lieutenant Gordon Flack, the Intelligence Officer, heard the CO of the Yeomanry remark, 'This is where they go to ground.' As several riflemen did throw themselves flat Major de Longueuil came across 'like a testy schoolmaster' and soon got them moving again. Shortly afterwards Gordon Flack went down himself, wounded by a rifle bullet.

Lieutenant Cyril Rand's platoon of C Company had made good progress through the woods to the north of the village. Here they came across a small brick building standing alongside the railway line that skirted Cambes. Lieutenant Rand sent a section forward to investigate and within a few minutes the section commander reported back that he had heard noises coming from within the building. The initial suggestion was to toss a hand grenade through a window and see what happened, but at this stage prisoners would be of useful value to the Intelligence Section. Also a rumour was circulating among the Division that £1 was being offered for each prisoner taken, although by the following September this was down to 2/6d a dozen. Three men were therefore positioned to cover the only door, while a smoke grenade was tossed through the window. From within there came the sound of shouting and a few seconds later three extremely distressed French farmers came tumbling out of the door. Apparently the Germans had allowed them to return to the village to milk their cows, a job that had been interrupted by the Rifles' attack!

A Company reached the far end of the village, moving doggedly through heavy mortar fire and suffered more casualties. Rifleman Hayes and Lance Corporal Lacy both received shrapnel wounds to the arm, while Lieutenant Ronnie Hall, commanding 8 Platoon, was killed.

As C Company reached the southern end of the village they came under fire from a Mk IV tank in a hull-down position presenting a difficult target for the anti-tank guns. The tank made no aggressive moves towards the riflemen apart from the occasional burst of fire from its machine guns and they in turn left it alone, while maintaining a wary eye on it! At about this time Lieutenant Bobby Diserens of 14 Platoon, C Company, was killed. He and Cyril Rand had been good friends for the last two years.

B Company had consolidated in and around the buildings in their area and established their HQ in a nearby farm. They were receiving the usual attention from German mortars so Major John Hyde sent Rifleman 'Sticky' Ryan to ensure that all platoons were digging in. On his return he stated the following: 'Sir, do you remember our difficulties on those Salisbury Plain exercises of getting the boys to dig in properly? You'll be glad to hear that, if they go on at their present rate, you'll have to indent for a ferret to deliver messages.' Experience is a wonderful teacher!

Throughout the action RSM Sam Fleming brought his Bren carrier forward loaded with ammunition. Ammunition resupply is the traditional role of the Regimental Sergeant Major in battle and Sam Fleming continued the tradition without thought to the shelling and enemy small-arms fire he attracted. As the carrier arrived at the designated spot the ammunition boxes were unloaded and if not required immediately were buried in a slit trench to protect them from the shelling. The RSM would then ensure that the position was well marked before venturing off for another load.

Captain 'Wigan' Wright the Battalion Medical Officer, with the able assistance of CSM Drumgoole, had set up the RAP in a Cambes chateau that was already filling up with wounded.

After the attack there was the threat of immediate counter-attack by the enemy, almost always a certainty when fighting the Germans. The rifleman began to dig in. The anti-tank guns were brought forward, towed by their carriers. As one gun was manoeuvred into position it was hit by a shell, killing Rifleman Stanley Bingham and wounding two others.

The riflemen had begun to settle in for the evening when an alarm was sounded and a body of infantry was spotted approaching the position; these turned out to be the men of the King's Own Scottish Borderers. Unsure of the outcome of the day's battle they were approaching with some caution. As recognition signs and passwords were exchanged a salvo of German mortar bombs landed and one particular 'Jock' dived into a convenient slit trench for cover. Greeting the occupants with the words 'Well Paddy, you old bastard, we never expected to see you again', he was surprised to see it was Lieutenant Colonel Harris and the Brigade Commander!

The expected counter-attack did not materialize as the enemy was too well situated in his prepared positions to the south of Cambes. He also knew the invaders/liberators would have to come to him.

The Rifles completed their defences, dispatched patrols and posted sentries. Now that the battle was done the most important thing was food. The majority of men had not eaten since breakfast, adrenaline having sustained them throughout the day. Now it was time for supper. The soldiers' diet in the field when fresh food was unavailable consisted of compo rations, a selection of tinned food which varied in taste and quality according to who was cooking or eating it. There was quite a selection that evening: tinned sausage and bacon, considered edible; stewed beef, best eaten with closed eyes; assorted vegetables, supposedly; sliced peaches, good when you could get them; and rice pudding, probably the most popular ration to come out of a tin.

There was also self-heating soup, a very hit-and-miss affair and as previously experienced, dangerous. And of course tea! Without tea there was nothing; without tea there could be no victory, no war. To this day there can be no finer drink to sustain a man in combat than a strong mug of tea made with condensed milk and at least two spoonfuls of sugar. There was almost a disaster in Cyril Rand's platoon when it was discovered that the man carrying the tea tin in one of the sections had been wounded earlier in the action and the vital ingredient was missing. Thankfully the remainder of the Platoon chipped in enough of the necessary leaves and the situation was saved. However, from then on each man was issued with his own ration of tea, milk and sugar, just in case.

At the end of the day the Rifles had suffered 11 officers and 182 other ranks, killed, wounded and missing. In this their first major battle of the campaign they had suffered 144 wounded, 11 missing and 44 killed since D-Day. The Rifles had acquitted themselves well, the number of gallantry awards bearing witness to exemplary behaviour in many cases. Captain James Montgomery and RSM Sam Fleming were awarded the Military Cross, while Corporal Charles O'Reilly received the Distinguished Conduct Medal.

10 June was a quiet day for the Rifles with work continuing on improving the Battalion positions as hectic air activity took place overhead. A tremendous artillery barrage from ship to shore began at 1615hrs, with some reply from enemy mortars. No casualties were reported within the Battalion area.

On 14 June at 2300hrs, the Rifles' Reserve Company of one Captain, six subalterns and 129 other ranks eventually came ashore. The landing craft supplied courtesy of the US Navy had spent some time chugging up and down the beaches looking for the correct landing place, her Captain completely lost. Lieutenant Jim Campbell, from Belfast, had been commissioned into the Royal Artillery in 1942, had transferred to the Rifles the previous January and now found himself standing in the prow of the LCI consulting his map and the Normandy beaches with equal intensity. In the end it was decided that they would go ashore and ask for directions, the point chosen turning out to be not too far from the actual landing. Little had changed since D-Day, including the depth of the water. As Rifleman Bobby Smyth, 5'3", stepped off the end of the ramp he promptly disappeared into water that was 6 feet deep. Thankfully his mate Rifleman Telfer, 6'2", was able to grab hold of his webbing straps as he sank and quickly pull him to the surface. Thus suspended he was carried safely to shore, although once on dry land the ordeal was far from over. As they made for the sand hills German aircraft paid a surprise visit and made a bombing run along the beach. On joining the Battalion Bobby Smyth was assigned to the Signals Platoon of Support Company, while Jim Campbell was given command of 18 Platoon D Company.

It did not take long for the riflemen to get used to the ways of fighting and surviving in Normandy. The slit trench became home; deep and narrow, sometimes with a roof of logs and earth, it provided cover from enemy bullets and shells, but not from the elements – when it rained the standard issue gas cape was the only protection for the infantryman in the field and it was not long before everyone was in need of a bath or shower. Living for an extended time in a hole in the ground and washing and shaving in a small mess tin did little for personal hygiene. In the rear area the Royal Engineers had constructed several shower units. These consisted of former oil drums perched on wooden supports, delivering a stream of water that ranged from tepid to hot, depending on one's place in the queue. Nevertheless, the chance to get a proper wash, however primitive the facilities, was one not to be missed. After his shower each Rifleman was issued with a new battledress that had been impregnated with a not-quite-odourless chemical that was intended to repel lice. It may have done, but it also dyed the normal khaki with a greyish tinge and caused near neighbours to be unsociable.

On 19 June the Rifles had several casualties from enemy mortaring. Rifleman Stanley Burrows suffered severe burns to his face and hands from the blast of an explosion, Rifleman Moreney was wounded in the chest and arms by shrapnel, while Lance Sergeant Andrew Stewart from County Down was killed in the same attack.

After so many years attempting to discover who was with the Battalion at any one time remains difficult if not impossible. Due to promotions, illness and wounds men moved from unit to unit with increasing frequency. Lieutenant Clifford Lyndon-Adams arrived with the Rifles on the day Sergeant Stewart was killed and was posted to the Mortar Platoon. He was wounded the following day, a day that saw the Rifles suffer many casualties from German artillery. The Lieutenant was kept in the RAP overnight and as he was being transported to the beach for evacuation to England he was killed by a direct hit from an enemy shell near Cazelle.

On 23 June Stanley Burrows' friend Hugh Crangle was killed. Crangle had been the third member of the group of friends known in the Battalion as the BBC – Burrows, Beck and Crangle. Hugh's brother Gerald had been killed serving with the Irish Guards in 1940.

John Hyde also remembered it was about then that one of his men suggested they should be renamed the 'Magnetic Division' as they seemed to be attracting all the armour.

For the following month things remained much the same – active patrolling, enemy shelling and home became a small hole in the ground. The Riflemen, among others, acquired the nickname 'slitters' because of their abode and along with the normal battle wounds the RAP had to treat such things as septic mosquito bites, diarrhoea, synovitis and various sprains. The very act of digging a trench was not without danger. One man remembered waking up in the morning to find that in excavating his trench his pick had grazed the side of a dead German, who by the smell had been there for some time. Not only that, but there was an unexploded 2-inch mortar bomb imbedded between the body's shoulder blades! One more swing of the pick would have meant serious injury or worse.

The nights were a strain on both eyes and nerves. On one particular night Rifleman Bobby Smyth was on guard when he spotted a suspicious movement to his front. With no answer to the challenge he fired and saw the shape crumple to the ground. With daylight came the realization that the 'enemy' had in fact been one of the Normandy dairy cows! Bobby's officer was not pleased, for not only was it a waste of ammunition, but in the summer sun the carcass would soon start to smell. As a punishment Bobby was told to bury the cow, so while the remainder of the Platoon looked on in amusement he set to work with his shovel. Thankfully the earth was reasonably soft, but it still took a long time to excavate a hole big enough for the animal. When he thought the hole was both wide and deep enough he persuaded two companions to help him roll the cow into the hole and with a mighty thud the body disappeared into the earth. Unfortunately a miscalculation had been made as far as depth and the cow's feet stuck up in the air well clear of the rim of the hole. This was a problem as the cow was much too heavy to lift back out of the hole in order to deepen it and to pile earth over the legs would create a blind spot in the defences. Bobby had the answer. Collecting together all the spare cigarettes in the Platoon he went off to find a solution to the problem – a Royal Engineer with a chainsaw! In exchange for the cigarettes it was the work of a few seconds to remove the four legs and these were quickly buried with the remainder of the carcass – problem solved!

In preparation for the assault on Caen the Rifles along with the remainder of 9 Brigade moved to an assembly area at Brieville on 7 July. Here they formed up behind 185 Brigade, who were to carry out an attack on Lebisey Wood. Once they had captured this objective they would in turn support 9 Brigade who would pass through them and move on, with the Rifles seizing the high ground on Ring Contour 60. From there they would descend into Caen.

Resting in their trenches that evening the Rifles were to witness one of the major blunders of the Normandy campaign. A force of 467 Halifax and Lancaster bombers dropped a total of 2,560 tons of bombs on the northern outskirts of Caen. Because of the danger of the aircraft 'bombing short', something that had happened before and would again, the RAF insisted on a safety margin of 6,000 yards between the target and the British front line. As a result of this a number of villages fortified by the Germans escaped and would cause disruption to any attack on the city. Nevertheless, as far as the Rifles were concerned the enemy was getting a good seeing to and that was all that mattered. Not that the RAF had it all their own way. From their trenches in Brieville the rifleman watched the Lancasters emerge from the pall of smoke rising above the city and make their way back towards the coast. Some aircraft trailed thick plumes of black smoke from damaged wings or fuselages, some fell slowly from the sky plunging into the French countryside between Caen and the coast, while one was seen to explode in an incandescent ball of fire.

Well aware that the German front line would be completely unaffected by the massive bombing raid the powers that be had prepared a tremendous artillery barrage. At 0400hrs on 8 July, 185 Brigade began its advance, huge fountains of earth preceding it as the guns fired in support. Despite all this the opposition was fierce and casualties in the Brigade were considerable so that it was the afternoon, approximately 1430hrs, before the Rifles were able to advance through Lebisey Wood and begin their own advance on

Hill 60. As they lumbered up the hill they were supported by the King's Own Scottish Borderers.

Following in the footsteps of 185 Brigade brought home the horrors of war. This was a recent battlefield and one that the enemy was not going to give up without the sternest resistance. Bodies lay everywhere, the dead, the dying, and in one particular case, the unrecognisable. Lieutenant Cyril Rand leading his platoon forward came across the bodies of two soldiers who had fallen in the path of a tank, the tracks of which had rendered both bodies into nothing more than shredded blood, bone and bits of uniform. There was no shame in the sound of retching that came from at least one of his men. Emerging from the wood the Rifles came under intense mortar, machine-gun and artillery fire as they crossed the open fields to their front.

The tall factory chimneys at Colombelles, still intact, provided the Germans with excellent observation posts for their 88mm guns and rocket batteries. In addition to the dreaded 88mm, 105mm field howitzers were a common feature in German artillery batteries as were Russian pieces of various calibre, captured on the Eastern Front and elsewhere. Previously an attempt by the Northamptonshire Yeomanry had been made to bring the two monster chimneys down, but without success. The 75mm shell of the Shermans simply bounced off the reinforced brickwork and even the shells from the Firefly's 17-pdr did little more than chip the stone.

With the ground bereft of cover there was nothing to do but plod forward, just as they had done at Cambes. By the time the Rifles arrived on their objective, Hill 60, they had lost 85 men killed and wounded. Cyril Rand's platoon had lost eight men, three of whom, all from the same section, practically disappeared when they received a direct hit from an enemy artillery shell. The cry went up for stretcher-bearers, but the Lieutenant realized that there would be little for them to pick up. Despite the intensity of the enemy fire the objective was finally reached and those Germans who remained were swiftly dealt with. The Battalion immediately took up defensive positions, frantically digging in to the soft earth. As this was happening A Company Headquarters received at least two direct hits from enemy artillery. The Company Commander, Major 'Digger' Tighe-Wood, was hit in the left arm by a piece of shrapnel, causing a serious wound and it was obvious that he would have to be evacuated from the field. He therefore turned command over to 'Charlie' Alexander. There was no decrease in the volume of fire and as even stretcher-bearers and medics were becoming casualties, volunteers were called for from the other companies to assist in bringing in the wounded.

This was the day it had been intended to enter Caen, but by the time the Rifles were ready to resume the advance the light was already beginning to fail. Nevertheless, Lieutenant Colonel Harris ordered Major John Hyde to take B Company, supported by two troops of tanks from the Northamptonshire Yeomanry, towards the town to probe the enemy positions.

Despite the cover offered by darkness they came under fire from enemy artillery and casualties were sustained, support from the Shermans being negligible owing to the devastation caused by the Allied bombing. The streets of Caen were denied to the tanks by huge mounds of rubble and deep bomb craters that were quite capable of swallowing a Sherman. Even the infantry found the going well nigh impossible.

As the infantry tried to penetrate the rubble it was quickly discovered that the Germans had left behind mines and booby traps in profusion. One tank of the Yeomanry did its best to assist – Yoke 3 Baker, commanded by Corporal Ken Snowden crunched its way through the streets followed on either flank by the men of B Company. In this case 'street' is a bit of an exaggeration as there were no streets, just mounds of rubble, each one like the last, with no signs or landmarks, just acre upon acre of rubble. As the Sherman clattered forward followed by the riflemen and the remainder of the troop, it suddenly reared up and despite severe braking by the driver dived forward into a bomb crater that swallowed it completely – not so much one bomb crater, but the amalgamation of several bomb craters, a huge excavation, big enough for several tanks.

Efforts to drive out the far side prove fruitless and after a hurried consultation between Corporal Snowden and John Hyde it was decided to try and reverse back out of the hole. As the riflemen hurriedly got out of the way, the Sherman roared into life and belching smoke and the occasional burst of Anglo-Saxon, 30 tons of tank slowly crawled back to the surface with a certain degree of dignity. With daylight fading it was decided to pull back both men and machines and wait for a new day.

Elsewhere in the battalion positions Rifleman Bobby Smyth discovered that being a 'short arse' had its compensations. On guard in a forward slit trench with a fellow Rifleman he was suddenly aware of the air above his head being disrupted by a passing bullet from a machine gun and the next burst set fire to a haystack behind the trench. Using the smoke as cover both riflemen made a hasty retreat to the company lines.

Before dawn on 9 July, two patrols supplied by A Company were sent out to discover the easiest way into the town. The first, under Lieutenant Wise and supported by a troop of tanks, took the road to Calix on the eastern side of the town. The second, under Lieutenant Brian Burges, went to St Julien to the north-west. Lieutenant Wise reached the village of Calix where the riflemen and tanks exchanged fire with enemy snipers and the Lieutenant was wounded in the head by a bullet. The patrol was later recalled.

Lieutenant Burges also reached his objective, but decided as things were going so smoothly to continue to advance into the city. At first all went well with only slight resistance which was quickly brushed aside, but things changed a little later and a burst of fire slightly wounded the Lieutenant and killed two of his NCOs (possibly Lance Corporal George Bradley and Corporal M. O'Beirne). As a result of this the patrol returned to St Julien, dug in for the night and rejoined the Battalion the following day.

This brings us to the question of which was the first unit to get personnel into Caen? In the regimental history Caves says that the Rifles entered the town just before 1100hrs and that Lieutenant Burges and his patrol were therefore the first Allied presence in Caen as liberators. However, surely John Hyde's incursion the previous evening was the first into Caen. Of one thing there can be no doubt – the 2nd Battalion Royal Ulster Rifles was the first unit to establish a headquarters in the city!

At 0930hrs the Rifles advanced into the city with B Company leading the way. Progress was slow, a sharp lookout had to be kept for booby traps and the occasional sniper's bullet caused delay. B Company had four bounds to report as they moved forward, codenamed 'Beer', 'Gin', 'Whisky' and 'Brandy'. As the Company inched its way forward there were repeated calls from Battalion for updates on their location, but as time went by and no 'bounds' were called in these requests took on an air of agitation. Suddenly out of the dust appeared a piece of intact wall with the sign 'Caserne Militaire' affixed. A quick translation – 'Military Barracks' – confirmed that Whisky, the third bound, had been reached, all indication of the others having been obliterated by the bombing and shelling of the previous days!

Casualties so far had been light although D Company had been shelled as it left its positions on Hill 60. Lieutenant Palmer and his Platoon Sergeant had both been hit by shrapnel and evacuated, leaving Sergeant Bonass to lead the Platoon.

Lieutenant Jim Campbell led his men through the rubble. 'It was just like scrambling over the Giant's Causeway.' That RAF bombing had done the Rifles no favours at all! The only troops to benefit from the destruction were the Germans – as at Monte Cassino it was proved that ruins were much easier to defend than intact buildings. While resistance from enemy infantry was deemed to be 'unorganized', it still had to be dealt with. German machine-gun posts would fire a few bursts before retiring, in many cases leaving their weapons behind.

Cyril Rand and D Company had reached an impasse. Artillery and mortars were falling all around and the Company was searching for cover in the rubble. As he lay on the ground he saw about 15 yards ahead some houses that had been hit and their contents blown all over the street. He noticed a round object about the size of a tennis ball glittering in the sunlight. Curiosity reared its head and having nothing else to do but lie and wait he crawled forward to investigate. It was a glass paperweight, not of any particular interest, but as he was about to return it to the rubble a mortar bomb exploded in the position he had just left, killing one man and wounding two more. Needless to say, the paperweight remained with him for the remainder of the war joining two other items Cyril Rand usually carried when he went into combat. The first of these was a small leather-bound bible, a gift from his mother, which he kept in the left-hand pocket of his battledress. The second was a Very pistol, carried in a leather holster worn so as to protect a vital part of his anatomy. While this may have singled him out as an officer to any observant sniper, he reckoned that in a major action he was only one among many and the odds were worth it.

Further into the town it was almost impossible to identify individual roads or streets. The city looked like the surface of the moon, with crumbled buildings, abandoned vehicles that had been tossed about by the bombing laying like broken toys and everything covered in a thick pall of dust. As D company reached the centre of the town there were occasional bouts of resistance, the odd sniper shot or burst from a machine gun. Once they had reached their objective the platoons were allocated defensive positions. It was impossible to dig in in the accepted sense due to the amount of rubble, but that same rubble was used to construct walls and weapon pits. Patrols were sent out to deter bothersome snipers and Cyril Rand accompanied one such patrol. Making their way through a terrace of houses from the inside they came to a closed door, from the far side of which could be heard the sound of voices, although the language was indecipherable. With Sten guns at the ready both Cyril Rand and his Corporal smashed through the door ready for anything, but the 'anything' proved to be an extremely startled French family of four sitting around a battered table. Once the initial surprise on both sides had subsided the liberators were offered refreshment in the shape of a glass of wine. Unfortunately the family did not possess any glasses and instead offered one rather dirty and cracked mug, the only drinking vessel they owned. Despite an initial refusal, the Major took a small sip at their insistence, in exchange handing the family a bar of chocolate – with the Entente Cordiale intact the patrol continued on its way through a hole in the far wall.

Later in the day Lieutenant Cyril Rand returned from a second patrol and was informed that a nearby shop was to be earmarked for Company HQ, but that no one was to enter the premises until the Royal Engineers had checked it for mines and booby traps. When this was done and the building declared safe Lieutenant Rand was relieved to hear it – he had brought his patrol through the same shop some thirty minutes previously.

By 1130hrs, Major Hyde and B Company had reached the Boulevardes des Allies, with the other companies near at hand and in close support. As the riflemen advanced further into the town the civilian population began to emerge from the cellars and soon the advance was transformed into a victory parade. The red, white and blue tricolour began to appear at various windows and soon crowds of French men, women and children were thronging the streets showering the riflemen with greetings and the not so occasional glass of wine.

Contact with the Resistance was made and thankfully with Major de Longueuil a fluent French speaker, relations between the Rifles and the Resistance went smoothly. While there were many who were more recent members of the Resistance, those in Caen had been fighting the Germans for a long time. As word of the invasion reached the city authorities some sixty-seven members of the Resistance held in the prison were cold-bloodedly executed. Those members met by the Ulster Rifles were more than helpful with regard to the location of enemy units, but there were also incidents that left a bad taste as far the riflemen were concerned. As soon as it was obvious that the Germans were gone for good, several members of the Resistance decided to administer justice to those who were known as collaborators, while women who were accused of sleeping with Germans were dragged out into the streets and had their heads shaved.

B Company had by now reached its final objective, Eglise de St Pierre. Here the Company second in command, Captain 'Billy' Baudains MM, went in search of a building for a headquarters. An apartment block, more or less intact, was deemed suitable and Company HQ was established on the ground floor, with the officers quartered on the first. Baudains had been commissioned in the field in 1943 and was proving as efficient an officer as he had been as a NCO. Realizing that a tidy soldier was an efficient soldier, he would often take time even in battle to clean his boots and keep his battledress in good repair. Despite having to make a slit trench his home for many weeks, he would put his trousers under his blanket while sleeping in order to keep them creased. Any man under his command quickly learned that care of weapons came before care of self. Baudains' calmness under fire was an inspiration to all those who served with him.

Later in the afternoon a patrol returned with a soot-stained lady who looked as if she had been 'dragged through a hedge backwards'. She explained that she was the owner of one of the apartments and had been using the cellar as an air-raid shelter. She further explained that if permitted to return to her home, she would in turn act as cook for the officers. It was decided that if anyone could make something that actually tasted nice from compo rations, they should be allowed to do so! When the officers of B Company sat down to dinner that evening it was a pleasant surprise to see that not only was the food tasty, but underneath the soot the hostess was also.

Moving through Caen the riflemen pushed forward until a line had been established along the River Orne, where any remaining resistance was mopped up. With the arrival of the Canadians on the right flank Caen was taken six weeks after it was intended, and which, from the beaches to the capture of the city, had cost the 2nd Battalion 400 casualties. For the next few days the Rifles formed part of the city garrison. In order to prevent looting guards were placed at various locations, one of which was the Church of St Etienne, a stately building that had escaped major damage apart from its imposing spire, now reduced to a blackened stump. Nevertheless, it commanded a vital road junction and was an ideal place to establish a guard post to deter looters. The Rifles provided a guard in the shape of Corporal Jack McMillan from Carrickfergus, Riflemen Stephen Glinchy, a Derry man and Charles Parkin from Lincolnshire. Armed with a Bren gun these three men formed part of a permanent guard until the Rifles moved on a few days later. At that time a friendship between the 2nd Battalion, Royal Ulster Rifles and the people of Caen was forged, a friendship that has lasted to this day.

Operation Goodwood – 'Our deepest tribulation, Troarn'

On 18 July the Rifles were on the move again, marching south a distance of one and a half miles to the village of Le Mesnil and from there a further mile to the east near Sannerville. This march was carried out in weather that had become extremely hot with little or no wind to cool the brow or clear the dust that seemed to be every-where. There were several cases of men fainting from heat exhaustion, but thankfully none were serious and the medical orderlies of the RAMC were able to treat them at the roadside. The issue of boiled sweets did a lot to alleviate thirst as they were more palatable than the tepid contents of water bottles.

At 1700hrs, Colonel Harris received word that 8 Brigade, with the assistance of the tanks of the 13/18 Hussars, had cleared all their objectives. It was now the turn of 9 Brigade and once more the riflemen prepared for action. B Company, led by Major John Hyde, again had the honour of leading the battalion forward, although this 'honour' was not appreciated by some of the rank and file! Support on the right flank was in the shape of the King's Own Scottish Borderers, while on the left were the Shermans of the East Riding Yeomanry; the initial objective was the 'Brickworks', half a mile north-east of Sannerville. The advance led through the village bisected by the Cours de Janville, a narrow stream, but still capable of stopping tanks and other vehicles. The bridge had been destroyed by the retreating Germans and was under fire from their machine guns and mortars. Obstacles such as this could easily be crossed courtesy of the 79th Armoured Division, so a Churchill tank adapted to carry a scissors-bridge was brought up and after a shell crater on the bridge approach had been filled in it quickly laid its metal bridge across the stream. With the bridge in position the riflemen charged across and any local resistance from enemy infantry and machine guns was swiftly dealt with. The enemy mortar teams quickly decamped with their weapons to the next line of resistance.

Then came the Brickworks itself, the Rifles arriving at approximately 1730hrs. While the enemy made initial withdrawals here and there, they did not stay away for long. On cue came accurate German mortar fire, driving the riflemen to cover, causing casualties and allowing the Germans to reoccupy some of their positions. B Company's scout section was caught in the open and its commander, Corporal McCullough, immediately ordered the men into the cover of nearby buildings. One member of the section had been hit and the Corporal remained with him in the open tending his wound until the arrival of stretcher-bearers. Then, between them, the seriously wounded man was carried into the shelter of the buildings.

Further along the street Captain Baudains was hit in the left arm by an enemy machine-gun bullet, but despite this he continued to organize a fire support plan until ordered to retire to the RAP, which he only did under strong protest. Some time later B Company reached its objective and was firmly ensconced at the

Brickworks. They were then relieved by C Company and shortly afterwards Major Hyde led the Company forward again, this time along the track north-east towards the junction with the main road into Troarn, the second of the day's objectives.

As the leading platoon of B Company approached the road junction they spotted two German 75mm guns firing from entrenched positions, but the Platoon was in turn spotted, a curt order was shouted and the guns immediately opened fire, causing casualties to the Platoon before it could find cover. Lieutenant Bobby Lyttle, although out of his own platoon area, immediately gathered together those few men available and organized a flanking attack on the first of the enemy positions. He ordered a Bren gun team consisting of Lance Corporal Sharp, Rifleman Charles and Rifleman McNally to cross the road and provide covering fire for the assault. As the three men made their way into position a fierce stream of enemy fire was directed towards them, but the enemy was shooting high. Once in position, a mere fifty yards from the enemy, the Bren gun team began to try and keep the gunners occupied while Bobby Lyttle with two other Riflemen charged towards the position. The attack was a success with one enemy gunner killed and six captured. Leaving the prisoners with the two riflemen, the Lieutenant immediately ran on towards the second gun position. This crew seeing the fate of their comrades immediately took to their heels with Bobby Lyttle close behind. Their capture was only avoided by the presence of an enemy machine gun firing from a dug-in position which caused the Lieutenant to break off the pursuit. Sten gun versus MG42 was an unequal contest in a fire-fight and Lieutenant Lyttle was forced to withdraw. At the end of the action the prize to the Rifles was six prisoners and two artillery pieces, not a bad few minutes' work.

By nightfall the Rifles had concentrated their companies in and around the road junction and had made contact with the 5th Cameron Highlanders who were to the north on the Escoville–Troarn road. Among the casualties treated in the RAP that day was Rifleman Glinchy, late of the St Etienne guard, hit in the neck by a piece of shrapnel from a German shell.

During the hours of darkness reconnaissance patrols were sent out and one under Lieutenant Purcell of C Company reported enemy activity some 600 yards to the east. There was little rest that night as trenches and gun pits were dug in expectation of the following day's action. During the hours of darkness the Germans also made their preparations as reinforcements consisting of the 3rd Battalion of 731 Grenadier Regiment and a squadron of Tiger tanks moved in alongside the 16 GAF Division, a Luftwaffe ground unit with its headquarters in Lille.

At 0300hrs on 19 July, Lieutenant Colonel Harris held an 'O' Group and informed the assembled officers that the advance towards Troarn would continue. D Company, under the command of Captain Alan 'Dickie' Bird, would lead. The objective was a small wood approximately half a mile down the road towards Troarn and the advance would be made with the support of a troop of Sherman tanks from the East Riding Yeomanry.

The Company moved off at 0630hrs and within a short time the objective had been reached without incident or casualties. As D Company waited for A Company to pass through them towards the next objective, enemy activity was reported from the area of a church on the left flank. It was therefore decided that before any further advance could be made this position would have to be eliminated. The church and a few surrounding houses lay off the main Escoville–Troarn road and could be approached from two directions, one running in an easterly direction and the second from the north-east, both meeting at the church itself. C Company took the first route and within a few hundred yards came under concentrated machine-gun fire. The leading section commanded by Corporal Brown did not hesitate, but charged forward and succeeded in capturing a German machine-gun nest with the bayonet. The result was 7 dead Germans, 13 prisoners and 4 machine guns. This was not the only machine-gun position in the area and lethal fire continued to harass the riflemen, with mortar bombs coming down and adding to the confusion. As the leading platoon came up Lieutenant Cyril Rand was knocked off his feet by a lump of shrapnel that imbedded itself in his left thigh. The weight of machine-gun and mortar fire was now such that C Company could make no further progress along this route.

It was now the turn of Captain 'Charlie' Alexander's A Company to try the second route. As the leading platoon made its way up the road using both sides for what little cover was available, it suddenly came under a hail of machine-gun fire at a range of some 30 yards, which immediately brought down four men. From their position on the road the tanks were unable to bring fire to bear. The Platoon Commander, Sergeant Sharkey, moved forward and with what can only be described as 'dash and elan' assaulted the machine-gun position, spraying it with rounds from his Sten gun. For once the weapon did not fail and in a few seconds the crew had been killed. This proved too much for the other enemy in the vicinity and they promptly withdrew. As the Germans fell back A Company and their supporting tanks followed up. The riflemen and the Shermans poured both small-arms fire and high-explosive shells into the enemy causing considerable casualties. Two enemy machine-gun teams were spotted running into a nearby barn, but several shells from the Shermans quickly set it on fire before any resistance could be offered. No one was seen to emerge from the burning building.

Such was the heat from the burning barn that the leading elements of the company were forced to withdraw 50 yards. The entire Company then withdrew and as usual the Germans returned to their original positions.

While attempting to determine in what strength the Germans now held the position around the church, an officer from the Yeomanry made a reconnaissance on foot, but a shot rang out and the officer was seen to fall. Lieutenant Brian Burges led his platoon forward in an attempt to recover him, but the Germans were waiting. As the riflemen approached the wounded tank officer they came under vicious machine-gun fire. Brian Burges fell with a fatal gunshot wound to the side, while six other members of his platoon were wounded, including Rifleman Johns with a gunshot wound to the jaw and Rifleman Donnelly who was shot in the left leg.

Despite all this A Company eventually made it to its original objective, a road junction some 800 yards out of the village, where an enemy anti-tank gun scored a hit on one of the supporting Shermans and knocked it out. As the crew bailed out of the burning tank and made for cover a machine-gun bullet in the thigh felled Trooper Brown. At once stretcher-bearers went out and he was safely delivered to the care of the Rifles' RAP.

The leading platoon, which happened to be Sergeant Sharkey's, put in a flanking attack on the position, but as the men moved forward they came under machine-gun fire. Sergeant Sharkey once more dashed forward and again the Sten gun did not let him down.

Several of the machine gun's crew were killed and ten prisoners were taken.

With the onset of darkness Lieutenant Colonel Harris ordered A Company back from the road junction in order to present a more compact Battalion position for the night. A standing patrol was established at the road junction, but had to be withdrawn as dawn broke due to pressure from the enemy who clearly wanted it back. Once again the St Etienne guard had suffered, and Rifleman Charles Parkin, who had travelled from the flat fields of Lincolnshire to the soil of France, was one of those killed.

20 July dawned with reasonably fine weather and it quickly became obvious from the initial reconnaissance carried out in the early morning that the Germans were not going to go quietly. The roar of Maybach engines and the scream of shells exploding in the Rifles' positions confirmed the presence of enemy tanks. Shells from the Rifles' own anti-tank guns and the M10 self-propelled guns of 20 Anti-tank Regiment, which was in support, promptly replied. The fighting continued throughout the day and casualties were heavy so that all over the battlefield the cry for stretcher-bearers was heard. In A Company Rifleman Avery and Sergeant Creaney were two of many wounded by the deadly rain of hot steel. Riflemen Tommy Keys from Belfast and George Martin from Soldierstown, County Antrim were two of those killed when German tanks appeared on A Company's front. In Support Company Sergeant Tom Corbett from Birmingham received multiple shrapnel wounds as the shelling continued. A direct hit killed Rifleman Billy Green in C Company and he was buried where he fell. In 20 Anti-tank Regiment the casualties were mounting at an alarming rate and many men were brought into the Rifles' RAP, Gunners Curle and Jones being two of several men suffering from the deadly effects of shrapnel. Through all this the imposing figure of RSM Fleming moved from place to place. With complete disregard for his own safety he organized the removal of the wounded to the RAP, the reinforcement of a part of the line weakened by casualties and the ample supply of ammunition where it was needed.

24 July was another day of near continuous shelling, heavy calibre stuff that even if it fell close to a slit trench could bury men alive. On several occasions Sam Fleming was on hand to help dig

these men out before they suffocated. The capture of the road junction was now the responsibility of a unit a bit bigger than the 2nd Battalion Royal Ulster Rifles. In fact the Rifles were not to be used in the next attack on Troarn. Their casualties in the action had cost them four officers and ninety-eight other ranks. Despite not being able to achieve their final objective they had performed well. Lieutenant Lyttle was awarded the Military Cross, the redoubtable Sergeant Sharkey the Distinguished Conduct Medal, and both Riflemen Charles and Reid the Military Medal.

On 30 July the Rifles were withdrawn from their positions at Troarn, being replaced by the 4th Battalion, Lincolnshire Regiment from the 49th Division.

August

Since D-Day the Battalion had been in almost daily contact with the enemy, with only brief spells out of the line. The Battalion was to be relocated at Cazelle where they were promised a full week out of the line for rest and recreation. But this was not to be. Both British and American forces made what can only be described as impressive advances and the 3rd Division was on the move again. Relieved of their task of guarding the bridgehead across the Orne, the Ironsides were detailed to act as a 'follow-up' division to the armoured spearheads racing across France.

On 3 August the Rifles found themselves in the town of Bieville, where two precious days were spent resting and generally getting both kit and weapons back into good condition. Since landing in France all moves had been achieved by marching, so it was a pleasant surprise to be loaded onto trucks for the next stage of the journey to the small village of Granville, some 10 miles north-east of Villers Bocage. This was a short stop, but at least a quiet night was enjoyed by all.

The following day they set off again, a journey of 30 miles to a hamlet a mile beyond St Martin des Besaces. Here C Company lost a man when a Crusader AA tank of 92 Light Anti-aircraft Regiment ran over a landmine. While the crew of the vehicle escaped injury, Rifleman Tom Williamson from Lisburn, County Antrim, who had been standing by the side of the road, was killed. This incident served as a grim reminder that even in what could be considered a safe area extreme vigilance was necessary at all times.

On 5 August, despite persistent shelling the Rifles suffered no casualties, although other battalions were not so lucky. Nevertheless, the RAP post was kept busy as even in war men become ill or have accidents. Rifleman Conboy complained of a sore throat and was discovered to have tonsillitis; Rifleman Cullen was treated for synovitis of the knee; while Rifleman Stevens had diarrhoea. Rifleman Wilkes lacerated his eye on a tree branch while moving about the Company area in the dark.

The following day, Sunday, the Rifles were not to be so lucky. While at the village of Vire/Montisanger, a barrage of enemy shelling that lasted no more than two minutes fell in the area. The result was that Company Sergeant Major McCutcheon, who had commanded the Mortar Platoon since D-Day, received shrapnel to his hand and shoulder. Sergeant Hodgkinson of the Intelligence Platoon was hit in the back, while Sergeant Pancott was hit in the leg. It was not a good day for NCOs and the riflemen fared little better; Patrick McGrory and Rifleman McNally were both admitted to the RAP with shrapnel wounds and later evacuated to hospital in England. Despite this being one of the most fearsome battlefields of the War, the more mundane ailments had to be seen to. When the seriously wounded had been taken care of, Rifleman Nelson was treated for impetigo, while Rifleman Williams had his boils lanced!

On Monday, 8 August Lieutenant Colonel Harris was ordered to lead his battalion against the village of Vaudry, situated to the east of the River Vire, the following day. This date bore some significance to the riflemen – on 9 June they had captured Cambes, on 9 July they had taken Hill 60 and entered Caen. It was about this time that Major Norman Wheeler joined the Rifles fresh from his adventures with Brigadier 'Trotsky' Davies in Albania.

As usual a reconnaissance was carried out by Lieutenant Colonel Harris and other officers of the Battalion along with those of the supporting arms. The plan was to advance on the village, capture it, pass through and consolidate on the Vire–Vassy road beyond. In conjunction with this, the King's Own Scottish Borderers would attack the high ground on the right flank of the objective. That night the Rifles moved to their assembly area at La Gallonerie where weapons were made ready, maps consulted and prayers said.

The night passed without incident and at 0600hrs the Rifles moved forward but the usual reception was not forthcoming – no machine guns, no mortars, just silence. A single explosion was the first resistance encountered and both Corporal Randall and Rifleman Foster of D Company went down with multiple shrapnel wounds to the legs. Everyone froze immediately as the word was passed around – minefield! As the stretcher-bearers arrived and carefully removed the wounded men to the rear the Pioneer Platoon led by Lieutenant Shimmin moved forward to lead the way. They carefully swept the ground with their mine detectors and eventually a lane was cleared towards the objective. The first men into the village were Captains Gaffikin and Gray, who had in turn been reconnoitring for the Pioneers.

By the end of the day casualties had been light. Apart from the men wounded by landmines several others had suffered gunshot wounds, including Rifleman Johnston of D Company, who was unlucky enough to be hit in the right leg by a burst of long-range machine-gun fire.

On the morning of 12 August, RSM Sam Fleming fell victim to random enemy shelling. His was a serious wound and required evacuation to England. In the same incident Rifleman Stanley Burrows from the Castlereagh Road, Belfast received injuries to his stomach and chest.

Two days later a member of B Company came to Major Hyde and informed him that an 'intact' Tiger had been discovered in the woods at Fleur. On examination the Tiger was indeed intact, possibly abandoned by its crew when the vehicle ran out of fuel. Major Hyde decided that this was an ideal opportunity to test the effectiveness of the PIAT against German armour, especially the much-vaunted Tiger.

The PIAT (Projectile Infantry Anti-tank) was the British infantryman's main defence against enemy armoured vehicles. It was a shoulder-fired, spring-loaded launcher that fired a 2lb bomb to a range of 50 yards. While of shorter range than the American bazooka or German Panzerfaust (Armoured Fist) its operation meant that there was no tell-tale flash when it was fired. Nevertheless, it was heavy and awkward to carry. In one case a weary, footsore Rifleman was seen struggling with the weapon while marching down a lane in Normandy. On seeing this, the platoon officer suggested he 'sling the weapon', and it was promptly discarded over the nearest wall!

Bringing three weapons to the wood they were set up within 50 yards of the tank and were made ready to fire. The principle of firing a PIAT was to 'aim', 'fire' and 'duck', as it was a well-known fact that the base plug of the bomb came straight back at the operator when it exploded! The PIAT crew duly took up a prone position behind a fallen tree trunk and fired at the tank, ducking down immediately. Wanting to see the effect of the strike of the bombs, Major Hyde was peering from behind the cover of his own fallen tree, but failed to take heed of Part 3 of the said rule. The result of this was that he was hit by the base plug in the chest and for him the War was over!

On 20 August the Rifles were informed that for the next week they would be in near constant training for an imminent assault crossing of a major river, accompanied by tanks. This was duly carried out, mostly in atrocious weather, the tanks coming from the 4th Grenadier Guards of 6th Guards Tank Brigade. The weather continued to be cold and wet, but at least there was the opportunity for a hot bath and the food was usually both on time and warm.

Operation Market Garden – The Right Flank

The Rifles arrived in Hacqueville, a small village some 8 miles to the east of Les Andelys-sur-Seine, on 3 September after an uncomfortable journey of 150 miles. All available transport had been centralized, with first call going to XXX Corps in preparation for its push up the 'airborne corridor' to Arnhem. As a consequence of this there were no troop-carrying vehicles available and the journey was made in basic 3-ton lorries, using compo boxes as seats. With the shortage of vehicles the men were packed in like sardines and were it not for frequent halts for calls of nature and the consumption of tea, things would have been much worse. It was something of a liberty to be told to sit to attention when passing through the various towns and villages 'in order to set a good example' to the natives. When the Rifles had settled into their billets a full training programme was implemented as a large number of reinforcements had been assimilated into the Battalion since the battles at Caen and Troarn and now it was time to bring everyone up to the same standard. Men had to be taught to operate as a section, platoon, company and battalion in order to recreate the machine that had performed so well since landing on D-Day.

On the morning of 16 September the Rifles again packed their belongings and piled aboard the trucks that would take them towards their next objective, the Escaut Canal, a drive of some 230 miles. The journey to the Canal brought back memories to many of the old soldiers and served as a history lesson to those who were of a younger generation. Names such as Amiens, Albert, Bapaume, Flesquières, Moeuvres, Cambrai, Valenciennes and Mons stirred emotions of the battlefields of the First World War, few of them pleasant.

At Louvain those veterans of the 1940 campaign recalled more recent battlefields and younger soldiers listened in awe to tales both tall and colourful. A party paid a short visit to Lezennes where they had spent nine months in 1939–40 and received a riotous welcome.

The Rifles arrived in Belgium at the village of Petit Brogel on the southern side of the Escaut Canal in the afternoon of 17 September. The men were tired for again it had been a tedious journey crammed into the back of the 3-tonners with nothing to sit on but the ubiquitous compo boxes. The Rifles were informed of their next task, an assault crossing of the Escaut Canal to broaden the bridge-head made by the 50th Division some 4 miles to the west.

At 0900hrs on 18 September Lieutenant Colonel Harris briefed his officers with regard to the forthcoming crossing. As part of General Richard O'Connor's VIII Corps, the 3rd Division, under General 'Bodo' Whistler was to cross the Escaut Canal at Lille Saint Hubert.* Here they would form a bridgehead and then advance to protect the right flank of the 'armoured spearhead' that was XXX Corps thrusting from the Dutch-Belgian border to the town of Arnhem, the prize of Operation Market Garden.

Supporting the 3rd Division was the 11th Armoured Division and 9 Brigade was elected to lead the assault across the 40-yard wide Canal. The Rifles were to be on the left flank of the original

* Modern spelling St Huybrechts Lille

road-bridge, the Lincolns on the right, with the King's Own Scottish Borderers held in reserve. The crossing would be made in assault-boats, with the KOSBs lending assistance in carrying the boats from the dropping off point to the south of the village. Once the infantry had established a foothold the Engineers would construct a Class 9 Bailey Bridge and later a Class 40 Bridge to carry the tanks of the 11th Armoured Division. The assault was to begin at midnight, after a reconnaissance had been carried out. Within the Rifles this was done in two ways. Whereas the enemy and a limited view of the Canal could be seen from the church tower in the village, the actual crossing point could not be observed due to intervening trees and buildings.

On the left flank, Lieutenant Firth led a small patrol from C Company down towards the bank. Crawling to within a few yards of the Canal the patrol discovered that between the towpath and the Canal was a ditch some six feet wide and ten deep, which was in turn half full of water. This would have to be crossed before any attempt was made to launch assault boats into the Canal proper. To the east of the Rifles' position another reconnaissance was undertaken. This time Captains Gaffikin and Baudains, dressed in 'borrowed' civilian clothes, boldly walked along the Canal bank in full view of any watching enemy. On their return the map was studied and a crossing place selected.

While this was going on all the officers had climbed the sixty-eight steps to the top of the church tower and made their own observations of the ground and buildings on the far bank. At 1630hrs Colonel Harris gave his final briefing and orders. Zero hour was to be midnight. The crossing was to be made in assault boats; each company was to have the use of seven with a further two held in reserve at the launching point and six at the off-loading point. The Pioneer Platoon would construct a Class V Raft and this would be used to ferry across the Battalion's jeeps and anti-tank guns.

The artillery of three divisions would support the attack and would bombard selected targets from H-hour minus 15 minutes until H-hour plus 15 minutes. After this they would be on call as required. A company of Sappers would be attached for the purpose of clearing any mines, preparing the northern bank to receive the Class 9 Bridge and in the construction of the bridge. They would also assist the Pioneer Platoon in the construction of the raft. The KOSBs would provide two officers and forty-eight other ranks to assist in carrying the assault boats to the Canal and then crewing them for the crossing.

At 2100hrs a final briefing was held at Brigade Headquarters. Lieutenant Colonel Harris then went down to Battalion HQ, situated in a house some 200 yards from the canal bank and ensured that all communications were in place and working. These consisted of a wireless link to Brigade via a 22 Set in Battalion HQ with a duplicate set situated 200 yards to the flank manned by Captain Perona-Wright, who also had a landline to Battalion HQ. Contact from Battalion HQ to the various companies was via 18 sets and to the crossing points via a landline.

By 2200hrs the assault companies, B and C, were in position, with A and D Companies in reserve. At 2315hrs the Rifles were ready to go, but where were the boats? Major Wheeler commanding Support Company was waiting patiently at the rendezvous point, but the Sapper NCO was nowhere to be seen. As the minutes ticked by the feeling of frustration rose. The men were ready, the artillery was ready but its fire plan would not wait. At last the boats arrived so without waiting for the carrying parties the men of the assault companies carried their own boats towards the Canal with more enthusiasm than skill and Rifleman Fred Anderson had to be taken to the RAP with a badly bruised back. Willing hands from the Pioneer Platoon also assisted and soon the boats arrived at the ditch before the towpath, where a halt was called. Here the boats were made ready for the crossing. This required them to be laid flat, the sides raised and wooden struts inserted to ensure the craft stayed rigid. At this point the British artillery began its bombardment of the German positions on the northern side of the Canal. Almost immediately German counter-fire landed among the assembled troops. This was mostly mortar fire, both plentiful and accurate, with Lance Corporal Farrell suffering a lacerated head from shrapnel. As the men assembling the boats went to ground Rifleman Green of B Company was seen ignoring the explosions and continuing with his work. This proved an inspiration to others and soon the assembly was again in progress.

The boats were now ready and with a rush they were carried

down into the ditch in front of the Canal, through the water lying in the bottom and up the other side. With much swearing, sweating and other cries of encouragement they were dragged up the 15-foot incline at an angle of almost 45 degrees, through thick scrub and plentiful nettle clumps. All credit must go to Lieutenants O'Neill, Barker and CSM Lutton, who led both vocally and by example. Once on to the towpath they splashed into the Canal to be swiftly rowed across the 100-yard stretch of water. Despite the darkness a straight course was held by B Company boats as Captain Gaffikin had taken a compass bearing from the launch point towards his Company objective. The riflemen were also assisted by the provision of 'Monty's Moonlight' – artificial light created by illuminating the clouds with powerful searchlights mounted on converted tanks.

To the left of the crossing point the men came under fire from German mortars and it was proving difficult to load the boats. In C Company's area Major de Longueuil took personal command of the loading and with sheer willpower saw to it that the boats got away. Despite planning to cross with his headquarters on the second wave, he decided to cross with the first and his presence did much to steady the men. Once in the water little opposition was met, save the occasional burst of machine-gun fire which did no damage. Landing on the enemy bank, C Company moved forward to their intended objective without meeting any resistance and soon had established a bridgehead some 500 yards deep. Shortly after reporting to Battalion HQ that they were in position, a runner arrived to say that enemy activity had been observed on the left flank and almost immediately the ripping sound of a German MG42 came from the woods 100 yards to the left as enemy infantry were seen forming up for an attack. Lieutenant Colonel Harris had been aware of the danger of this flank from the beginning of the operation and had detached two dismounted sections of the Carrier Platoon to bolster C Company. Despite this added firepower the German infantry penetrated the Company position making it all the way to Company Headquarters, where in the confused fighting Captain Leslie Laving, the second in command, was killed. For a brief time it looked as if the Headquarters would be overrun, but Major de Longueuil quickly rallied as many men as were available and a swift counter-attack forced the Germans back to the woods.

The enemy left behind two dead and many wounded were observed being carried away. An immediate wireless message to Battalion HQ updating them on the situation and requesting reinforcements brought D Company swiftly across the Canal. D Company dug in for the remainder of the night and would continue to its original objective as dawn broke.

On the right flank B Company was fighting its own battle. Having crossed the Canal without incident they advanced to their first objective, a pathway 200 yards from the Canal bank. Despite sporadic machine-gun fire and mortaring no casualties were sustained and within a few minutes the advance continued, still following Captain Gaffikin's compass bearing. The second objective, a point on the main road just north of the village, was reached without incident. Here the Company dug in and reconnaissance patrols were sent along the main road to the north as far as the railway line and to the south towards the village. Both patrols quickly returned and reported some enemy activity at the level crossing, with more in the village. The enemy in the village were clearly oblivious of B Company's presence as a party of German medical orderlies in the process of evacuating a number of casualties towards the railway was intercepted and captured, much to their surprise.

When contact was made between B Company and Battalion Headquarters Captain Gaffikin reported that he was perfectly willing to enter the village and clear out the enemy, but felt that he should have a firm base to operate from in case of an enemy attack from the direction of the railway. As a result of this the CO sent forward A Company under the command of Major Sweeny and informed Captain Gaffikin that on his arrival the decision was to be made as to which Company was best placed to enter the village.

At 0345hrs, A Company successfully crossed the Canal without incident and was met by two riflemen from B Company, who led them into B Company area. While the two commanders discussed the situation it became evident that as B Company was already established, Major Sweeny's men would have the honour of assaulting the village. As the Company made its way southwards into the village the leading platoon under Lieutenant Betty flushed out a party of five German soldiers occupying a drainage ditch to the side of the road, who promptly surrendered. Approaching the first house they were met with sporadic fire. Lieutenant Betty gave the order and the swift return of rifle and Bren gun fire ensured another expeditious surrender of the occupants and ten more prisoners were added to the night's bag.

Daybreak was shrouded by a thick blanket of early morning mist and as the riflemen continued with their advance the sound of horses' hooves was heard approaching from the village. Out of the gloom came two heavily laden farm carts crewed by a motley collection of Germans armed with a less than motley collection of weapons. A quick glance showed machine pistols, light machine guns, Panzerfausts and Panzerschrecks, while the clink of glass on glass betrayed the presence of something other than military hardware. Again the presence of the Rifles was unknown to the enemy. As the ambush was sprung the Germans leapt from the carts with surprising agility and within a few seconds had their weapons in action and were returning a steady fire. This resistance did not last long. Sergeant Peel led a section in a flank attack and with a few well-placed hand grenades the battle was quickly over. Several more prisoners were added to the bag.

Further resistance came from the next objective, another house, but again well-directed Bren gun fire induced surrender and another five enemy were taken prisoner, among whom was a member of the Royal Engineers who had been captured the previous night while on a reconnaissance. This was the last piece of resistance and soon the Company had reached the Canal and declared it free of enemy. On returning to the north of the village Major Sweeny received new orders from Lieutenant Colonel Harris to reinforce the still exposed left flank. He therefore led his Company to a position between C Company in the centre of the woods and the north bank of the Canal. D Company was to the north of C Company in the area of the railway. During this move A Company came under enemy machine-gun fire and a bullet wound to the head killed Lieutenant Morgan.

On the Canal the bridging operation was in full swing without interruption. The Battalion jeeps were ferried across the Canal along with the 6-pdr anti-tank guns at 0900hrs on 19 September. The guns were all in position by 0930hrs, a section being deployed with C, B and D Companies. By now the Class 9 Bridge was in operation and the Battalion Bren carriers also crossed. By 1000hrs the Rifles were as prepared as possible for any attack. The night's action had netted them 44 prisoners, 4 enemy killed, a small calibre anti-tank gun, 12 machine guns, 8 mortars, some 50mm mortars, a collection of anti-tank weapons and a large number of machine pistols, rifles and ammunition. Against this the Rifles had lost three men killed – Captain Laving, Lieutenant Morgan and Corporal Henry Steadman. A further thirteen men were wounded.

On the right flank of the Rifles the Lincolns did not have such an easy time and heavy casualties were sustained.

Unlike the experiences of 1st Airborne Division fighting in and around the suburbs of Arnhem to the north, communications within the 3rd Division and particularly within the Rifles worked extremely well. Throughout the battle Battalion Headquarters, situated on the south bank, was able to maintain contact with all units on the northern side.

Major de Longueuil received a well-deserved MC for his skillful handling of C Company, whose actions did much to ensure a successful outcome to the crossing. Rifleman Green's behaviour during the assembling of the assault boats merited a Military Medal.

With fierce fighting taking place on the north bank of the Canal and the Class 40 Bridge still not complete, General O'Connor decided to attempt to send reinforcements via the newly captured 'Joe's Bridge' at the Grote Barrier. At once C Squadron, Inns of Court Regiment, 2nd Fife and Forfar Yeomanry and the 1st Herefords moved to the left along the Canal towards the bridge.

With permission from XXX Corps granted the three armoured units crossed the Canal at 'Joe's Bridge' at 1430hrs and advanced some 8 kilometres before making a right turn towards the 3rd Division, although this move had to be abandoned when it was found that the Germans had blown the bridge between the villages of Borkel and Schaft. There was no alternative but to continue along with the vehicles of XXX Corps towards Valkenswaard, arriving at 1900hrs. Meanwhile back at Lille Saint Hubert the Class 40 had been completed at 1930hrs and the attack was ordered for the following day.

At 0900hrs on 20 September, the 11th Armoured Division attacked across the Canal, while 29th Armoured Brigade attacked from Valkenswaard and the village of Leende was successfully taken at 1300hrs.

The Rifles advanced as part of the 3rd Division and by the end of September were situated in the village of Cuyk, some 5 miles from the German border. The major obstacle between them and Germany was the Meuse, but before that river could be crossed there was another battle to fight – the worst was yet to come!

The 3rd British Infantry Division was tasked with the eradication of enemy resistance in the area of Overloon, Venray and Venlo, resistance that was described at the various briefings as a 'pocket' – it was to be a very deep pocket indeed!

'Now is the winter of our discontent'

By the beginning of October the glorious summer had well and truly come to an end and one of the fiercest winters for a long time was beginning across all of Europe. On 12 October 9 Brigade moved to St Anthonis, a village 10 miles south of Cuyk, where they were briefed for the attack. 8 Brigade advancing and capturing Overloon would open the assault, 9 Brigade would clear the woods to the south and west of the town, while 185 Brigade passed through 8 Brigade and captured Venray.

At 0900hrs on 13 October Major Charles Sweeny led his A Company towards their objective. Heavy enemy mortaring and shelling fell, mostly on the Overloon–Oploo road. In order to lessen the chance of sustaining casualties Major Sweeny kept his Company well to the north of the road. Once they reached the north of the wood they crossed to the left in order to meet a company of the South Lancashire Regiment who were supposed to be on the northern edge of the wood. No Lancashires were found and A Company continued on to occupy its objective. Following up on A Company was D Company led by Major Bird; they successfully passed through A Company positions, but soon ran into difficulties. Not only were the Germans going to be troublesome, nature was now on the side of the enemy.

The woods were difficult in the extreme, one minute almost impenetrable, the next the riflemen found themselves stumbling out into small glades and clearings bereft of any cover, with the exception of ankle-deep leaves and discarded German equipment, evidence of a hasty retreat. Not all the enemy had left. There was the crack of a sniper's rifle and Sergeant Cochrane of B Company was brought down with a bullet in his left foot. A few seconds later Rifleman Pickavant, also of B Company, was shot in the chest and Rifleman Johnston of D company was hit in the stomach. The clearing out of these snipers was both dangerous and tedious, but some men excelled at it. Sergeant Schofield led his Platoon towards one suspected position and with a short burst from his Sten gun produced a German corporal only too ready to surrender. Three more surrendered to the Platoon in short order, while several more were seen to flee towards the enemy lines.

As the Battalion moved south the woods took on a more orderly appearance, although medium-sized pine trees and a thick blanket of undergrowth made the going difficult in the extreme – jungle warfare without the heat. An added difficulty was that the enemy was using a number of captured weapons and this made locating them that much harder. Was the burst of Bren gun fire to your flank being fired in support or against you? Several tracks meandered through the wood, adequate for infantry, but useless for vehicles due to the very soft going and the constant danger from landmines. Added to this was the fact that neither wood nor tracks bore any resemblance to the maps supplied. Even when a revised trace from a recent air photograph was used it was still hard to find one's way.

As a result of this progress was slow and it was some time before D Company could report its objective, approximately halfway through the wood, secure. This advance had been subject to enemy mortaring and Lieutenant Curran had been severely wounded by shrapnel in the head and neck. Just as the Company reached its objective the mortaring slackened off, but not before one of the last shells hit Rifleman Guy, killing him instantly. In return D Company had a confirmed kill of one enemy and had taken six prisoners. Having met no opposition of any strength, Lieutenant Colonel Harris ordered D Company to continue their advance towards the final objective, while C Company, under Major de Longueuil would take over their position in the wood. This went ahead without incident and soon D Company was digging in on the left-hand forward edge of the wood.

Captain Gaffikin led B Company towards the right-hand corner of the wood at 1400hrs, passing through both A and C Companies without incident. He then contacted Major Bird at D Company to ascertain the situation to the front. With no sign of enemy A Company resumed its advance through the wood but on reaching a small clearing the Company came under attack from small arms and Panzerfausts. The leading platoon instantly deployed to meet this threat, but before the manoeuvre could be completed the enemy had withdrawn at a rapid rate.

While the Company again prepared to advance the sound of tanks was heard and two Mk IVs were observed crossing the Company front in a south-easterly direction. The anti-tank teams were brought forward, but found that they were out of PIAT range. Captain Baudains, second in command, used his skill with the .303 to keep the tank commanders' heads down. Whereas rifle bullets will do no damage whatsoever to the 90mm armour on a Mk IV, the effect on hitting a human skull is obviously quite different, a fact well known to all tank commanders. With the smack of the bullets hitting the turrets, hatches were slammed shut instantly, thereby greatly restricting their visibility. As a result the Germans had no idea where the fire was coming from and were forced to withdraw.

The RAP was kept busy with Rifleman Clayton of B Company being one of several men to be treated for exhaustion. As the Battalion settled in for the night there was a problem in bringing up much-needed supplies of ammunition, water and food. Because of the state of the sandy tracks and the fact that they had not been swept for mines, no vehicles could use them and all supplies had to be manhandled forward. This work had to be carried out by men whose day had begun at 0300hrs that morning.

The Lincolns passed through the Rifles' positions on 14 October and attacked wood 'Y' as German mortars and artillery fell with monotonous regularity and casualties mounted. A salvo from a Nebelwerfer fell on the headquarters of the Anti-tank Platoon, wounding Captain Gray, the OC, and mortally wounding Lieutenant Rapkins, the second in command. Shrapnel to the chest killed Rifleman Kenneth Erskine, who was twenty-two years old and recently married to Agnes. In A Company shrapnel wounded Corporal Biggs in the buttocks as he lay in the open, while Rifleman Crawford was hit in the chest and in C Company Rifleman Roberts was hit in the face.

Due to the continued difficulty in bringing up supplies, the forward companies took turns in going to the rear behind Battalion Headquarters to eat their food. This was deemed more sensible than totally exhausting already tired men by carrying the food forward.

During the hours of darkness a bulldozer was brought up and working almost non-stop managed to clear a passage through to the southern end of the wood, although it was still not possible to reach either B or D Companies with a wheeled vehicle.

On 16 October, the CO received orders that the Rifles, along with the remainder of 9 Brigade, were to relieve a unit of the 11th Armoured Division. Once in position they were to act as a block against any enemy counter-attack towards Overloon, while the remainder of the 3rd Division attacked towards Venray. In order to effect this relief the Brigade was forced to carry out a route march of some 4 miles – in peacetime conditions no more than a stroll, but for tired men, along tracks that had been waterlogged by incessant rain and churned to liquid mud by various tracked vehicles, it was real hardship. An advance of one thousand yards per day was considered good going.

For the remainder of the month the Rifles had a comparatively quiet time. The enemy was loath to come to grips at short range and contented themselves with shelling and mortaring on a daily basis, this becoming increasingly heavy between 1700hrs and 2100hrs. Thankfully the Riflemen suffered few casualties due to being well dug in and with their trenches having ample overhead cover.

Most infantry regarded the Nebelwerfer as a dreadful weapon due to the horrendous noise its rockets made in flight. More commonly known as the 'Moanin' Minnie', many men said it was the noise more than the explosive effect that caused the problems. The Rifles took a more pragmatic view. According to Rifleman Bobby Smyth the noise told you that the rockets were on their way and it was time to lie down. Also, as the rockets were launched from a circular mount, they were inclined to fall in the same pattern, so, if you were either inside or outside this pattern you were relatively safe. That was the theory anyway.

The Rifles moved to the village of Veulen a mile south of Venray on 1 November. Here they spent some time waiting to see the outcome of the Allied offensive further to the south. One afternoon a recent reinforcement arrived in the Signal Platoon with a wooden box under his arm, which he had recovered from the ruins of a nearby house. Asking other members of the Platoon if it might contain anything valuable he was quickly told to take it away, carefully. The wooden box turned out to be a German schu mine. Mines and booby traps were a constant worry, both in open fields and in ruined towns, the schu mine being especially difficult to deal with. Its wooden construction meant it was practically impossible to be found by mine detectors of the Royal Engineers and the first indication of their presence was usually when someone or something got blown up.

While the Battalion was receiving reinforcements in adequate numbers, there was a continuing problem. Since the initial losses in Normandy riflemen had gained experience on a daily basis, but this had been traded off against the fatigue of combat and the near constant draw on reserves of courage. Reinforcements reaching the Battalion had freshness and courage as yet untested, but lacked experience. The secret was to keep them alive long enough to gain the experience that would turn them into good soldiers. Morale had suffered on certain occasions, especially during the month of August, and there had been several reports of self-inflicted gunshot wounds, and even some cases of shell shock. The Rifles were not alone in this and other battalions suffered to the same extent. Thankfully the treatment of such cases had improved since 1914–18.

It was now the turn of the Rifles to attack. On advancing it was found that the enemy had gone, leaving behind a series of road-blocks, minefields and booby traps. These combined with the weather conditions, mud, rain and fog, ensured that any pursuit was difficult in the extreme. The system of leapfrogging by battalion was carried out, but no contact was made with the enemy.

The Rifles were ordered to relieve part of the 15th (Scottish) Division who had driven up from Horst through Teinray to Blitterswijk and this was carried out on 26 November.

Blitzwick

The Rifles moved into the area Blitterswijk–Mierlo on 27 November, A and D Companies being positioned in Blitterswijk,

B Company in Megelsum and C Company in Meerlo. The weather was described as 'fine but cold' and there was some enemy shelling, Battalion Headquarters being hit between 2300hrs and 2345hrs, resulting in four casualties. B Company was also hit with the destruction of a 15cwt truck and two men wounded, although the War Diary does not record their names or the nature of their wounds.

On arriving, Lieutenant Colonel Harris was informed that all was not as it should be and a considerable number of enemy still remained on the Allied side of the 'canal' in the area of Wanssum. It was to be the job of the Rifles to clear out this 'pocket' of enemy, thereby ensuring a straight line on the east bank of the Meuse.

The German position was well defined – a single coil of barbed wire running from the canal across the Helling–Mierlo road 700 to 800 yards south of Helling. From here it swung away to the north-east towards Blitterswijk, crossing the Wanssum–Blitterswijk road half a mile west of Blitterswijk, before carrying on to the north to the Meuse. While the wire would prove little in the way of a barrier, it was known that it was well protected with mines and booby traps. The following days were spent in reconnaissance and preparation for the attack.

At 0500hrs on the morning of 30 November, C Company, along with the Pioneer Platoon, moved out from its positions and advanced towards the wire. Leading the Company was Major Edward Murphy, going into action for the first time with the Rifles. He had recently arrived in the Battalion from a staff appointment at Second Army Headquarters and was as fearful of letting the men down as he was of the enemy.

As the Company closed with the wire Lieutenant Shimmin and his pioneers cut the wire, disarming those mines and booby traps necessary to create a viable breach. The leading platoon made its way through the gap and advanced up the road towards Helling, closely followed by the Pioneer Platoon. For the time being Major Murphy held the remainder of the Company at the wire. This was not a good night for an attack as not only was the air clear, carrying sounds easily across the flat, open countryside, but a fair wind kept the clouds moving across the sky allowing a full moon to break through, lighting up the area like a searchlight. Those present reckoned that visibility was about 150 yards.

The vanguard platoon, under the command of Sergeant Hammersley, approached some houses to the south of the village and found them clear of enemy. As they moved on the silence was broken by the now familiar sound of MG42s firing across the open fields. Sergeant Hammersley's men and the Pioneers were caught in a crossfire. From the village directly ahead bullets spewed out of a downstairs window, while from an orchard on the left flank tracer bounced and whirled towards the now prone riflemen. The Platoon was pinned to the ground, and efforts to either advance or retreat resulted in men being hit.

Major Murphy, watching from the wire, decided to commit a second platoon in a left-flanking attack, sending them along the bank of the canal. As this platoon drew level with the leading platoon it in turn came under fire from two machine guns situated on the western side of the orchard. The Germans had the ground well and truly covered by interlocking arcs of fire.

The Major ordered the Company 2-inch mortars to lay down covering fire, but the Germans were well dug in and the small calibre high-explosive shells had little or no effect on them. Major Murphy then ordered the withdrawal of the two platoons of riflemen and the Pioneers. This task was given to Rifleman Beattie who promptly set off towards the left-hand platoon. With the message safely delivered he then went towards the vanguard platoon and delivered the order to withdraw to Sergeant Hammersley.

The Major asked for smoke to be put down by the Mortar Platoon to cover the withdrawal and as the smoke bombs detonated they gave off a fleeting red glow. Seeing this the Germans assumed it was signal flares being fired by their own troops and immediately fired a salvo of high-explosive bombs in support. During this salvo Sergeant Hammersley was seriously wounded and was evacuated by stretcher-bearers. In the confusion it would appear that there had been no time to pass the word to the other sections of the Platoon or to the Pioneers and both Lieutenant Shimmin and his platoon became prisoners, with only five members of Hammersley's platoon returning safely to the Company lines.

Through his binoculars Major Murphy had observed a number of riflemen being taken to the rear of the enemy positions under escort, one carrying a Red Cross flag. A little later he was able to recognize Lieutenant Shimmin and Sergeant Raffaelli, the Pioneers' second in command also being taken to the rear.

Things were going better on the right flank. Major Bird had led D Company out of Blitterswijk at 0415hrs towards the night's objective, a ruined mill. In the village their positions were occupied by A Company, who were to provide a firm base. By 0500hrs they had reached the barbed wire and here the Pioneers under the command of Corporal Tony Genovese began to clear a gap. On this stretch of the wire there were no mines, but the Pioneers found explosive charges placed in the centre of the barbed-wire coils. Unable to reach them, there was no alternative but to cut the wire and pull it to one side thereby detonating the charges. This was done without injury to the men and, surprisingly, without causing any reaction from the enemy.

The leading platoon, under the command of Lieutenant Hancock, made its way through the cleared gap to be followed by the second, led by Lieutenant Jim Campbell. As Campbell's platoon cleared the wire a machine gun opened up from close range but despite the hail of bullets aimed at the riflemen there were no casualties. Jim Campbell's reaction was to order a bayonet charge directly towards the muzzle flash of the enemy weapon. This tactic was completely successful and when the riflemen arrived at the machine-gun post they found the enemy had gone, although the weapons, an MG42 and a Panzerfaust, were lying abandoned.

In the meantime, Lieutenant Hancock's platoon was also under fire. Lying between them and the mill was a wood and from here a stream of machine-gun bullets was aimed at them. Zigging and zagging into the wood the Platoon moved from position to position, with first a hand grenade and then a quick charge with the bayonet. Despite being wounded on two occasions, Lieutenant Hancock, with the able assistance of Corporal Harrigan, repeated this tactic as they moved through the wood. On reaching the final position it was found that once again the enemy had flown, albeit in a great hurry judging by the amount of weapons and equipment left behind.

The third platoon through the wire had also received the attention of enemy machine-gun fire, but without casualties. Now all three platoons concentrated at the mill before going on to the second objective, the western edge of the wood, several hundred yards to the north-west of the mill. The third objective, another wood lying to the south, was a different matter entirely for it was reported that it was occupied by two or possibly three machine-gun positions, all well concealed and protected.

The only 'artillery' available to precede the attack came from the Company's 2-inch mortars and PIATs. Bombs from both were directed at the enemy, but it took a good old-fashioned bayonet charge to make the enemy take to his heels. The German soldier at this time seemed quite capable of taking any amount of shelling and bombing, but his reaction to the bayonet was something else. While D Company took no prisoners, all those capable of moving having run away, their weapons collection was now most impressive. Six MG42s and an equal number of Panzerfausts, along with copious amounts of ammunition, were added to the Battalion's hoard.

The Germans were not slow to react and soon a barrage of shells was being delivered from the far bank of the Meuse as D Company dug in and waited for the expected counter-attack.

Post-action reconnaissance showed that the enemy had been forced to cede ground, but had managed to retain a perimeter to the east of Wanssum, where they had regrouped and were once again preparing to give a spirited defence. In this action C Company lost 6 men killed, 4 wounded and 12 missing. The Pioneer Platoon lost its commander and seven other ranks missing, while the Battalion lost a further four men killed that night – Riflemen Harold Banton from Burton-on-Trent, Herbert Capell from Herefordshire, James Dick from County Durham and John Gale from the Isle of Man.

At 0100hrs on 1 December, it was a cold and clear moonlit night with visibility at 200 yards and a far from ideal time to launch an attack. Nevertheless, the Rifles were once again on the move and the second battle for Wanssum was about to begin. The leading platoon of B Company had advanced some 300 yards from the start line when it came under fire from a machine gun firing from the direction of the village, to be joined shortly after by three more. In this crossfire the Platoon was pinned to the ground unable to move either forward or back. The 2-inch mortar was brought into action in an attempt to silence the machine guns, but these were well dug in and the small bombs had little effect, if any. To add to the confusion two of the enemy positions were equipped with Bren guns and for a few moments the riflemen thought they were being fired on by their own side. From the enemy position two signal flares climbed into the night sky and immediately down came the German defensive fire from their own mortars.

Back at the start line Captain Gaffikin reviewed the situation. He had a further two platoons and had intended to send one of them on a left-flanking attack, but the amount of enemy fire from both machine guns and mortars made this impossible. Any further attack would require artillery support. He then observed the leading platoon make another attempt to advance, but it was again driven to ground and suffered more casualties. The enemy had their machine guns set to fire at below waist height, ensuring that a standing figure had little or no chance, and even those attempting to crawl were vulnerable. A runner was sent forward with orders to withdraw.

The leading platoon eventually made it back to the Company lines, but only after an exhausting crawl all the time under intense and accurate machine-gun fire. Total casualties to the Company were six killed and thirteen wounded, among whom were John Aubne from Durham and John Lewis from Birmingham.

Alan Bird's D Company fared little better. The leading section had just crossed the Blitterswijk–Wanssum road, heading for the wood on the far side, and had just dropped into a gully when they came under fire from at least two MG42s. The Section Commander, Corporal Carroll, was hit immediately, along with one other man. The others were forced to lie flat in the bottom of the gully to avoid the fire and would have stayed there if it were not for the actions of a member of the following section. Lance Corporal Rossiter, seeing the plight of Corporal Carroll's section, bolted across the open ground and into the gully. Hoisting the wounded NCO on his shoulder he called for the men to follow him and hurried back to safety, all the time under fire from the enemy machine guns.

By now it was obvious to Lieutenant Colonel Harris that any further attempt to continue the attack would only result in further casualties. After consulting with Brigade Headquarters it was decided that an attack would be launched the following day using two battalions of infantry supported by both artillery fire and two squadrons of Churchill tanks.

The attack did not materialize on 2 December after information was received from a civilian at Battalion HQ in Mierlo that the enemy had retreated across the Meuse. This at first seemed doubtful. During the hours of darkness a German patrol had approached a position of D Company, but due to the vigilance of Rifleman Irwin had been fired on. Fire was returned, but it quickly became apparent that on this occasion the Bren gun had the upper hand and the enemy patrol commander fired off a signal flare to bring down covering mortar fire to allow him to withdraw his patrol. Later in the night the sound of a wounded man was heard so Rifleman Irwin crawled forward in the darkness and successfully brought the wounded man back into the Company position.

A careful reconnaissance was therefore made towards the town and was able to report that it was indeed clear of enemy troops. That afternoon the Brigade advanced and moved into the town. The 'battle' for Wanssum had cost the Rifles dear. Seventy men had become casualties, including a large number taken prisoner. Several nights later a German patrol entered the town and went down into the cellar of Battalion HQ where they found Captain Sturgeon and his signaller, Rifleman Brankin, asleep. Both men were taken prisoner.

For the remainder of December the Rifles took time to rest and recuperate. Major Tighe-Wood returned to A Company after recovering from his wounds received at Caen. Major Sweeny, who had done a fine job as caretaker commander, was posted to Field Marshal Montgomery's staff. The Field Marshal was fond of Irish officers and had many serving as both staff officers and commanders. He was not so fond of married officers and in December 1944 proved just how petty he could be in this matter.

The Rifles' War Diary records that 31 December was a very cold day, but it was not only the weather that was bad, for a message from HQ informed Lieutenant Colonel Harris that he was being transferred to the Far East and was to hand his Battalion over to John Drummond of the 1st Battalion. It would appear that the romance between Tommy Harris and Anne-Marie had come to the attention of Montgomery and he was not pleased. As a result of this Harris found himself transferred away from the two loves of his life, his battalion and his new wife.

'A Happy New Year' – 1 January 1945

The year 1945 began with a bang! As the first chime struck twelve German small arms, mortars and artillery delivered an absolute symphony of noise and fire on the Rifles' positions. It was almost as if the frustrations of the past few weeks were being released in one gigantic display of temper and lasted for about five minutes, before dying away. The remainder of the night was quiet.

The following morning at 1000hrs, German fighters, a rare sight in the skies of late, swooped down on the Rifles' positions and the remainder of the 3rd Division, but 92 Light Anti-aircraft Regiment was awake and ready. Seven German aircraft were destroyed, with five others being recorded as 'probably' destroyed, while the Regiment 'shared' in two more.

Throughout Belgium and Holland Allied airfields and other positions were getting the same treatment. The first few weeks of 1945 were going to be more interesting than the last of 1944! To the south the Americans were engaged in the largest land action since landing in Normandy the previous June. Twenty-five German Divisions, eleven of them armoured, were fighting it out with US infantry, tanks and aircraft of the 1st and 3rd Armies in an action that would become known as the 'Battle of the Bulge'.

The 'battle patrol', recently reformed, would have the pleasure of providing the first incursion into enemy territory in the New Year. Lieutenant Hancock from D Company and Lieutenant Hogan of A Company were appointed as commander and 2ic respectively, and would cross the river at Lottum, a village on the west bank of the river.

Prior to this Captain Baudains had taken a patrol to Grave on the Meuse, where the riflemen had been indoctrinated into the discipline of boating on a much rougher stretch of water than would now be required.

The old military maxim that time spent in reconnaissance is never wasted was not ignored. Lieutenant Hancock spent an entire day in a forward observation post some 400 yards from the crossing point sketching the ground and making any other notes of relevance. Lieutenant Colonel Drummond, now well settled into his new home, requested and received permission to fly over the ground courtesy of the RAF, a flight that showed a small creek from which the patrol's boat could be initially concealed and then launched. At Battalion HQ members of the Pioneer Platoon constructed a sand model of the area using information from aerial photographs.

It was planned that the actual crossing would be done under cover of a barrage. For several nights prior to the crossing a combination of fire from the artillery, 4.2-inch and 3-inch mortars and streams of machine-gun fire poured across the river for about ten minutes on each occasion.

In the event that anything might go wrong and the patrol came up against opposition it could not deal with, an escape plan was devised. If necessary the artillery would fire a 'box barrage' inside which the patrol would withdraw, while the mortars delivered harassing fire into the village of Lomm. Added to this a considerable weight of small-arms fire could be directed onto various targets at the direction of the patrol commander when required. This group was commanded by Captain Baudains, who was also in contact with the Royal Artillery forward observer, Major Nicholson, and Lieutenant Colonel Drummond.

The objective of the patrol was a hamlet called Hoeken, which was situated between the east bank of the river and the village of Lomm. Here the patrol would determine if the enemy held the hamlet during the hours of darkness and if so in what strength. If possible a prisoner was to be brought back.

The boat to be used by the patrol was brought to the creek and concealed on 30 January. At 0200hrs the next morning the battle patrol launched their craft out of the creek and into the river. As the first shells in the covering barrage blasted from the guns the oars were dipped into the water, the boat surged across the river and after five minutes of strenuous paddling squelched into the east bank of the river. It only took a few seconds for the two officers and seven other ranks to disembark, not onto dry land as expected, but a mudflat. Immediately all were almost waist deep in thick gelatinous mud and it was only with extreme difficulty that the actual bank was reached. Here the patrol flopped down, their breath rising like clouds of steam – not the most auspicious beginning, soaking wet and covered in mud on a January night!

Undaunted, the barbed wire lining the bank was cut and Lieutenant Hogan and three men armed with Bren guns dug in to the mud, to provide a firm base, while Lieutenant Hancock led the remaining four men towards the hamlet, some 250 yards from the river bank. To describe it as a hamlet is probably an exaggeration for just five houses made up Hoeken; they lay parallel with the river and their gardens stretched about 75 yards down towards the water. A hedge that formed an enclosure approximately 100 yards long surrounded them, to the south of which lay the remnants of an orchard; between this and the hedged enclosure a track ran up towards the south end of the hamlet. Lieutenant Hancock led his men up towards the track to be greeted by the sound of jack-boot on gravel coming from the southern end of the orchard. Taking cover, they watched as several pairs of boots marched past within a few feet of where they lay. At the same time a rattling cough was heard coming from the direction of the orchard. The men waiting with the boat confirmed the direction of the cough and the first enemy position had been located.

Lieutenant Hancock gave the order and the riflemen got to their feet, moving towards the houses. Just before the first house, or the last, depending on where you were coming from, the men once again lay down in the snow, making themselves as comfortable as possible. This house was obviously the guardhouse for the river outpost. As a Belfastman would say, 'It was a bit like Royal Avenue.' The door was constantly opening and closing and the noise from inside betrayed a sizeable detachment. Footprints in the snow led hither and thither, including towards the 'coughing' post.

After a short time Lieutenant Hancock had the men on the move again to the halfway point along the hedge and they forced their way through and into the garden. As the last man squeezed through two German sentries marched past the spot, but were gone before the riflemen could turn around and grab them. Clambering back through the hedge the men lay down and waited for the pair to return, but they didn't. Having lingered for a considerable time Lieutenant Hancock brought the men back to the track between the orchard and garden. No sooner had they arrived than two more sentries came out of the house and marched across the garden the patrol had just vacated. This was getting ridiculous! After a total of four and a half hours of crawling and lying about in the snow, Lieutenant Hancock reckoned that their duty had been fulfilled. It was very cold and with only four men at his disposal any attempt to bring a prisoner back by assaulting the guardhouse was out of the question.

The patrol made its way back to the river bank and after the correct exchange of recognition signals, the party made their way safely back across the river. Although no prisoners were taken, the patrol had crossed into enemy territory, observed his positions and routines and had returned unscathed and undiscovered, an ideal reconnaissance.

The information gathered was put to good use, when on 4 February another patrol was sent across the Meuse. Again a prisoner was the object of the mission and this time A Company was to supply the personnel. Lieutenant Bevan and ten men made up the patrol. Conditions were somewhat different than the last time. The night was pitch black, so it was decided to leave earlier, at 2000hrs, and to use 'artificial moonlight' as an aid. The weather had got slightly warmer and a thaw meant that the river was considerably swollen with the extra water. This came to light when the boat taking the men across fouled on the wire that had been cut by Lieutenant Hancock on the previous patrol.

Nevertheless, the men were able to disembark, thankfully avoiding the mud, and soon the secure base of three Bren guns had been set up under the command of Sergeant Bonass. Lieutenant Bevan led the patrol towards Hoeken avoiding the 'coughing' position, from which, by the sound of it, the same soldier was in residence, although this time he seemed a little nervous and loosed off a burst from his MG42 every now and then for no apparent reason.

Hoeken was if anything even busier than the last time. At one stage the patrol saw a soldier carrying a shovel of burning coals from one house to another, probably to start a fire. The men moved into the orchard, just in time to see three Germans marching down towards the river. Initial disappointment was overcome with the realization that the same three would come back, but before this could happen, another two Germans came from the direction of the houses. With the thought that two were as good as three and easier to deal with, the men were challenged, disarmed and quickly bundled towards the river bank. Again the recognition signals were exchanged and all were back in the battalion area by 2320hrs – a successful patrol and two dejected prisoners, all in just over three hours, another useful reconnaissance.

This patrol proved to be the swan song of the Rifles' time on the Meuse for the campaign was moving on as the Allied forces lumbered forward. In the previous seven days British XII Corps had been engaged in an offensive to position Allied forces along the entire length of the Roer. While of a limited nature it boded ill for the enemy for once the Roer was crossed the plain of Cologne would be open to Allied armour and towns such as Krefeld, Munchen-Gladbach, Bonn and the city of Cologne itself were within reach. 3rd (British) Division was withdrawn into reserve, being replaced by the 52nd (Lowland) Division.

By 6 February the Rifles had a new home. Headquarters, along with Support Company, A and B Echelons, was situated in Thildonk, a small Belgian village situated a mile from the main Louvain–Malines road. Along the road itself were the rifle companies, A, B and D on the roadside, with C about half a mile to the west. Billets were described as the best since the campaign began. After a winter of static warfare it was obvious that the Rifles would need a period to return to their usual sharpness. Morale was not at its usual level and there had been much sickness among the men. All ranks were rusty and courses were run for both junior and senior NCOs, as well as physical and weapon training.

Elsewhere, the Canadian First Army was making good progress in the Reichswald, despite one of the worst winters in living memory. The towns of Goch and Cleve were both captured by 20 February.

On 21 February the Rifles were on the move again, destination Goch and the relief of the Jocks of the 15th (Scottish) Division. From here they were tasked with continuing the advance. Stores, equipment and riflemen piled into the 3-tonners, made themselves as comfortable as possible and began their trek towards the next battlefield. Once more the familiar names of 1940 came and went as the lorries trundled along the roads – Louvain, Diest (Deist), Burg Leopold, Helmond and St Anthonis. At the Meuse they crossed with dry feet thanks to the Royal Engineers who had built the longest Bailey bridge in the world up to then. As they crossed the land frontier into Germany itself, the border was marked by massed batteries of 25-pounder guns in action on either side of the road.

At the end of the journey there were no welcoming billets, just a dark and dismal spot in a forest under the gaze of Schloss Calbek, an edifice unlikely to win a prize for architectural beauty – a poor billet for men who had crossed two countries and into a third in a single day, although some credit was due to the drivers!

In the early hours of 22 February, remembered as a gloomy day, first blood was drawn in the Third Reich by a sentry in A Company. An unidentified noise, no answer to the challenge, a single shot and the outcome was a dead pig. For the next few days little of any interest to the riflemen occurred and there was even time to rest and catch up on letters to and from home. At Brigade Headquarters the battalion commanders were briefed on what was to be the Division's next battle. On the left flank the 3rd Canadian Division was to attack Udem; on the right the 53rd (Wessex) Division was to attack Weeze; the 3rd (British) Division was tasked with clearing some 5 miles of woodland stretching from the outskirts of Goch towards Kervenheim. 9 Brigade was to advance as far as the Udem–Weeze road, with the Rifles being responsible for the final consolidation of the position.

On 26 February the Battalion was ordered to secure the Brigade start line and prevent any enemy intrusion prior to the advance the following day, the start line being a track that ran across the Brigade front 200 yards ahead of the forward positions.

Captain Baudains led out a patrol of the Carrier Platoon to reconnoitre the track and to discover if it was mined or otherwise occupied. As the patrol made a cautious advance they came across the bodies of three men lying beside the track. On closer inspection they proved to have belonged to a British tank unit. As Captain Baudains was attempting to identify their unit he spotted the unmistakable shape of a German helmet peering over the top of a bank not 30 yards away. Making a hasty withdrawal to his patrol, he quickly organized a flanking attack on the enemy position. As the 2-inch mortar fired a mixture of smoke and high explosive, the remainder of the patrol moved round and charged the enemy with three Bren gunners firing from the hip. While this may not be the most accurate way to fire a Bren gun, the effect of three streams of .303 bullets slamming into the enemy trench produced the right result. Two prisoners were taken and as they were being marched back down the track they were quick to point out the presence of mines, both anti-tank and anti-personnel. When questioned by the

Rifles' Dutch interpreter the prisoners were able to supply both the location and numbers of mines in this particular area.

The morning of Tuesday, 27 February dawned cold, misty and damp. The Lincolns, followed by the KOSBs passed through the Rifles' positions and on towards their objectives, the troops advancing in the wake of a creeping barrage from the supporting artillery that slowly worked its way forward towards the enemy positions. At 1000hrs, the Rifles followed, D Company on the right flank and A Company on the left. Immediately in front of the riflemen were the Churchill tanks of the Scots Guards, whose guns took out any suspected position with high-explosive shells and seemingly endless machine-gun fire. Such was the weight of fire directed at the enemy that they were still cowering in their slit trenches when the Rifles arrived to take them prisoner. The 'bag' was a mixed bunch of Hitler Youth who cried in frustration at being captured, old men of the Volksturm who seemed glad that it was all over, and here and there a scattering of paratroopers calmly accepting the fall of the dice.

The attack sped forward with prisoners being taken on a regular basis. On one occasion Lieutenant Purcell and his platoon of C Company made a daring assault on the cellars of a house, forcing the occupants to surrender. And so it went on, the advance and various small actions happening with speed and professionalism. Casualties were two officers and sixty-four other ranks, the majority caused by enemy shelling prior to the actual advance. One of those killed was Rifleman John Beck, aged twenty-one, from Yorkshire. Roy Purcell was subsequently awarded the Military Cross.

In March 1945 the Rifles were given responsibility for a front of some 3,000 yards, between Calar and Rees. This was a large area to cover and there was little time for either rest or recreation. Nevertheless, 17 March was celebrated after a fashion. While no parade could be held and alcohol was in short supply, food was abundant and the Rifles enjoyed an exceptionally good meal. It was obvious to all, from Rifleman to Commanding Officer, that the next hurdle was to be the Rhine. All around could be seen the build-up for what would combine the largest airborne operation of the War and a massive assault across the last great water barrier in Germany.

On 24 March the Rifles were briefed on what was to happen in the coming battle. At precisely 1700hrs, the artillery began to fire on targets on the far side of the Rhine and for the next four hours the firing from the Allied guns was non-stop.

The Rifles moved out on 27 March and crossed the Rhine at Rees. Once across they relieved a battalion of the 51st (Highland) Division, situated some 5 miles on the far side of the river. The move itself had caused some consternation as a few days before, the Rifles' transport had been sent back to St Anthonis in order to clear the road for the assaulting troops and the crossing was made mostly on foot. As darkness fell the KOSBs passed through the Rifles' position and occupied the village of Werth.

In the early hours of the following morning the Lincolns took the lead and advanced towards the high ground to the east of Bocholt, but as their leading units came to the River Aa they came under fire. Some probing was done with aggressive patrolling, and this proved that the opposition would require more than one battalion to overcome.

At 1700hrs on 29 March, Lieutenant Colonel Drummond received orders to attack across the river, zero hour to be midnight. No intelligence was available with regard to numbers of enemy, where they were located, minefields or even the width and depth of the river. The first thing to be done was to establish a firm base from which to operate. Captain Bevan and C Company were sent to clear the area that would be used as the start line. A search of those houses and farms in the immediate vicinity uncovered four enemy soldiers who were more than willing to co-operate. Apparently sick and tired of the war, they had simply waited to surrender. Added to this was the discovery of two friendly civilians who spoke good English and from whom it was revealed that the Aa was some 10 to 12 yards wide, 2 feet deep, with steep banks. On the far side of the river was an earth embankment.

To add to their knowledge of the river, Lieutenant Leslie Harris actually waded across, up to his knees in cold water. This not only confirmed the depth of the water, but the Lieutenant was also able to report no sound of the enemy on the far bank. It was therefore decided that assault boats would be used for the crossing and Captain Baudains led the Carrier and Pioneer Platoons down to the river to clear away any mines and make a route for the boats. At the same time the Intelligence Section marked out a start line with white tape 200 yards back from the river. At 2200hrs the first of the boats was brought down to the river bank on the back of a Bren carrier, but it took a full hour's work by the Carrier Platoon with the assistance of a platoon of C Company to get all the boats in position.

With a little more time required for preparation, zero hour was put back to 0100hrs, the plan being that A and D Companies would be the first across. A Company was to advance straight to a point some 700 yards beyond the river, while D Company was to consolidate a bridgehead and guard the left flank. B Company would then cross behind D, pass through and take over the defence of the left. Meanwhile C Company, Battalion HQ and the Carrier Platoon would occupy the ground behind A Company.

After A Company crossed the river they climbed the steep embankment on the far side and discovered the first of the enemy, who although dug in, were not alert and were quickly captured, with no casualties on either side. The Company continued and next came across two horse-drawn carts that were making their way to the rear. Opening fire the riflemen wounded two men and captured another two. The wagons were loaded with three mortars and a full complement of ammunition.

On the left flank D Company had formed their bridgehead. Within a few minutes there was firing from the flank and a group of enemy charged towards the Company position. The German patrol soon realized that they had bitten off more than was chewable and the prompt action of Sergeant Cochrane and his platoon soon had them in the bag. The Sergeant then sent a runner to inform the Company that this had been a patrol action and not a counterattack as first suspected.

Meanwhile, on the west bank of the river Battalion Headquarters and the Carrier Platoon were preparing to cross. Suddenly shots rang out and within a short time three men had been hit including Rifleman John McQuillan who was killed. Captain Baudains spotted the sniper and with a 2-inch mortar he fired six bombs in quick succession, not only marking the sniper's position for the men on the east bank of the river, but also keeping the German's head down long enough to stop him doing any further damage. He was dealt with by a patrol from D Company.

In B Company area the leading platoon under Sergeant Tipper

had reached its objective without incident. Here several houses were cleared and between twelve and fifteen Germans captured. With the prisoners sent to the rear Sergeant Tipper ordered the Platoon to dig in. As the riflemen set to work in pairs with pick and shovel a German Warrant Officer emerged from the shadows of one of the buildings and pointing his pistol at an unsuspecting Rifleman took him prisoner. Where his partner was at this time is not known. As the two men slipped away an alert Rifleman Hayes spotted them. Issuing a challenge and not getting a satisfactory answer, he opened fire with his Bren gun, killing the German immediately and wounding the Rifleman. It was generally agreed that a flesh wound from a .303 was better than a spell in a German POW camp.

Total casualties for the Rifles on the west bank of the river came to 6 men wounded, while the Germans lost 59 prisoners to the Rifles, and 2 killed, along with a large amount of weapons and equipment. Sergeant Cochrane was awarded the Military Medal for his part in defending the left flank during the initial crossing. The following few days were spent in resting and cleaning weapons and uniforms, the billets at Bocholt proving adequate, as was the food.

On 3 April the Rifles were on the move again and for the following two days travelled along the axis of the Guards Armoured Division. In the event that the tanks got held up the Brigade was to take the lead and clear away any enemy resistance, but as it was, when resistance was met it would take the entire Division to clear it away.

Lingen was a town that was steeped in the doctrine of the Third Reich, and was also a garrison town and the home of several officer cadet training units. It was the personnel from these, along with the 111 Battalion Grossdeutschland Brandenburger Training Regiment and a detachment of several hundred paratroopers who set about defending every street and house with fanatical devotion.

The tanks and armoured infantry of the Guards Armoured Division had captured intact the bridge across the River Ems, some 2,000 yards to the west of Altenlingen. Here Captain Ian Liddell of the 5th Battalion Coldstream Guards had earned the Victoria Cross by personally disconnecting the fuses to the demolition charges.

The Rifles would not be involved in the town fighting at first, having been detailed to relieve the 2nd King's Shropshire Light Infantry from their defence of their bridgehead over the Ems Canal. While the KSLI went off to help clear the town, the Rifles moved into the bridgehead. As they crossed the Class 40 Bailey bridge, constructed by 17 Field Company, Royal Engineers, they lost two vehicles to enemy shellfire.

The following two days were spent in combat with elements of the German 7th Parachute Division. Fatal casualties to the Rifles were Riflemen William Gourley from Coatbridge, John Ingham from Bury, Malcolm McMillen from Belfast, Geoffrey Reading from London and William Bennett from Kent.

The Rifles advanced into Lingen on 6 April. The plan was that C Company was to capture the crossroads on the outskirts of the town, not by a direct advance, but by using a right-flanking attack along a secondary road. A Company, advancing straight up the main road towards the crossroads, would follow. As they progressed they would clear the houses on both sides of the road and drive the enemy towards C Company ensconced at the road junction.

D Company would then pass through C and consolidate some way forward. They in turn would be followed by B Company, who would clear any houses left by C Company on its advance.

John Drummond told Captain Barry that C Company was to get to the crossroads as quickly as possible and bypass any opposition too strong, leaving this for B Company. To assist Michael Barry, Drummond assigned a troop of Sherman tanks and three Churchill Crocodiles.

The Crocodile was a variation of the basic Churchill infantry tank. It weighed almost 40 tons and towed an armoured trailer that carried the fuel for the flame-thrower, which replaced the hull machine gun and had a range of between 100 and 200 yards.

Lieutenant Purcell's platoon was the vanguard. At first all went well and the Platoon advanced through the rubble-strewn streets without meeting any opposition. All at once an MG42 opened up from a house approximately 100 yards ahead on the right-hand side. The Platoon immediately took whatever cover was available and returned fire. Depending on his leading section doing their job, Roy Purcell ordered his next section to take the enemy held house using a left-flanking attack. As quickly as it began the firing stopped and the Platoon was able to advance but as they reached the crossroads they again came under machine-gun fire. This time the enemy had waited a little longer and the range was down to 75 yards, added to which there was sniper fire from the houses on the far side of the crossroads. Such was its volume and accuracy that both sections were now pinned down. Corporal Watkin and his section made a daring rush for one of the houses, but a stream of bullets cut him down and wounded several other members of his section. Roy Purcell and his third section were no luckier and also found themselves pinned down by the withering machine-gun fire.

Michael Barry came forward and was discussing the hold-up with Lieutenant Purcell when groups of about half a dozen figures were observed advancing towards them through the rubble. At first it was thought they were the leading sections withdrawing, but then the shape of the helmets identified them as the enemy. They were paratroopers and were armed to the teeth with the best weapons available. Some men carried an MP40, the standard sub-machine gun of German troops, while others were armed with the FG42, an assault rifle specifically designed for German airborne troops. Fitted with a twenty-round magazine, its rate of fire was 750 rounds per minute. Against the .303 it was a winner in close-quarter battle. These paratroopers from the 7th Parachute Division had fought on the Russian Front and at Monte Cassino, and were experts at street fighting.

Nevertheless, experience and superior weapons do not make a man bulletproof and the combined fire from the .303s and the section Bren gun was directed towards the running figures. The first man was brought down by the combined fire, while others fell to the marksmanship of Rifleman Scott who personally brought down three of them before they could get too close. Despite this two of the enemy managed to get into the Platoon HQ area and in the ensuing melee Michael Barry was fatally wounded before both the attackers were themselves killed.

As the enemy fire continued to rain down on C Company, it looked as if the advance had been stalled. A few minutes later the second in command, Captain Charlie Alexander, arrived with Roy Purcell and was informed of the situation. Spending a few precious minutes to study the situation, he returned to Company HQ and radioed for assistance from the Crocodiles.

As the tanks moved forward they left the road to form an extended line, the ideal formation for their attack and the deployment of the flame-throwers. Unfortunately the Germans had an ally as nature played her hand and within a few seconds all three vehicles, each weighing 39 tons, had ploughed up to their belly in the boggy ground that ran alongside the road.

Undaunted, Captain Alexander ordered Lieutenant Fairman to bring his platoon forward and with the support of a Sherman Firefly to advance against the houses occupied by the enemy. As the Platoon advanced the Sherman fired solid shot over their heads to pierce the house walls and deter the machine-gunners. But bad luck still dogged C Company. The first few shells shattered the branches of some trees that the Platoon was passing under, showering the men with splinters of wood, almost as deadly as steel. This proved just too much for the riflemen and with casualties sprawling on the ground they dived for cover. Again the advance had been stopped.

Lieutenant Fairman spent some time reorganizing his men, but they had only gone a short distance when once again the sheer volume of machine-gun and mortar fire drove them to ground.

Watching this Captain Alexander issued orders to Lieutenant Leslie Harris, commander of his third platoon, to advance along the main road on the right-hand side only. Supporting fire would come from the two platoons already ahead and from the supporting Shermans.

The tanks had learned their lesson by now and all shells went where they were intended. With their Besa machine guns blazing almost constantly they hosed down the houses, covering every window and doorway with fire which, combined with that from the other two platoons, allowed Lieutenant Harris and his men to move from house to house with complete success. When they finally reached their objective they had collected twenty-five prisoners.

Now it was A Company's turn. To their surprise resistance was only a fraction of that experienced by C Company – a few scattered shots and then a hasty withdrawal to the next house in the street. About halfway along resistance faded away completely. With their line of retreat now blocked by C Company the Germans seemed to have lost the will to continue and soon prisoners were being passed back to Battalion HQ at a prodigious rate. As A Company closed the distance with C Company a patrol led by Lieutenant Songest was sent forward to make contact and warn of the imminent arrival of the other riflemen, but after only 200 yards through the rubble they were forced to ground by machine-gun fire from one of the houses that had caused so much trouble for C Company's leading platoon. Having taken casualties in his small command, Lieutenant Songest realized he had neither the weaponry nor the personnel to engage in a protracted firefight. Detailing a few men to accompany him, he made a rush for the house under the cover of fire from his remaining men and a smoke grenade. With bullets from the enemy MG42 literally dancing around his feet the Lieutenant tossed a grenade through a window and with a well-placed kick opened the door. The riflemen, hot on the heels of their officer, plunged into a storm of smoke, flame, dust and bullets. Casualties were sustained on both sides, but those of the Germans were fatal. As the dust cleared the patrol took stock. Lieutenant Songest had been grazed in the neck by a bullet. The enemy dead were left lying in the house, while some sixty prisoners were collected from this house and several others. The road through to C Company was now clear.

By now D Company had advanced and passed through C Company, and had reached its own objective. When orders were received by the CO to secure a position 600 yards to the south of D Company, Major Cummins (Cummings) and B Company were allotted the task, taking with them a troop of Sherman tanks. The position was duly reached and occupied; all seemed quiet. Across the street from one of the forward positions stood a solitary house backing on to a large wood. As this house overlooked the approaches to the position from Company HQ it was decided to send a patrol to ensure it was clear of the enemy. Lance Corporal Glover drew the short straw and, gathering his men, advanced across the road towards the house. With all attention on the house and the immediate area, a burst of machine-gun fire from the woods came as a complete surprise, Glover being one of those hit. Despite his wound, he remained on his feet and in command. The men took whatever shelter was available and under cover of smoke grenades prepared to withdraw. Giving the order to retire Glover led his men back into the Company area in good order and was able to give a coherent report on the enemy position.

Major Cummins detailed Lieutenant McCrainor's reserve platoon and two of the Sherman tanks to take care of the troublesome machine gun. Once again the Shermans proved their worth, punching high-explosive shells into the trees. As the riflemen charged in after the brief, but accurate bombardment, they caught the Germans completely by surprise in their emplacement. In the fierce melee that followed, one enemy soldier was killed, two wounded and one taken prisoner; the supporting infantry fled back into the woods. As the riflemen continued further they came under fire from two separate positions, but by now the trees were so close together that the enemy machine-gunners did not have a clear field of fire and no casualties were caused. Unaware of the enemy's strength, Lieutenant McCrainor reported back to Battalion HQ. Lieutenant Colonel Drummond was advised that the enemy in the trees was probably part of the parachute unit that the Rifles had already encountered in the town. With the limited visibility, the inability of the Shermans to force a way through the woods and the quality of the enemy, it was decided to withdraw the Platoon to its Company position.

This was the last action fought by the Rifles at Lingen. It had been a hard, bitter fight with little or no quarter offered on either side. The resistance offered by both the fanatical members of the Hitler Youth and the sheer professionalism of the paratroopers had in many cases stopped the attack in its tracks. Bombing and massed artillery had killed some enemy, but equally had provided them with the ruins from which they could snipe and ambush almost at will. Only the deadly flame-throwing Crocodiles had really disorganized the enemy – all else had been a matter of boot, bayonet, grenade and sub-machine gun at close range. In the end it was the infantry who had taken the contested ground and had held it. On 6 April, the Rifles lost ten men killed and over thirty wounded. Among the dead were Captain Michael Barry, Rifleman Ronald Allwood from Leicestershire, Rifleman David Kane from County Tyrone and Colour Sergeant Frank Dicken, who had previously been wounded at Cambes in June 1944. Among honours gained was the award of the Military Cross to Captain Charlie Alexander.

It was time for a rest and the Rifles found themselves in the village of Diepholz, a hundred miles away from their recent scene of conflict. While the population was not exactly welcoming and a vigilant watch was the order of the day, and night, the billets were at least clean. There was time to catch up on the all-important mail and carry out repairs to uniforms and vehicles.

On 13 April, the Rifles moved 40 miles to the village of Harpstedt, from where a carrier patrol under the command of Lieutenant Leslie Harris was sent out to reconnoitre the road towards Delmenhorst. As the vehicles moved north they were fired on by a small group of enemy infantry in the woods to the side of the road. Fire was returned and one of the ambush party was killed, while another, although wounded, managed to escape into the trees. Lieutenant Harris dismounted part of the patrol and gave chase, but as they moved into the woods a couple of hundred yards from the roadside there was an enormous explosion – a concealed landmine had been detonated as the riflemen passed. Lieutenant Harris was killed instantly along with seven of his men, including Corporal Fitzgeorge from Essex, and Riflemen Carruthers from Glasgow and Shaw from Belfast. A barrage of mortar and machine-gun fire was directed at the road immediately following the explosion. This prohibited any attempt to recover the bodies and after a short while the carriers and surviving riflemen were forced to withdraw under the weight of fire, having sustained no further casualties. Two men managed to stagger back to the carriers despite severe wounds, while three were later reported missing.

Bremen

On 17 April the Rifles gathered themselves together and moved to their concentration area to the north of Barrien.

The next day the watery sunshine gave way to early darkness as the Rifles moved up behind the Lincolns for the night. After a few hours fitful sleep they were on the move again to capture Moordyke, some 1,500 yards further on. Despite the fact that the Lincolns had previously covered this ground, Lieutenant Colonel Drummond was taking no chances and forward reconnaissance patrols were deployed. The enemy had been forced back onto his home ground and some units, thought to be fanatical Hitler Youth, were turning to fight like cornered rats. A nasty night-time surprise was averted when a patrol under the command of Corporal Holt of B Company searched some burnt-out houses and discovered a German officer and fifteen men hiding among them and surrounding ditches. These however, were not fanatics and it only took a few warning shots to bring them into the open with their hands up.

At 0700hrs on 19 April, the attack against Moordyke was launched. All went well and soon D Company had reached its objective, the main crossroads in the village. On requesting a prisoner tally, Major Bird was informed that since crossing the start line the Company had sent back some fifty prisoners, all other units involved in the attack enjoying a similar experience. By 1300hrs, the Rifles were well ensconced on all objectives with the weapons haul including machine guns, Panzerfausts, pistols and sub-machine guns. An added bonus was finding three abandoned 20mm anti-aircraft guns. These weapons, mounted on a light two-wheeled carriage, were deadly when deployed in a ground role and their capture meant fewer casualties in any future engagement. Their crews were not the normal Luftwaffe troops, but Hitler Youth, many of whom cried with frustration when captured, ashamed that their fight for Führer and Fatherland was over. The Rifles dug in and with the usual brewing of tea rested as the remainder of the Brigade passed through and continued on towards Huchting.

Relief in the form of fellow Celts came with the arrival of a battalion of the 51st (Highland) Division on 21 April, although Rifleman Meyerstein of Support Company would probably have objected to such a description.

The Rifles moved to Barrien where they were introduced to the Buffalo. Having already experienced water travel on several occasions they considered themselves old hands, but the Buffalo was something else entirely. While some of the officers had watched a demonstration in February, this was the first time the riflemen had actually set foot aboard the vehicles – or were they craft? This ignorance in what was then the cutting edge of river-assault technology was soon put to rights by the men of the 4th Royal Tank Regiment, who set forth with a will to instruct the PBI (poor bloody infantry) on how to cross water with dry feet.

The Buffalo – or as it was officially known, Landing Vehicle,

Tracked (Unarmoured) Mark IV – had been born in the Everglades of Florida, where the United States Government had developed a vehicle for use in hurricane and swamp rescue. From this a military version was designed and first used by the US Marine Corps. Many versions were built, including an armoured vehicle mounting a 75mm gun that was used in the Far East. The Buffalo that the Rifles' boots clattered on and off during rehearsals was the 2½-ton version which was capable of carrying a jeep, a Bren gun carrier or thirty riflemen. It was also armed with one .50 calibre and two .30 calibre Browning machine guns.

As the next target for the Rifles was to be Bremen, which lay south of the Weser and east of the Ochtum Canal, the Rifles set to with a degree of enthusiasm in their new role. Time and time again they practised loading and unloading until they had it as perfect as it was going to be. One rifleman had to be constantly censured by his platoon sergeant for using the phrase 'getting up the Buffalo' as opposed to 'getting on the Buffalo'.

Although the Ochtum Canal provided little in the way of defence to Bremen, the deliberate flooding of its banks had created a man-made lake some 2,000 yards across, varying in depth from ankle deep to drowning – thanks to the RAF. The route the assault was to follow lay partly across a dummy airfield which had been build earlier in the War by the Germans. This had obligingly been bombed on at least one occasion by the RAF and the craters left by this attack meant that what should have been several feet of water was likely to be very deep indeed.

Captain Harris, who had been designated as Buffalo Squadron Leader, had another problem on his plate, the matter of navigating across 2,000 yards of water in the dark without any form of land-marks. It was then brought to his notice that the RAF failed to do any damage to the 'dummy' airfield control tower and enough of it was visible above the water to provide adequate guidance. Meanwhile, having carried the Highland Division across the Rhine and the Canadians across the Issel, the tank men were determined that the Ironsides would get across with dry feet.

The objective for the Rifles was a point just to the south of Kattenturm, a village to the north of Brinkum and south of Bremen. The southern side of the village was enclosed by an earthen bund (dyke) that kept the flood waters out of the village and it was this bund that had been selected as the 'debuffing' point for the riflemen. As the loading ramp for the Buffalo was at the rear the vehicles would have to drive up to the bund, turn 180° and reverse hard against the bund to allow the men and vehicles to unload.

Intelligence was able to offer very little information on the expected opposition. Phrases such as 'it can be deduced' and 'one must suppose' were bandied about in lieu of hard facts. Air reconnaissance had shown that the Kattenturm Bridge was still intact, but again it had to be 'supposed' that it was prepared for demolition. There was also evidence of slit trenches and gun positions, but no sign of their occupation. It was further 'supposed' that some form of resistance force would be deployed on the southern side of the bridge, although patrols from 8 Brigade had managed to get within 200 yards of the crossing and had seen no one. Assuming that the Germans would have left nothing less than a company as a garrison, and that this would be adequately supported by artillery, preparation went ahead for the attack.

By 24 April, Captain Harris, Buffalo Squadron Leader, no extra pay, but an imposing title, had amassed a 'flotilla' of forty-seven Buffaloes for the assault. This meant that the entire fighting strength of the Rifles could cross as one unit, with only some administrative vehicles to come across in a second wave.

That morning all officers of the 3rd Division had been briefed by the GOC with the plan for the capture of Bremen. As far as the 2nd Battalion Royal Ulster Rifles was concerned they would capture Kattenturm and seize the bridge, hopefully intact. The afternoon was spent in final preparations for the crossing. The Buffaloes had a number displayed on all four sides, written in white chalk, with riflemen, carriers and jeeps being allotted to each one in turn. By the time darkness fell each Rifleman knew his Buffalo and the crew who would be responsible for carrying him across. There remained a few hours in which to try and grab some sleep, something to eat and perhaps write a letter home.

At 2100hrs, in the sinking sun of a warm spring night the Rifles gathered themselves together and climbed aboard their assigned Buffaloes. To the tune of the usual songs the ungainly vehicles trundled forward; at a distance it was difficult to tell which end was which. On reaching the forward assembly area at the village of

Leeste the engines were switched off and the Rifles 'debuffed' to stretch their legs for an hour and enjoy a mug of hot sweet tea laced with a tot of rum. Darkness had fallen completely when the word was passed down the convoy. With a roar the seven-cylinder Continental engines burst into life and the convoy was on the move again. As the Buffaloes moved down to the water the Brigade Commander, along with a motley collection of war correspondents, stood waving them good luck. Some of the gestures waved in reply were rather different.

Despite the noise of forty-seven engines roaring out there was no chance whatsoever of it being heard by the enemy. The covering barrage, which had been going on for the past several nights, had begun at 2200hrs and would increase as the craft reached the water.

On the convoy's left the 'pepper pot' could be observed falling on the enemy shore. This was a collection of 4.2-inch mortars, Vickers machine guns and Bofors 40mm anti-aircraft guns firing in the ground role and directed towards enemy positions, both known and suspected. Overhead the riflemen could see bursts of three tracer shells fired by a single Bofors gun; these passed by repeatedly and were assisting Captain Harris to keep a straight course across the water.

Out on the water, illuminated by moonlight and tracer shells, the convoy formed into two parallel columns, with C Company leading the way, having crossed the start line at 2400hrs. A and D Companies followed at 0200hrs, following the line of buoy lamps that had been dropped by the leading vehicles. There were no losses on the crossing from enemy action, although one Buffalo became bogged on the canal bank some distance from the shore and had to have its load transferred. The Buffalo carrying the Adjutant and his 22 Set was also marooned for a time before the crew was able to manoeuvre it free and make it safely to shore. Admiral Nelson would have been proud of the seamanship of Captain Harris and his tank men as they delivered the Rifles onto the enemy shore.

C Company was the first to come in contact with the enemy. When still 50 yards from the bund on which they were to land, two red flares soared into the night sky, followed by long bursts of machine-gun fire and the flash of Panzerfausts erupting from the bund. There were no casualties and the Buffaloes made the final surge towards dry land. As the vehicles turned in the water and reversed their ramps against the bank, each platoon was in the exact spot as planned. Sergeant McAleavy's platoon launched themselves at their objective, an enemy gun position, and after a brief flurry of small-arms fire, six Germans were taken prisoner. On the right flank Corporal McCullan led his section against a second gun position and met with equal success. With these two positions now in the hands of the Rifles the enemy guns were turned through 180° and fired towards the village of Arsten until all ammunition was expended.

'Digger' Tighe-Wood's A Company had now landed and Sergeant Bonass was one of the first to be wounded, by a fragment from a projectile fired by a Panzerfaust. As the riflemen closed with the position the enemy seemed to lose the will to fight at close quarters and quickly surrendered. These turned out to be mostly Volksturm troops, the German equivalent of the Home Guard. As A Company continued along the bund it soon became obvious that the initial opposition was to be the exception and not the rule. The Germans had dug trenches and foxholes all along the bund which was only 12 feet wide so any chance of making a flank attack was slim. The only option was to go at it head on and hope that speed would win the day. The enemy retaliated with machine guns and Panzerfaust. There seemed to be no shortage of the latter and the flash from the rocket launchers was soon familiar to the riflemen, particularly as it gave a split second of warning and allowed the men to throw themselves flat with the rocket passing overhead. A Company's leading platoon made good headway along the bund, but care had to be taken that no enemy position was overlooked. Rifleman Loughran was crawling towards an enemy foxhole to deal with it using a hand grenade when he was shot from behind by a German sniper. Rifleman Mellon pulled him into cover as machine-gun bullets splattered around both men.

One particular position offered determined resistance. This was a large house 20 yards behind the bund that was more than adequately defended by both machine guns and Panzerfausts. Lieutenant Songest and his platoon spent some time exchanging fire with the house, but were coming off the worst for it, with the Lieutenant being wounded along with several of his men. Refusing to be evacuated he continued to command his platoon and requested support.

Major Tighe-Wood brought up a second platoon to put in a flanking attack, but this was not required. From Lieutenant Songest's platoon Corporal Lambourne led his section forward in a gallant rush and despite fanatical resistance within the house the Riflemen prevailed and the enemy withdrew.

When the remainder of the Platoon came forward the reason for the ferocious defence was revealed. In a concealed position in the front garden of the house was an 88mm gun in full working order. Thankfully its position was such that it had been unable to traverse far enough to the left and had therefore been unable to fire on the Buffaloes as they crossed the water.

A Company continued with the attack, but it was obvious that the main line of resistance at Kattenturm had been broken. Nevertheless, there was still some bloody fighting to be done and the Company advanced with both speed and elan. Rifleman Wilkes was caught in the explosion of a Panzerfaust, suffering injuries to his face, but refused to be taken to the RAP, just one more injury in a catalogue of misfortunes. He had suffered from tonsillitis and exhaustion while at Cambes the previous July, with his tonsillitis returning to haunt him at Troarn. Lance Corporal Dalton found himself in command of his platoon with all other NCOs wounded. As the advance continued the prisoners and captured weapons made an impressive list: forty POWs, the 88mm gun, three of the deadly 20mm flak guns and a large number of assorted small arms. Against this the Company had one officer, Lieutenant Songest, and twenty-four other ranks wounded, few of the wounds being serious.

While all this was going on C Company had landed and established a firm bridgehead. As the ramps of the Buffaloes slammed down on the bund, jeeps, carriers and anti-tank guns drove inland, directed by Captain Gray, who as well as commanding the Anti-tank Platoon, was acting as the Battalion Landing Officer and was responsible for finding a route inland for the Rifles' vehicles.

D Company had advanced in concert with A, but the German defences lacked depth and with the exception of some sniping, were easily dealt with and the Company advance was unopposed. Battalion Headquarters followed close behind D Company and as the eastern end of the village was reached HQ was established for the duration of the battle.

B Company had also made it ashore without incident and when D Company reported all its objectives clear B Company passed through their lines and made for the prize, the Kattenturm Bridge. At 0300hrs B Company Commander, Major Cummins, had ordered Lieutenant McCrainor to take his platoon forward with all speed and to bypass any opposition that did not present a serious threat. The bridge was constructed of stone and spanned the river for a distance of about a hundred yards.

As Lieutenant McCrainor's platoon advanced, with Corporal Holt's section acting as vanguard, they came under fire from machine guns positioned alongside the road and from a large house situated on the left flank. Holt's section went for the machine gun by the roadside and swiftly dealt with the enemy, a few shots and some close-in bayonet work doing the trick. Simultaneously another section rushed the house and dealt with the occupants in an identical manner. As they reached the crossroads just before the bridge, the opposition proved too much for the Platoon and obeying orders the Lieutenant slipped his men around the flank of the crossroads and continued towards the bridge.

With their boots firmly on the bridge the riflemen swiftly crossed and deployed on both banks, preventing any attempt to blow it up by the defenders. Now that the enemy party at the crossroads found themselves cut off, they surrendered, leaving any still fighting along the bund to be dealt with less urgently.

When the group defending the crossroads was eventually disarmed it was found that it included four officers, between twenty and thirty other ranks and one camp follower! Their weaponry consisted of the usual collection of machine guns, Panzerfausts and sub-machine guns, along with a plentiful supply of ammunition.

On the bridge the Royal Engineer attached to the Rifles uncovered two aircraft bombs that had been intended to destroy it and made them safe. The Germans had also constructed a near-impregnable roadblock on the bridge itself. After being examined by the Sappers for booby traps a bulldozer was brought forward and began to demolish it with some difficulty.

Dawn was breaking on 25 April when the news was passed back to Headquarters that the bridge was in safe hands and intact. The Rifles had won a great victory at the Kattenturm Bridge, but this would not have been possible without the back-up of the Buffaloes.

On being interrogated after the battle one of the German field commanders admitted that the attack had been expected to come along the road from Brinkum, hence the sighting of the 88mm gun captured by Corporal Lambourne. The Germans felt that their flank was secured by the flood waters and the assembled prisoners had greeted the sight of Captain Harris and his Buffalo flotilla with amazement.

26 April was a sad day for the Rifles after their great success. Major Alan Bird left D Company lines in a Bren carrier to make contact with 51st (Highland) Division in Huching. Travelling with him were Lieutenant Hancock, Lance Corporal McCoy, and Riflemen McGlennon and Stevens. Rifleman McGlennon had been awarded the Military Medal for his actions in Normandy on 9 June 1944. As the carrier made its way out of the position and along the road towards Huching there was a tremendous explosion, which blew it and its entire crew to bits. It was later established that a German magnetic mine had been placed at the side of the road, the explosion killing men who had served together through some of the most bitter fighting seen by the Rifles since landing in Normandy almost a year earlier.

When the German surrender was announced on 8 May 1945, the Rifles were resting in the village of Delmenhorst, near Bremen in Lower Saxony, a village famous for its jute, woollens and linoleum – not that the riflemen showed much interest.

With the onset of peace came more responsibility. Jim Campbell, now a Captain, was commanding a camp of 'displaced persons' at Gelsenkirchen. A local Belfast sports club had sent the Rifles a number of footballs and one of these had ended up with Jim. Matches were organized between the riflemen and the DPs, mostly Russians – so good were the Russians that the call went out to the other companies in the Battalion for their best players to enable the Rifles to win the odd game. After such games it became traditional to exchange gifts of alcohol. Jim's father worked for a distiller in Belfast and would send him out the occasional bottle for medicinal purposes, but the Russians made their own! After the game a few glasses would be raised and lowered as each side celebrated or commiserated. Jim Campbell was not regarded as one of life's hell-raisers and was remembered in the Mess as a quiet, reserved type, not given to outbursts of rowdyism. On one particular day a hard-played match had ended in a draw, necessitating the downing of several glasses by both the Irish and the Russians. A few hours later Lieutenant Colonel Drummond arrived on a tour of inspection. Finding all in order he had a few words with Captain Campbell and left to continue on his way. As Drummond got into the staff car he was heard to remark, 'Jim's very talkative today.'

The Rifles had fought a hard war and they had fought it well.

PART TWO

1st (Airborne) Battalion The Royal Ulster Rifles

On the day war was declared, the 1st Battalion was on operational duties at Razani on the North-West Frontier of India. One of these duties involved keeping the road open for convoys and protecting them from attack by hostile tribesmen. The occasional punitive patrol was launched against some of these tribes, after one of which Lieutenant B.J. Fitz-Donlea was awarded the Military Cross.

With the outbreak of war on 3 September the Battalion was aware that it would be returning to play its part in the forthcoming campaigns in Europe, although it was to be June 1940 before any homeward move was made. The Battalion travelled to Bombay and here all baggage was loaded aboard the troopship SS *Karanja* by local coolies, something that was to have severe repercussions later in the voyage.

On 4 June, the *Karanja* made up a convoy with four other troopships and sailed from Bombay. These ships carried a battalion each of the Royal Scots Fusiliers, Royal Welch Fusiliers, South Staffordshire Regiment and the Oxfordshire and Buckinghamshire Light Infantry. In conjunction with the Royal Ulster Rifles, the battalions were to return to the UK to form two Regular Independent Brigade Groups, that would eventually help defend the south coast of England in the event of a German invasion post Dunkirk. Their only escort for the voyage home was the cruiser HMS *Kent* armed with eight 8-inch guns. The rumour-mongers on board had a great time passing round the news that a German pocket battleship was waiting just over the horizon.

The convoy had been at sea for six stormy days when at 0400hrs on 10 June smoke was seen pouring from the *Karanja*'s aft hold. By this time it was pitch black and while the sea had calmed, there was a following wind and soon the ship was engulfed in thick smoke. With the threat of enemy submarines and even the supposed pocket battleship it was impossible for the *Karanja* to leave the convoy – the fire would have to be fought on the move. While maintaining a speed of 17 knots the ship's lifeboats were swung out and the Battalion mustered on deck, ready to abandon ship if necessary.

A volunteer fire-fighting party was assembled consisting of Captains Otway and Ridgeway, twelve other ranks from the Battalion, the ship's chief officer, a cadet and several Lascar sailors. The first job was to break into the hold. The railings around the hatch covers were cut away with axes and the covers, by now red hot, were lifted clear. Water was then hosed onto the lower deck to make it cool enough to stand on. When this was done the party descended to repeat the process all over again. While the sea water cooled the decks nothing could be done about the thick smoke or the lack of oxygen and the men were only able to spend a short time below decks before having to come up for a breath of clean air.

By splitting the party into two groups and with liberal supplies of tea, the fire was fought to its source. It was later discovered that an Italian-manufactured incendiary bomb, no doubt placed by a sympathetic coolie in Bombay, had started the fire. The remainder of the voyage was uneventful. The *Karanja* would later take part in the landings in Tunisia as a Landing Ship Infantry (LSI) and would end up burnt out on the beach.

In June 1941, the 1st Battalion was in training at Hereford as part of a Brigade Group in the anti-invasion role. The following month an Indian Animal Transport Company was attached to the Battalion and was stationed, appropriately enough, at Hereford racecourse. With the Battalion only recently returned from India there was no shortage of volunteers to work with the mules, but the issue of horses seemed inappropriate. Whereas mules were adept at carrying heavy loads and if treated properly worked reasonably well, horses were more temperamental and and were totally unsuited to both the loads and terrain. Exercises were carried out in the Black Mountains of south Wales and while this toughened up the men, a succession of bites and kicks proved that once and for all horses were unacceptable as pack animals.

In October, Lieutenant Colonel Campbell, the Commanding

Officer, was informed that the Battalion, along with the other infantry battalions in the Brigade, was to convert to an airborne role and would henceforth be going into battle by glider. This news was met with obvious delight by all ranks who were experiencing a degree of frustration at being left out of the war so far. Those officers who had previously applied for a transfer to the Far East rushed immediately to have the applications cancelled.

On 7 December 1941, the day the Japanese attacked Pearl Harbour, the Battalion arrived in the Newbury area of Berkshire, the primary objective being to concentrate all those units of what was now the 1st Airlanding Brigade. Netheravon airfield, which was close by, was to be used for glider training. On conversion to the airborne role, all ranks of the Battalion had been offered a transfer to another unit if they so wished. No records remain to show how many took advantage of this offer, but personal reminiscences show there were very few indeed, although some men were transferred for medical reasons, usually to do with their ears. When Rifleman Stanley Burrows told his mother that he was going to be flying in a glider, she thought this far too dangerous and wrote to the CO telling him of Stanley's ruptured eardrum. A transfer to the 2nd Battalion swiftly followed and he finally landed in Normandy from the sea.

At the beginning of 1942, an order was received from Divisional Headquarters to the effect that no rank would be allowed to remain in the Division if his conduct were to be assessed as less than 'Good'. The wisdom of such an order, even sixty odd years later, is yet to be fully explained, especially as it had serious repercussions on the Battalion. Being a regular unit and having, even at this date, a high proportion of long-service men, it was naturally to be expected that a brief glance at conduct sheets, under the terms of King's Regulations, would reveal that a number of riflemen would be assessed as having characters below the standard required. The cost to the Battalion as a result of this nonsensical order was in excess of 140 men posted to other units of the Royal Ulster Rifles. The departure of these trained and experienced men can only be described as deplorable. At least one rifleman, whose worth was in no way doubted, approached the Adjutant at the railway station and in tears asked if a reprieve could not be granted, even at this late hour.

This loss was happily offset by the arrival of an excellent draft of young soldiers from the 70th Battalion. This draft was possibly the best ever received by the Battalion during the War and reflected the greatest possible credit on the training staff of the 70th Battalion. Young soldiers they definitely were. On one route march carrying full packs, the Battalion passed through a village in Wales, where the women yelled abuse at the officers and NCOs for allowing children to carry such heavy loads.

Initial flying training was carried out in the Hotspur glider, a small, uncomfortable aircraft with no view out for the men; crashes were frequent, although the Battalion suffered no fatalities. With a load of only seven soldiers and a pilot, it was obvious that a bigger glider was required and this came in the shape of the Horsa Mk I and II.

In April the Battalion was issued with the maroon beret and moved to Bulford Fields Camp, not the best place it had ever been billeted in. Nevertheless, it was closer to Netheravon, rifle ranges were at hand and the Horsa glider arrived making training a lot simpler. This glider could carry a full platoon and soon both officers and men had settled into their new role. As well as the constant training the riflemen were used as a demonstration battalion and were often issued with new bits and pieces of equipment to try out.

In early 1943, the Battalion had a change of commanding officer, when Lieutenant Colonel Robert John Heyworth 'Hank' Carson took over from Lieutenant Colonel Campbell. Carson had been born in India in 1909, the son of an officer killed in the First World War. 'Hank' had been educated at Charterhouse and then at the Royal Military College, Sandhurst, and was commissioned into the Royal Ulster Rifles in 1929. Before the War he had served at Aldershot, Belfast, Palestine, Egypt, Hong Kong and the Isle of Wight, and later Armagh and Ballymena. From 1942 to 1943 he commanded 70th (Young Soldiers) Battalion RUR.

Training continued and if there was energy to spare a man could represent the Battalion sport. During 1943, the football team lost only three matches during the whole season, while the boxing team suffered only one defeat in four years. In January 1944, a proportion of the Battalion went to Ilfracombe in Devon to either learn or practise swimming. Despite the weather this was a pleasant change from the daily routine and would undoubtedly come in useful in the near future. At the same time a number of officers and men made exchange visits with an American airborne division and much useful information was learnt on both sides.

On St Patrick's Day, Major General R.H. Lorie presented the shamrock and wished the men 'good luck' in their forthcoming battles. The following May the Battalion was inspected by their Majesties the King and Queen, accompanied by Princess Elizabeth.

In the spring of 1943, the 6th Airborne Division was formed, command going to Major General Richard 'Windy' Gale. Divisional Headquarters was located at Syrencot House, Figheldean in Wiltshire. Gale arrived on 7 May and such was the speed of organization that he was able to issue his first Divisional Routine Order just seven days later.

The Division would eventually consist of the 3rd and 5th Parachute Brigades, 3rd Parachute Squadron Royal Engineers and 224 Parachute Field Ambulance. The 1st Battalion Royal Ulster Rifles and 2nd Battalion Oxfordshire and Buckinghamshire Light Infantry were transferred from the 1st Airborne Division and, along with the 12th Battalion Devonshire Regiment, would form the 6th Airlanding Brigade. Command of the Brigade went to Brigadier the Honourable Hugh Kindersley who had previously commanded a tank battalion of the Scots Guards in the Guards Armoured Division. The following June saw the addition of the 53rd (Worcestershire Yeomanry) Airlanding Light Regiment, the 3rd and 4th Airlanding Batteries and the 2nd Airlanding Light Anti-Aircraft Battery. Other Divisional units came from the Royal Signals, Royal Engineers, RASC, RAOC, REME, RAMC, Intelligence Corps and Corps of Military Police – an army in miniature. By the beginning of June 1944, the 1st (Airborne) Battalion Royal Ulster Rifles was trained and ready for war. For the landings in Normandy Lieutenant Colonel 'Hank' Carson commanded a battalion rated as second to none, having assumed command in 1943, when the Battalion was stationed at Chilton Foliat. He was judged to be a competent officer, shy and reserved in his off-duty manner, and not given to the more raucous Mess parties. Carson married Letty McGonigal, the sister of Eoin, a fellow Rifles officer who was later killed serving with the SAS, and Ambrose (later Sir Ambrose) of No. 12 Commando, SAS, and 1RUR in Palestine in

1945–6. Rifles officers marrying each other's sisters was something of a tradition within the Regiment.

Carson's second in command was Major John Dean Drummond who had been commissioned into the Regiment in 1931. A former pupil of Beaumont College, Windsor, Berkshire, Drummond had previously served in Egypt and Hong Kong, being promoted to Lieutenant in 1934 and Captain in 1939. Adjutant of the 2nd Battalion when it went to France in 1940, he was evacuated from Dunkirk in June and appointed GSO 3 (Operations), Headquarters IX Corps, until 1941. Promoted to Major in May 1941, he served with the 8th Battalion from 1942 to 1943. Captain Bob Sheridan filled the post of Adjutant, while the Regimental Sergeant Major was 'Scoop' Griffith. Born in County Monaghan, 'Scoop' had enlisted at Gough Barracks, Armagh, in 1934, just after his sixteenth birthday. He had seen previous service in India, Palestine and on the North-West Frontier and had the reputation of being a crack shot.

Padre John Johnston administered to those Presbyterians in the Battalion. Born in south Dublin, he was the son of a farmer turned Presbyterian minister. Their church was burned down during the Easter Rising in 1916, but this did not stop John from attending Trinity College, Dublin, where he excelled at rowing and rugby and gained a first-class honours degree in Divinity. He went on to Cambridge where he gained another first in Theology. Padre Johnston served with the Battalion until 1945.

Captain James McMurray Taylor from County Fermanagh cared for those members of the Church of Ireland, while Father Hourigan, a former Irish rugby international, took care of the Roman Catholics in the Battalion.

The Battalion consisted of Headquarters Company, four rifle companies and Support Company. HQ Company contained the Reconnaissance and Pioneer platoons. Each rifle company was comprised of a headquarters and four platoons, and was supposed to contain six officers and 150 other ranks, which they rarely did. Support Company contained a machine-gun platoon of four Vickers machine guns, a mortar platoon of four 3-inch mortars and an anti-tank platoon of eight 6-pounder anti-tank guns. In addition each company headquarters contained two 3-inch mortars.

Major Charles Vickery, a native of Kent, commanded A

Company. He had enlisted in the Regiment in 1940 and quickly rose through the ranks, being a Company Sergeant Major by 1940 and commissioned after the return from Dunkirk. Within Company Headquarters were Colour Sergeant O'Connor and CSM Beggs, while the cooking was done by Rifleman Cordner. Within the ranks were Corporal John Brunton, one of the many volunteers from neutral Eire, and Sergeant John Coyle from Ballyscullion, County Londonderry. From Belfast came Corporal Bill McConnell, who would eventually become RSM, Sergeant McCully, known to all as the 'Brown Bomber', one of the finest boxers in the Battalion, and Rifleman Samuel Glass, an ex-member of the 70th (Young Soldiers) Battalion.

On 1 June, at Broadwell Transit Camp, Sergeant Dwyer was killed instantly when a No. 75 grenade exploded in B Company lines.* Lieutenant Seale was fatally injured, while Major Warner, the Company Commander, and nine other ranks were injured. Because of Warner's injury Major Gerald Rickcord arrived three days later to take command of B Company. Born in 1913, the son of a naval commander, Rickcord was educated at Douai and Sandhurst. Commissioned into the Rifles in 1934, he served with the 1st Battalion in Egypt, Hong Kong and India. For a time he served as ADC to the Governor and C-in-C Hong Kong, and in Ceylon. Rickcord returned to the UK in 1939 and was posted to the Depot at Gough Barracks in Armagh. From there he went to the 10th Battalion Royal East Kent Regiment (The Buffs) as Adjutant, serving with them from 1940 to 1942. During this time he also commanded a battery of 117 Light Anti-Aircraft Regiment during the Luftwaffe air raids on Coventry. This was followed by courses at the Senior Officers' School, Brasenose College, Oxford, the Staff College at Camberley and the School of Land Warfare. On returning to the Battalion he took command of B Company.

Rickcord's second in command was Captain Harry Croft, a

---

* The No. 75 (Hawkins) Grenade, named after its designer, was first issued in 1941 and approved for general issue in 1942. It is perhaps inappropriate to call it a grenade; as it was in fact a small anti-tank mine resembling a flat screw-topped talcum powder tin. Designed to be laid flat under the tracks of a tank or if attached to a piece of cord pulled across the path of an advancing vehicle. It could also be thrown.

Londoner, one of several in the Company, including Rifleman Cohen, who had been trained as a sniper. Lieutenant 'Mickey' Archdale from Hampshire, who would leave a detailed diary of his time in Normandy, commanded 12 Platoon. Sergeant William Baker would be promoted in Normandy and transferred to D Company as CSM, at twenty-two the youngest in the British Army at the time. Lance Corporal Alexander Connolly, born in Eire, had been working in a factory in Coventry when war broke out and had left a good job to join the Regiment, probably following a family tradition. From County Armagh came Rifleman 'Shots' Bryans, again from a long line of soldiers. From Ballywalter in County Down came Rifleman Harry Gunning, whose brother had opted for the Merchant Navy. In 20 Platoon Sergeant Harry Pegg was admitted to hospital with an infection in his leg due to a previous injury on a training exercise. Sergeant James Cramer was brought up from the Reinforcement Company to take his place, but Harry Pegg was a quick healer, one of the men in the Battalion who was parachute trained and soon returned to his platoon. Cramer then persuaded a young and inexperienced rifleman to drop out and so 20 Platoon went to war with two sergeants.

Frederick Robert Armstrong 'Darkie' Hynds, came from Station Road, Sydenham, Belfast, having joined the regiment as a band boy and previously served in Shanghai, Hong Kong, Palestine, Egypt and India. As a Company Sergeant Major in India he was commissioned as a Captain. Promoted to Major, he commanded C Company in Normandy.

The Company runner was Lance Corporal Samuel 'Sando' Barr who came from Belfast and was well known as a boxer. His superb fitness made him ideal for the job. The Company stores were in the hands of Colour Sergeant Richard Boyce, a Londoner who was known to all and sundry as 'Fenian Dick'. He had originally enlisted in the Royal Irish Regiment and was a man of considerable experience. He was also considered to be a very good chess player, his main opponent being Sergeant 'Cushy' Hunter, a Dubliner.

D Company came under the command of a 'tall, thin, wiry subaltern'. Major A.J. 'Tony' Dyball had originally served with the 2nd Battalion London Irish Rifles and had led a group of approximately sixty men to India in early 1940 to bring the 1st Battalion up to strength. Lieutenant 'Jack' Chapman from Ballymena,

County Antrim commanded 19 Platoon. He had been educated at RBAI and Queen's University Belfast, before enlisting in the 1st Battalion, Royal Irish Fusiliers. He had seen action in Tunisia, especially at Point 437, Djebel el Mahdi. Here his platoon of the 'Faughs' fought a fierce action against a well-armed and entrenched enemy. At the end of the action the Platoon had captured nineteen prisoners, but in return had sustained very heavy casualties, Chapman being severely wounded in the head. On recovering from his wounds he transferred to the Royal Ulster Rifles. Also in 19 Platoon was Sergeant Robert Cotter from Carrickfergus, County Antrim. At thirty years of age he had already served for twelve years. His father, Edwin, had been killed in the First World War. Lance Corporal Thomas Chambers served in 20 Platoon and came from Broughshane, County Antrim; he was 25 years old and had already seen seven years service. His wife Sylvia and baby son lived in Swansea, Wales.

Major Ronnie Wilson, a former solicitor from Portadown, County Armagh, commanded Support Company. The son of a solicitor, he had obtained an honours degree before the War and had lost his brother in 1943, killed in action while serving in Bomber Command. Wilson had served as Motor Transport Officer (MTO) prior to Normandy, when he had handed over command to Captain Dean Steadman.

On 25–26 May 1944, the Battalion, less 'E' (Reinforcement) Company, left Kiwi Barracks, Bulford and was despatched to the two invasion airfields, Blakehill Farm and Broadwell. Here both the weather and perimeter security was very good and all entertainment was within the barbed-wire fence surrounding the airfields. Briefings were carried out twice a day so that each man was fully aware of the larger picture and what both his platoon and the Battalion were to achieve.

There was also an opportunity to visit the 9th Parachute Battalion, which had been neighbours at Bulford. This battalion contained many Ulster Riflemen, from its commanding officer, Terence Otway, Major Gordon Brown, Lieutenant Mike Dowling and numerous other men. Otway had been seconded from the Battalion to replace Lieutenant Colonel Martin Lindsay and would lead his unit against the Merville Battery on D-Day, a position capable of bringing fire down on Sword Beach.

119

Operation Mallard – D-Day, 6 June 1944

The Battalion was provided with a 'fat less' meal in order to prevent or reduce airsickness while airborne in the gliders. Tea and water were provided on board the Horsas and all ranks were instructed to drink as much as possible before landing. The remaining old Indian veterans recalled the words of Kipling's poem *Gunga Din*, 'when it comes to slaughter you will do your work on water.' Although the weather was reported to be cloudy with a slight wind, even a slight wind could cause problems for men prone to airsickness. Captain Wilfred Tallentire, from Banbridge, County Down, a glider pilot, had some experience of airsickness on training flights prior to Normandy. This was his answer to the problem.

As the time approached for the invasion of Europe it was deemed necessary to acquaint all Air Landing Troops with glider transport. How to get in, how to get out and above all to cope with the motion of flight. For weeks troops endured familiarisation, as the exercises were delightfully named in true military style. Airsickness became a problem. By the very nature of the Horsa glider's construction, claustrophobic feeling was created, even before flying commenced. Add to this impasse the sensation of rumbling along the runway unable to see what was really taking place induced, if not fear, at least a degree of apprehension. This induction would be followed by a flight of some duration often in turbulent weather causing the glider to lurch and yaw, thus creating untold problems.

The soldiers with few exceptions were anxious for the excursion to end. Suddenly a snap followed by the dying off of wind noise as the Horsa lost speed, now in free flight. Then horror of horrors down tilted the nose at an alarming angle. Was this to be the last moment in the wretched machine? Oh No! The approach flight was suddenly apparent, one felt to be at an angle nearly vertical. At last levelling off and the comforting sound of the wheels rumbling on mother earth.

It was apparent that troops on landing from a glider were not in tiptop form, indeed the reverse was evident. Worried minds were at work in high places trying to resolve this thorny problem. Parachutists on the other hand came to the scene of action feeling elated and in high spirits. The situation worried officers for not only was the mental condition weak, many had been actively sick en route. Something had to be done to combat this malady.

First attempt to control the sickness came in the form of an issue of paper bags, one to each man prior to entering the glider. Dispose of same on landing. In the appropriate place. So stated the order. This scheme was a disaster.

'What's this for?'

'Oh, that's to be sick in.'

A good idea, I'll have to be sick. Auto suggestion; call it what you may. Twenty-four men sat side by side each with a paper bag, waiting. It didn't take long. Mind over matter speeded up the process. Suddenly one bag was used, then sat on the floor and promptly burst. The chain reaction was quick and devastating. In a moment of time every man was sick. So, paper bags were disused, instead four gallon petrol tins were placed in strategic spots. All went well until suddenly the aircraft lurched tilting the already used tin. In a flash everyone was sick.

Now nearly all the pilots chewed gum, available in the canteen. Hence a certain glider pilot thought up an idea. To collect Wrigley 'chicklets', unwrap them and put into a tin.

The next training flight with troops was to be a night cross country to last about two and a quarter hours. As time drew near for take off, those in charge debated the strength of the wind. Was it too strong, too gusty and so forth? All the while the troops to be carried lounged around as service men do. The glider pilot made himself known, listened to their question and doubts. These men of the Royal Ulster Rifles were in little concern about sickness.

'Is it going to be rough, Sir?'

'De ye think we'll be sick?'

It was obvious the flight was going to be rough. The pilot knew there was no point in saying otherwise. What he did say was:

'Don't worry. It will be bumpy of that there is no doubt, but you will not be sick.' Here he went on to wax lyrical as to the preventative powers of the magical tablets, they taste just like chewing gum, but they are special brand new anti-sick sweets, and so on.

'Where did ye git them?'

'Ah! Here's the secret. No one here has ever seen these.'

'They're laxatives,' a Belfast doubter said.

'No they're not, give me yours.' He swapped and chewing commenced. They were convinced.

During flight soldiers sat face to face, rifles between knees, chewing steadily, every one of them, and no one was sick. After such a flight exercise someone of self-importance debriefed pilots. A lot of stock questions finishing with state of morale and how many sick.

'None Sir.'

The officer looked up. 'I don't believe you.' The pilot repeated his statement and asked if the officer would like to speak to any that had been on board. The request was refused or his nibs declined.

Naturally a plan of this sort was impossible to keep secret. It soon got around about the wonder tablets. Questions were asked, vague answers given, but the panacea was soon to fall asunder. The Commanding Officer collared the wonder pilot and wanted to know the ins and outs of the mystery. Two days later, there appeared in standing orders for Glider Pilots that they were to ensure that all personnel whilst in flight were to chew Wrigley's Chewing Gum. We were back to square one!

By 1700hrs, the Battalion had moved to the airfields at Broadwell and Down Ampney. Here last-minute preparations were made and the men boarded their gliders for the flight to Normandy. Aboard their Horsa and ready for take-off were Staff Sergeant Harry Howard and his co-pilot Sergeant Holman. This was to be their first flight to Normandy and both men were keyed up with excitement – a sentiment shared by the platoon of Ulster Riflemen who filed aboard and strapped themselves in for the journey to France. As the Dakota tug gained speed along the runway the Horsa took off first and Howard brought the glider to a position just above the tug's slipstream. Suddenly the Dakota's undercarriage collapsed and the aircraft ploughed along the runway in a shower of sparks and grey smoke. Howard immediately disconnected the towrope and cleared the crashing Dakota with feet to spare. As he flew overhead Howard could see that the pilot had skidded his aircraft to one side, so as not to block the runway for the following tug/glider combinations. Experience had taught Howard not to jettison the Horsa wheels on take-off – they were fitted with hydraulic brakes, which gave a degree of control on landing, unlike the glider centre skid, which did not!

As the glider wheels touched down Howard could see the perimeter fence coming closer and with gentle pressure he turned the Horsa to the left and onto the grass, where both he and Holman gave a deep sigh of relief. The remarks from the platoon in the back were something else altogether. Within a few minutes an RAF tractor arrived and began to pull them back to the dispersal area, a trip of two miles around the perimeter track. The Horsa was quickly attached to a new tug and with some judicious flying the combination was able to rejoin the main force heading for France.

The Battalion crossed the Channel on an uneventful flight, although described by many as slightly bumpy. The French coast came into view at 2045hrs and as the glider train crossed the beach-head light flak was experienced. At 2100hrs, six minutes early, the first glider of the 6th Airlanding Brigade to touch down on the soil of France was glider No. 1 with Major Gerald Rickcord and B Company Headquarters; they made an uneventful landing on Landing Zone N at Ranville. As the remaining gliders of the Battalion and Brigade Headquarters came in to land there was light mortaring and machine-gun fire from the edges of the landing zone. Some difficulty was experienced with the tails of those gliders carrying vehicles, but a few frantic minutes work with axe and saw ensured an egress of the vehicles concerned.

The glider carrying the Medium Machine Gun Platoon ploughed to a stop and was caught in a shower of mortar bombs. The deadly shrapnel pierced the thin canvas fuselage and within a few seconds it was on fire. Crew and passengers all made it clear of the burning aircraft without injury.

At 2102hrs, the Horsa carrying 18 Platoon, B Company came to a halt against a brick wall after hurtling across a landing zone still covered in anti-glider poles that tore a huge hole in the wing. As Lieutenant Michael 'Mickey' Archdale, born and bred in Hampshire, emerged from the glider he met up with Lord Lovat, commander of the 1st Special Service Brigade. Lovat described the situation as 'sticky', probably an unnecessary comment as mortar bombs were peppering the landing zone.

Rifleman Joe McClatchey, also of B Company, made it safely to cover along with his friend Rifleman Junior Greer. In May 1941, McClatchey and Greer had walked from Portadown to Belfast to enlist. The recruiting sergeant was not satisfied that the two boys were old enough and a quick telephone call to the local RUC Barracks confirmed their real ages. Nevertheless, Joe's older brother had lost an arm in a factory accident some time earlier so on returning home Joe had borrowed his birth certificate, this time going to Omagh where he had successfully joined up. Junior Greer had arrived in the Depot soon after.

Elsewhere the remainder of the Brigade came in. On Landing

Zone W the Ox and Bucks, Devons and various elements of Divisional troops landed. There was also the arrival of the 6th Airborne Armoured Reconnaissance Regiment, which flew aboard Hamilcar gliders, each glider carrying a Tetrarch light tank. Two tanks were lost immediately when the giant Hamilcars crashed on landing and the remainder were immobilized when their bogies and sprocket wheels became entangled in the rigging lines of the numerous discarded parachutes. It took quite a time for the crews to get their vehicles mobile again, usually by using sharp knives and blow torches. Nevertheless, that evening they could claim that they were the only tank regiment within the history of the British Army to have brought their vehicles into battle by air.

Shortly after landing Lieutenant Alan Malcolm commanding 20 Platoon, D Company, along with Sergeant Harry Pegg and the Lieutenant's batman, Rifleman 'Duffy' Dunlop, went on a reconnaissance patrol. This was not without its dangers, for as well as expected enemy soldiers, the Royal Air Force was in the process of dropping supply canisters without the aid of parachutes. These metal containers came down on and around the dropping zones in free fall and would easily have caused injury or death to anyone unfortunate enough to be hit by one. The patrol escaped injury and was able to report back that there was an inordinate amount of mechanized vehicles in the vicinity, which subsequently turned out to be German self-propelled guns.

Battalion Headquarters was established at Ranville Farm buildings by 2200hrs, all personnel being accounted for except for Rifleman John Woodburn from Manchester who had successfully escaped from the glider caught in the mortar fire, only to be shot by a sniper a short time later. The nineteen-year-old from Manchester was the Battalion's only casualty on D-Day.

Stand-to for the Battalion was at 0500hrs the following morning, with an 'O' (Orders) Group at 0815hrs. When Lieutenant Archdale's platoon was ordered to take up a position on the left flank of B Company, Rifleman Hill was wounded in the opening few seconds of the attack, one of the first casualties before the Platoon reached the stone wall surrounding Longueval.

Major 'Darkie' Hynds with his C Company occupied a small hill feature called Ring Contour 30, which lay to the south of the Battalion area. This hill overlooked future Battalion objectives and was to be the scene of some bitter fighting. Major John Drummond, the Battalion 2ic, was also with C Company, as was a Forward Observer Bombardment (FOB) who was in contact with the cruiser HMS *Arethusa*, lying offshore.

C Company, along with the Battalion Anti-tank and Machine Gun Platoons under Lieutenant Harry Morgan, remained on the Ring Contour and were in a position to give covering fire while the remainder of the Battalion moved to seize the first objective, the village of Longueval, which was bordered by woods and apple orchards, and perched on the banks of the Orne. The assault was to be carried out using a right-flanking attack, with support from the Battalion's own 3-inch mortars situated south of Ranville. This attack was a complete success, encountering little or no opposition, but the situation soon changed as the Germans got their second wind.

With the capture of Longueval completed, D Company under Major Tony Dyball and Battalion Headquarters dug in to provide a firm base, while A and B Companies went on to assault Ste Honorine. Like many other towns and villages in Normandy, a stone wall surrounded the objective, providing cover both from fire and view.

During this time C Company and its support elements were receiving a colossal amount of attention from enemy mortars and self-propelled guns of the 200th Assault Gun Battalion situated in and around the second objective, the village of Ste Honorine. This unit, commanded by Major Alfred Becker, was equipped with armoured vehicles fitted with both 75mm and 105mm howitzers. Becker was the talented son of a mechanic and his considerable skills ensured a quick turnaround in field repairs. Artillery support could not be called for as the FOO from 3rd Division was unable to come forward due to the weight of enemy fire and the FOB could not make wireless contact with the *Arethusa*. The Battalion's 3-inch mortars were therefore all the support available! At 1130hrs, rather late, the two companies attacked and quickly penetrated the enemy defences in and around the village. Somehow this delay had not been communicated to C Company, the mortars or machine guns and consequently the supporting fire plan had gone ahead as planned. By the time A and B Companies crossed their start line and advanced on Ste Honorine, the mortars and machine guns were running low on ammunition, just when the covering fire was needed most.

As the two companies closed in on the village through the cover of a smoke screen those men on the Ring Contour saw seven German 75mm self-propelled guns advancing from the north-east towards the village. A radio warning was passed to Battalion Headquarters, but failed to get through. As the men of A and B Companies neared the village losses were sustained from enemy machine guns and mortars.

'Mickey' Archdale's 12 Platoon, B Company had a horrendous time as they crossed the wall into the village. The enemy seemed to be everywhere and was very difficult to spot. A mortar bomb fatally wounded Sergeant John Coyle from Londonderry, while shell fragments to his legs paralysed Corporal Jefferson; Corporal Walkingshaw was severely wounded by machine-gun fire and 'Spud' Murphy fell victim to the ever-present mortar bombs. With the loss of so many NCOs command and control of the Platoon was proving extremely difficult.

There was an immediate counter-attack by infantry supported by tanks and self-propelled guns. With only PIATs and Gammon bombs as anti-tank weapons the Airborne men were forced to give ground and a withdrawal was ordered back to Longueval at approximately 1500hrs. Archdale's Platoon found themselves trapped by accurate sniper fire and with German tanks closing in it looked like surrender was the only possibility. It was then that Rifleman Charles Feeney came into his own. With total disregard to both shellfire and snipers he skilfully began throwing smoke grenades to cover the withdrawal of the Platoon, and by the time they were back in their original starting place by 1000hrs, Archdale was shocked to see that he only had eight men fit for combat.

In the meantime C Company continued to receive more than its fair share of enemy fire. Lieutenant Morgan, in command of the Machine Gun Platoon, was wounded, as was Lieutenant Dean. Corporal McCayna was killed, while Colour Sergeant Boyce was among those wounded. As it was now clear that any attempt to capture Ste Honorine with the strength available was doomed to failure, it was decided to consolidate the entire Battalion at Longueval, including C Company from the Ring Contour. This difficult manoeuvre under fire was successfully carried out and the

Battalion took up positions around the village, unfortunately having to leave their dead behind. Despite being concentrated into quite a small area, the defences were such that observation from the enemy was difficult and the men were well dug in. The ground directly behind the Battalion sloped steeply down towards the River Orne, allowing a degree of reverse slope, which also posed a threat to the German flank. The position was known to all outside the Battalion as the Anzio Beach Head, an allusion to the position in Italy where Allied forces had suffered horrific casualties. During the afternoon a shell that fell close to Battalion HQ killed Lieutenant Boustead, while Lieutenant Morgan was reported as 'missing'.

The casualty list for the day was 16 men killed, 69 wounded and over 40 reported as 'missing in action'. Among the dead were Lance Corporal Patrick Barry from London, Rifleman Percy Godson from London, and Rifleman Thomas Hankey from Dublin. The weather was reported as 'warm and fine', which was small comfort to the injured men.

At 0300hrs on D+2, Lance Corporals Henry and Mullins of 12 Platoon, B Company, arrived back in the Battalion area. They had stayed with Corporal Jefferson after he had been wounded and when darkness fell had placed him on a groundsheet and dragged him foot by foot back to 'Red Location Station'. Here he had been left and Lieutenant Archdale immediately sent out a patrol to bring him in to the RAP. The patrol was observed by the Germans and came under heavy mortar fire forcing them back to the Company lines. At 0900hrs, a further patrol, including Corporal Thompson and Rifleman Gunning, was sent out to bring in Jefferson. Despite the area being infested with enemy snipers this was achieved, but Corporal Thompson was wounded. Although Corporal Jefferson was found, he had died of his wounds some time during the night.

The remainder of the day was mainly spent in strengthening the defences. A reconnaissance patrol was ordered out from D Company at 1400hrs, their destination Colombelles. This was a small village close to a steel works that had two tall chimneys, giving a commanding view over the approaches to Caen. Sergeant Harry Pegg was part of the patrol and was present when two elderly French civilians were questioned about enemy strengths. According to the Frenchmen the German soldiers numbered approximately

100 and belonged to the 21st Panzer Division, but no tanks had been seen for some time.

Later in the day a salvo of artillery shells fell on part of the Battalion defences destroying one of the anti-tank guns, killing five men and wounding nine others. One of the wounded was Captain Jimmy Browne, hit by shrapnel close to Company HQ in an orchard. Jimmy was not one of the Battalion's sportsmen, much preferring more academic interests, not to mention good food and wine. As the stretcher-bearers struggled to bring his generous frame to the RAP a strongly built French farmer lent a welcome hand. While being treated Jimmy complained that he had trained for four years for a war in which he had lasted forty-eight hours. Harry Pegg was among those who assisted with the recovery of the wounded, a wheelbarrow being used to convey many of the injured men to the RAP. Those killed were Lance Sergeant Charles Allen, Rifleman Patrick Mullins, Rifleman Edward Payne and Rifleman Starr. Corporal Raynham of the Signals Platoon was taken to the RAP, but died of his wounds.

At 1725hrs a body of German infantry, estimated at platoon strength, was observed forming up behind Battalion Headquarters. RSM Griffith and Captain Sheridan engaged them from the attic window with Sten guns, while various clerks from Battalion HQ joined in with their rifles. The enemy patrol was forced to move to the flank where they were similarly engaged by B Company and the Germans eventually withdrew having failed to inflict any casualties on the Battalion.

Captain Robin Rigby arrived at Battalion Headquarters at 1825hrs and informed them that the shells that had fallen on the Battalion area earlier in the afternoon had come from British guns! When Captain Rigby had discovered this he had swum the river and canal in an attempt to have the firing stopped and in so doing had almost been captured by the Germans. He subsequently recrossed both water obstacles and arrived at Battalion HQ dripping wet. He was then reclothed with items supplied from the Todt Organisation. There can therefore be little doubt that the anti-tank gun crew and men lost by the Battalion was the result of friendly fire.

At 1930hrs the Battalion was briefed that another attack was to be made on Ste Honorine. Lieutenant Archdale noted in his diary that all ranks were quite shaken by this order, including himself. Corporal Edwards, of his Platoon, was taken to the RAP suffering from shell shock. At 2100hrs the order was rescinded until a proper reconnaissance could be made, there was much relief all round and most men managed about three hours sleep.

By 2315hrs the total casualties suffered by the Battalion on its third day in Normandy were 5 other ranks killed, 17 wounded and 9 missing.

On 9 June plans were made for another attack on Ste Honorine and the 12th Parachute Battalion arrived in Longueval to assist, but this attack was finally cancelled when adequate artillery support could not be found.

Breakfast consisted of 'compo' rations, but in B Company they had acquired some fresh sausages, which went down well with freshly brewed tea, and morale rose throughout the Company. In the days to come those men in the front line would find that their rations were pilfered by those employed on the beach in unloading the supply ships. Elsewhere Rifleman Joe Cullen earned a reputation for making excellent chicken soup from 'wounded' hens.

At 1000hrs D Company was split into two fighting patrols, each of approximately fifty men. The patrol under the command of Captain Donnelly was to proceed to Ste Honorine, but was cancelled due to a lack of artillery support. The one led by Major Dyball, which was to proceed up the river to Colombelle and then on to Ste Honorine, had a degree of success. As the patrol approached the village on the main road a French lady riding a bicycle intercepted it. A member of the patrol, Lieutenant Milliken, acting as interpreter, was informed that 'les Boches' were close by. The patrol immediately took cover by the side of the road and watched as a German staff car drove past. Remaining in cover the men waited and a few minutes later the car returned. This time there was a loud explosion from a hand grenade thrown by Major Dyball, followed by bursts of Bren gun fire being answered by the ripping sound of a German MG34. A party of German infantry, estimated at twenty men, had been ambushed by the other end of the patrol and almost wiped out. The patrol was now under fire from supporting machine guns firing from some distance away and there was the sound of a German armoured car approaching. Major Dyball therefore ordered the patrol to disengage, causing problems to those men who had to cross a road swept by enemy fire. The patrol lost one man wounded and two killed, Rifleman McIlroy and Rifleman Prosser, both from Belfast.

At 1400hrs, Lieutenant Chapman and 20 Platoon were ordered to sweep the woods to the rear of Battalion Headquarters in order to clear out bothersome enemy snipers. Chapman had been a former student at Queen's University, Belfast, where he had studied dentistry. A short time later a report was received that the Regimental Aid Post was under fire and medics attempting to load casualties onto the medical jeeps were being sniped at from close range. Lieutenant Colonel Anderson, the officer commanding 195th Field Ambulance, who had been working in the RAP, was shot by one of these snipers, despite the preponderance of Red Cross flags and his own Red Cross armband. Both Majors Drummond and Hynds witnessed this shooting. Later a RAMC nursing orderly was also killed and another platoon of the Rifles was sent into the woods to clear the snipers out. When the Reconnaissance Platoon arrived at the relevant corner of the wood they soon put a stop to the shooting. Later D Company was ordered to maintain standing patrols to ensure that the enemy did not return.

Corporal Steward of the Reconnaissance Platoon arrived at Battalion Headquarters to report that Lieutenant Campbell had been wounded in the previous action and was lying in the open to the north of the road that ran behind the position. Any attempt to recover him had been prevented by accurate small-arms fire. Captain Rigby ordered a smoke screen to be laid using the 2-inch mortars, under cover of which the Reconnaissance Platoon advanced and successfully recovered the luckless Lieutenant. As this was going on a German self-propelled gun arrived on the scene and began to lob shells into the smoke, as a result of which Rifleman McIlroy was severely wounded, but he too was taken to safety. Both men were removed to the RAP, but despite the best efforts of the medical staff Rifleman McIlroy later died of his wounds. Lieutenant Campbell was transferred to the Base Hospital.

Lieutenant Quinn spotted a self-propelled gun in the woods to the rear of Battalion Headquarters at 1705hrs, possibly the same one that had fired on the Reconnaissance Platoon. With permission from the CO, he ordered the gun crew to load a sabot round into the 6-pounder, the first time this type of ammunition was used in the Normandy campaign.

Ten minutes later the gun had been positioned and opened fire. At this point the gun was quite close to the building being used as Battalion Headquarters and no warning had been given to those men inside. The muzzle blast shattered what few panes of glass remained and brought down several ceilings. Those men on their feet and not holding on to something sturdy were thrown to the floor. It was the considered opinion of the occupants that the house had received a direct hit from enemy artillery, a view that was reinforced when the gun fired a second round and various ranks were seen to leave the building with indecent haste.

Although the sabot rounds did substantial damage to the trees between the gun and the target, no hit on the enemy vehicle could be confirmed! Nevertheless, all small-arms fire ceased and enemy infantry were observed withdrawing from the woods. The only enemy interference for the remainder of the evening was some sporadic mortaring.

In B Company's area two German prisoners were brought in, both very young, who proved to belong to the 736th Coastal Division. Lieutenant Reg Ellis, serving with Support Company, brought four more prisoners later in the day. When captured each man was armed with a light machine gun, rifle, pistol and hand grenades, which showed that in the defensive battle being fought by the German Army, there was no shortage of weapons or ammunition.

At 2300hrs, Lieutenant Archdale, Corporal Henry and six other men were detailed to go to a nearby farm to protect one of the Battalion's anti-tank guns. It was a quiet night apart from the noise of anti-aircraft fire, as German aircraft made attacks against the beaches.

The next day, 10 June 1944, dawned cold and cloudy, with the promise of sunshine later on. It had been a quiet night with only occasional mortaring, which had caused no casualties. At 0700hrs, the guns of the British 3rd Division delivered a concentrated artillery barrage on Ste Honorine. There was no reply from the enemy and the remainder of the morning was spent in resting and general cleaning. That afternoon M. Davoisne, the owner of the house that held Battalion Headquarters, delivered some interesting news. The Frenchman had become an invaluable source of information to the Battalion, going out each day and questioning the local population as to the location and strength of the Germans. His long conversations with Lieutenant Fogt, a fluent French speaker, were a reliable source of facts and figures. Today he revealed that some 300 German reinforcements had arrived in the area of Colombelles. Meanwhile communications to the various Brigade positions and rear area were proving difficult due to telephone cable being cut by enemy shelling. That evening the Germans began to stir and mortaring began again. Rifleman John Stogdale from Blackburn in Lancashire was killed.

It was now five days after the landings and the smell of decaying cattle and men was becoming overpowering. Despite the best efforts of both Allied and German troops to bury both their own and enemy dead, there were just too many bodies. Those of the famous Normandy dairy herds lay in thousands, rotting in the hot summer sun. Attempts by the Battalion to bury those cattle close to their positions by day were hampered by both mortaring and snipers; only during the hours of darkness could parties of men go out to retrieve the dead, to be brought in and buried by the Battalion padres. Rifleman James Hutchinson remembered that on most nights the padres' words came out of the darkness, 'I am the resurrection and the life'. The graves of those members of the Battalion buried in Normandy were each marked with a bunch of ox-eyed daisies, a flower that would forever be associated with Normandy, as the poppy was with Flanders.

At the farmhouse occupied by Lieutenant Archdale and his patrol, the farmer seemed to accept the loss of his dairy herd philosophically. He had built an air-raid shelter in his vegetable garden and he and his wife would retire there whenever there was any shelling. When some German fighters appeared early that morning, a mixture of ME109s and Focke Wulf 190s, a patrol of Spitfires attacked them and within minutes two of the German aircraft had been shot down, an event watched by the Riflemen in the farm as they ate their breakfast.

The following day, 11 June, was the first Sunday in France for the men of the liberating armies. At 0100hrs the entire Battalion came under a heavy barrage of mortar bombs, with men being wounded in both B Company and Battalion HQ. This was followed by machine-gun fire and the sound of tracked vehicles was heard in front of B Company positions. There was no sleep for the remainder of the night and a welcome breakfast was served at 0700hrs. The remainder of the morning was relatively quiet, with some firing coming from east of the Battalion at 1300hrs. A Royal Artillery FOO with B Company called down fire on Ste Honorine and claimed hits on two separate machine-gun positions. At 1900hrs, Lieutenant Archdale, Sergeant White and Lance Corporal Irvine went out on a patrol to try and find the location of the mortars that had been fired during the previous night, but despite a thorough sweep of the area nothing was found. Later in the evening the Padre held a short service, which was well attended.

On Tuesday, 13 June a further attempt was made to capture Ste Honorine. This time the Battalion had the assistance of the 5th Battalion Queen's Own Cameron Highlanders, on loan from 51st Highland Division. Lieutenant 'Jack' Chapman and his 19 Platoon of D Company were ordered to clear the orchards before the village, this being the start line for the Highlanders. Several German snipers were quickly dealt with and the Platoon prepared to defend the flank of the FUP. As they waited they came under enemy mortar fire, the Lieutenant and most of his Platoon Headquarters becoming casualties. As the survivors moved back Chapman was hit and lay for a while in the bullet-swept field until rescued by Major Ronnie Wilson of Support Company. The Platoon Sergeant, Bobby Cotter, from Carrickfergus, County Antrim, was so severely wounded he was evacuated to England and did not return to the Battalion.

Meanwhile Lieutenant Alan Malcolm, Sergeant Harry Pegg, Lance Corporal Chambers and another Rifleman had also moved forward to the FUP, leading the Highlanders into position. This attack was supported by a heavy artillery bombardment, but unfortunately one gun was firing short and shells began to fall among the riflemen. Among those killed was Lance Corporal Thomas Chambers from Broughshane, County Antrim.

The Highlanders succeeded in capturing Ste Honorine, but were later forced to retire after suffering heavy casualties and a strong counter-attack by German infantry and self-propelled guns.

That evening D Company was forced-marched to assist in the

defence of Breville where the 12th Parachute Battalion was having a hard time in holding off enemy attacks at Breville. The following morning Sergeant Harry Pegg witnessed the cost of the battle. Less than one hundred men of the 12th Battalion were still on their feet, all others being casualties, with dead paratroopers and enemy lying among the houses, the surrounding fields full of dead cattle and horses and everywhere the permeating smell of decaying flesh.

The Battalion was relieved from the defence of Longueval on 14 June and moved to Breville. This was carried out on foot during a very hot day and took the men past their old landing zone. At Breville the village was still strewn with dead Germans, with most of the buildings destroyed by artillery. Nevertheless, the area around the village was considered good ground and the Battalion dug in. 12 Platoon was assigned to an orchard and by 1500hrs were well dug in, with scavengers deployed to see what was available in the nearby farmhouses. Despite the buildings being absolutely wrecked by the shelling, the men recovered two chickens, a supply of potatoes, pots and pans for cooking and cushions to add a little comfort to the slit trenches. There was also a plentiful supply of cider to wash down the evening's chicken stew.

Friday, 16 June dawned with all ranks on edge after a night of confused firing from several directions. At 0900hrs two enemy soldiers appeared before B Company positions with their hands raised, and were identified as a Pole and a Lithuanian, foreign 'volunteers' who had deserted. As they were being escorted to the rear a party of eighteen Germans appeared and were also taken prisoner, having apparently been out hunting for the first two men! At 1015hrs Lieutenant Richard Quinn, a Londoner, was doing his rounds of the Anti-tank Platoon positions when he was shot and killed by a German sniper.

The next few days at Breville were relatively quiet for the Battalion, although there was sporadic shelling, and time was spent in burying the many German bodies. The weather was still very warm and the smell quite unpleasant.

On Monday, 19 June a section of the Reconnaissance Platoon was in the process of moving to a nearby wood in order to establish an OP when they came under machine-gun fire and Corporal Robert Riley from County Durham was hit. Sergeant Hardy, the patrol commander, ordered his men to withdraw for a short distance and sent for assistance. Lieutenant Malcolm was sent with 19/20 Platoon of D Company, now formed into one unit due to casualties, to cover the evacuation of the wounded Corporal and the remainder of the Reconnaissance Platoon. However, when they arrived, Malcolm's men found the wood empty and on approaching Corporal Riley saw that he appeared to have died from his wounds. Malcolm's men were reluctant to move the body, well aware of the German habit of using booby traps. Intending to clear out the enemy machine gun the Platoon moved into the woods towards the offending position. As the attack went in the Platoon came under fire, not only from their intended objective, but from at least three other machine guns and mortar fire from the direction of Breville. Casualties were incurred and on attempting to withdraw they were pinned down. Lieutenant Malcolm in turn sent a runner to Company Headquarters for assistance to evacuate his wounded, but in the meantime the Lieutenant was able to disengage his platoon and return to D Company lines, having failed to recover Corporal Riley's body. The Platoon also left behind the bodies of Riflemen 'Curly' Johnston from Newtownards, County Down and Timothy O'Connor from County Kerry, both killed in the exchange of gunfire.

At first light the following day a reconnaissance patrol led by Lieutenant Bryan went to the wood, but could make no contact with the enemy. Two German soldiers killed the previous day had been taken away, but Corporal Riley's body was still there. That afternoon another patrol was sent into the woods to recover the bodies of Corporal Riley and Rifleman Keogh, another casualty from the previous day, and this was achieved without any interference from the enemy. Another patrol under Lieutenant Milliken reported enemy in the village.

In B Company, Lieutenant Archdale's platoon lost the services of Rifleman Feeney when he was transferred to a special sniper team under the command of Major 'Killer' Johnston. An enemy shell hit the house being used as an advance dressing station, but no injuries were suffered.

An enemy self-propelled gun fired on the Battalion area on 22 June and Captain 'Windy' Windebank, commander of the Pioneer Platoon, had a close shave when a shell landed on the lip of his trench. Lieutenant L.J. Burke, who had returned to the Battalion that day after being wounded on 15 June, had been close by but escaped injury. In fact the Lieutenant would not be wounded again until 3 April 1945. The next day, as the men were brewing tea, a large number of enemy leaflet bombs, many of which failed to open, fell all across the Battalion area. No shortage of toilet paper was reported.

Sunday, 25 June. Lieutenant Archdale and his platoon watched as a large number of American Flying Fortress bombers crossed their position, heading for Caen. The day was reasonably quiet and in the afternoon all ranks got some sleep. The Lieutenant was briefed for a night patrol and as he and his men prepared to move out at 2200hrs, it started to rain. At 2330hrs the patrol crossed the Company boundary and made its way into enemy territory. It would be his last patrol as some time during the night the Lieutenant was killed by enemy action.

June gave way to July and when Captain Bobby Gordon was promoted to Major and appointed to HQ 6th Airlanding Brigade, the Battalion strength was reported to be 34 officers and 576 other ranks.

Wednesday, 5 July had only a few seconds to run when an abrupt enemy mortar barrage caught Rifleman Huddy of the Reconnaissance Platoon in the open and he was slightly wounded. German mortaring was a constant menace in Normandy and caused most of the casualties to the Battalion. At noon the following day five German mortar bombs landed in Support Company area, the only casualty being Rifleman Eagle, who was wounded. One of the bombs set fire to a trailer carrying explosives and Lance Corporal Walsh of 4 Platoon showed great presence of mind and courage in tearing off the blazing canvas cover and extinguishing the fire. An hour later Corporal Edward Dempster of 19 Platoon was killed, again by an enemy mortar bomb. Dempster, from Belfast, would be remembered as a fine footballer and was one of those riflemen who were parachute trained. At 1400hrs Lieutenants Bennett and Cranston joined the Battalion as replacements and were posted to B and A Companies respectively. Their arrival was timely as the following day more mortar bombs fell and shrapnel wounded Lieutenants Monroe and Kinsella. That evening, as a result of a propaganda broadcast made to any Russians serving with the Germans opposite the Battalion's positions, the Germans replied with a 'broadcast' of heavy calibre shells!

On 8 July Major 'Killer' Johnston took command of B Company for a time. Eric Francis Johnston came from Newcastle in County Down and had been educated at Campbell College, Belfast before attending Sandhurst. Commissioned into the Regiment in 1937, he had served in Palestine and on the North-West Frontier, where he had earned his unfortunate nickname. This had come about when a sentry had spotted what he believed was a sniper in a tree some distance from the camp. Johnston, a fair shot, had borrowed a .303 and brought down the sniper with a single shot. Unfortunately the sniper turned out to be anything but and although a diplomatic incident was averted, the nickname had stuck.

The following day the Battalion began by having a reasonably quiet day. A German sniper wounded Belfastman Sergeant Jackie McAlpine as he moved across a stretch of open ground. The stretcher-bearers were left alone as they brought him into the RAP. Rifleman Bob Hoey of the Army Catering Corps, attached to the Battalion, was the cook in C Company. Having set up his 'kitchen' in a barn, Bob, a native of Carnalea, County Down, was preparing the evening meal. It was a warm day and this combined with the heat from the stoves, caused Bob to discard his customary steel helmet. From out of nowhere came a single enemy mortar bomb, which exploded on the roof of the barn. A shell splinter hit the Rifleman in the head killing him instantly. Bob Hoey died on the day his twin sons were born.

On 11 July at Ste Honorine the graves of eleven men previously reported as 'missing in action' were discovered. These included Lieutenant Morgan and Sergeant George McCayna, a Londoner. The following day Lieutenant Cranston was buried in Ranville, having been killed two days earlier.

Lieutenant Colonel Carson attended a lunchtime investiture at Divisional Headquarters on 16 July, where General Montgomery presented the Military Medal to Riflemen Charles Feeney, from Dublin and John 'Doggy' Gilliland, from Newtownards, both men being decorated for their bravery under fire at Ste Honorine. That evening the NAAFI supplies of beer and whiskey arrived, the first since D-Day. As darkness fell German bombers raided the area, but were driven off by anti-aircraft fire. Some bombs fell to the west of the Battalion area and German infantry were seen to be marking their bomb line by firing green flares.

As daylight was breaking on 18 July a large force of British bombers was seen flying over the Battalion area and dropping bombs to the south-east in the direction of the Bois de Bavent and Troarn. From the rear heavy artillery barrages began to fall on suspected enemy positions and the sound of tank engines could be heard all around – it was obvious that a major Allied attack was under way. From the wireless traffic it appeared that the fighting was both confused and fluid. As Lieutenant Maginnis stood in the doorway of B Company Headquarters he was struck by shrapnel from an enemy mortar and fatally wounded, the only casualty of the Battalion that day. He was buried the following day in Ranville Cemetery. The following few days and nights were quiet despite some shelling by British artillery! A reinforcement draft of sixty other ranks arrived in the Battalion and began the process of fitting in, one of the first lessons being how to dig a trench.

Allied anti-aircraft batteries in and around the beachhead were numerous and the barrages put up were tremendous, few German aircraft succeeded in carrying out either bombing runs or strafing attacks. Nevertheless, gravity dictates that what goes up must come down. It was mid-morning on 25 July when the daily grind of Battalion Headquarters was rudely interrupted as the nose cap of a British 3.7-inch anti-aircraft shell pierced the roof of the tent and buried itself in the ground. No casualties reported.

The only event of note for the remainder of the month occurred in D Company positions when one of the Battalion snipers was badly wounded by his German counterpart and evacuated to the Main Dressing Station. Unfortunately the War Diary does not record his name.

As August began the area occupied by D Company, to the left of the Battalion, was handed over to the 12th Devons, allowing one company at a time to be returned to the reserve area for a complete rest. The enemy continued to launch mortar attacks, but the Battalion was well equipped to answer this bomb for bomb and the Germans soon realized that discretion was the better form of valour!

On 5 August two enemy soldiers were discovered right up against the barbed wire surrounding the Battalion positions. When approached one opened fire and was promptly killed. The second was taken prisoner and brought before the second in command, Major Drummond. Refusing the offer of water to drink, he arrogantly demanded whiskey! No doubt the knowledge that an Irish regiment had taken him prisoner allowed him to assume that this would be plentiful. It goes without saying he was totally unsuccessful, as was his attempt to mislead the Battalion regarding the layout and numbers of his own unit. The following few days passed without any undue action by either side, with the exception of near constant shelling and mortaring by both sides. Lieutenant O'Hara Murray returned to the fold along with some sixty reinforcements, many of whom were ex-members of the Battalion who had been wounded previously.

During the early hours of 9 August a standing patrol of C Company reported the sound of horse-drawn transport coming from a chateau opposite their position, but the target was not engaged due to a shortage of ammunition. At 0900hrs a barrage of shells landed in B and D Company areas and Lieutenant Alan Malcolm was wounded and evacuated. In the same incident Sergeant Harry Pegg received a slight wound but was able to return to duty after being treated at the RAP. Both men were very lucky as the shells were between 105 and 150mm.

Two days later Lance Corporal Milne who had been 'missing in action' since 7 June during the attack on Ste Honorine, returned to the Battalion. He had escaped from the Germans and rejoined 33 RHU attached to 101 RF. Also on this day the reconnaissance party from the Princess Irene Netherlands Brigade Group arrived, with the Brigade due to take over the Battalion's positions the following day.

Having been relieved by the Princess Irene Brigade the Battalion travelled to an allocated rest area close to Colleville sur Orne. Here Battalion Headquarters managed to ensconce itself in the underground headquarters of a German flak network, a position that lacked nothing in refinements for a headquarters and surprisingly had not suffered any battle damage, possibly because it had not been defended by its former garrison. The remainder of the Battalion had to make do with what was available outside the complex. The following few days were spent in resting, swimming and other means of recreation in glorious summer weather, with an almost holiday atmosphere prevailing.

On the morning of 16 August Brigadier Kindersley inspected the Battalion and after lunch General Gale addressed the officers and NCOs giving them an account of the Division's activities and strength since D-Day. He stressed in particular how important had been the long, bitter defence of Longueval and its consequence on the campaign so far. That evening Lieutenant Colonel Carson led a reconnaissance party to Amfreville, where the Battalion was to relieve the Devons on the following day. On completing this they returned to Battalion Headquarters to be told that intelligence indicated that the enemy to the Brigade front might at any moment withdraw, and a move would immediately be made to follow up. This was to be known as Operation Paddle and would involve the Brigade pursuing the enemy as closely as possible.

At 2230hrs, the message 'Prepare to Paddle' was received and a speedy excursion was made to Brigade Headquarters to procure the obligatory maps and aerial photographs. Just after the witching hour, the Battalion was briefed on the operation, weapons were made ready, rations issued and prayers said. At 0130hrs, the following morning the telephone in the Battalion Duty Officer's office rang and he was informed that there had not been the expected change in the enemy dispositions and everyone was to go back to bed! Transport would arrive later in the morning to take the Battalion to the Devons' positions to effect the changeover.

By 0545hrs it was all on again, the Battalion was roused from its short sleep and wearily climbed aboard the limited transport available to ferry them to Le Plein. In the vanguard was the close pursuit force consisting of C Company, the Reconnaissance Platoon, Pioneer Platoon and one section from 249 Field Company Royal Engineers. This force arrived at Le Plein at 0830hrs, closely followed by the remainder of the Battalion.

At 1300hrs, the Battalion was ordered towards Cabourg. On their way forward they passed through the Devons, located close to Conneville, and a short time later the Ox and Bucks, at Descanneville. But this was no lightning advance – the road and surrounding countryside had suffered from extensive cratering due to the attention of the Royal Air Force, whose maxim in Normandy continued to be 'more is better'.

Nevertheless, other forces were on hand making holes in mother earth. The Pioneer Platoon reached Le Petit Homme and was within 800 yards of the enemy when the road disappeared to their front in a massive explosion. When the Battalion reached the hamlet, Lieutenant Colonel Carson was ordered to detach one company in order to cut off any enemy retreating from Franceville Plage. B Company drew the short straw and as they proceeded to deploy, it quickly became evident that the enemy had not only cratered the road, but had also spent time in sowing a very effective minefield. Immediate casualties to the Battalion were Lieutenant Bennett and four other ranks.

The Battalion continued its advance along the coast road towards Cabourg, deftly making their way around two more craters, courtesy of the Royal Engineers. Mines were everywhere and progress was restricted to the main road. Good progress was made and with the exception of a brief exchange of small-arms fire between the Reconnaissance Platoon and an enemy rearguard at Le Homme, the outskirts of Cabourg were reached without incident. It was during this time that the Battalion Padre was responsible for taking some Germans prisoner. The Padre, along with Rifleman Jim Hutchinson acting as bodyguard, were travelling along a track when they were flagged down by a French farmer. Using a combination of sign language and schoolboy French it became clear that the farmer wanted the two men to follow him. Thinking that perhaps they were being taken to see some Allied evaders both men went along, although Hutchinson kept his finger on the trigger of his rifle. Arriving at a large barn the farmer opened the door to reveal about a dozen German soldiers, their arms neatly stacked in the corner. Ordering the prisoners outside the Padre was nonplussed as to what to do next, but his problem was solved by a patrol of the Devons who arrived a little later. On returning to the Battalion and making his report the Padre was informed that this was the largest single batch of prisoners captured by the Battalion so far in Normandy.

It was in Cabourg itself that the enemy had decided to make his main stand, the Battalion was stopped in its tracks and despite attempts to launch flanking attacks, the Germans held firm. Lieutenant Colonel Carson had orders to pursue the enemy closely, but not to become embroiled in a slogging match. As daylight was now fading he decided to concentrate the Battalion in the area of Le Homme and Les Panoramas for the hours of darkness, the Battalion dug in on the sides of the road and standing patrols were set up on the flanks. Tea was soon brewed, rations cooked and trenches made as comfortable as possible for the night.

As dawn broke over the Normandy countryside on 18 August a patrol made its way out from the Battalion area, their objective to test the right flank of the enemy with a view to a possible attack. In the meantime the Battalion position was adjusted to allow for this. With mines having been detected and lifted to allow for any advance, the Reconnaissance Platoon was again sent forward to try and discover the whereabouts of the enemy. Accurate and heavy machine-gun fire caused the Platoon several casualties, as did landmines, including Rifleman Richard Jarman. Such was the camouflage employed by the enemy that their positions remained concealed and eventually the Platoon was ordered to withdraw. For the following two hours a party under the command of Captain Robert Martin of the Mortar Platoon went out several times to recover the wounded of the Reconnaissance Platoon. The patrol that had been sent out at dawn returned to report that the enemy flank could not be turned due to the presence of enemy strong points, minefields and flooded ground.

A planned attack using tank support had to be abandoned when the leading tank was blown up by a mine while attempting to negotiate one of the troublesome shell craters. The destroyed tank now sat astride the only mine-free route for supplies and a ferrying operation had to be brought in to get food, water and ammunition around the blockage. This worked with what the War Diary described as 'reasonable success'. Later that morning Belgian Engineers declared the route clear. Just after midday the Battalion water cart came up and as it passed the damaged tank it detonated another mine and was in turn destroyed. On re-examining the scene the Engineers discovered that some of the mines were as much as four feet deep due to the rubble piled up from the cratering of the road. Again the Engineers went to work and by dusk both the damaged tank and water cart had been bulldozed aside and the route was once more clear.

In the meantime Lieutenant Colonel Carson had been ordered to hold his position, but maintain contact with the enemy without bringing on a major confrontation. As the day came to a close and darkness descended Lieutenant O'Hara Murray led out another patrol to probe the enemy positions. Despite a fierce exchange of small-arms fire at close range no casualties were caused and the patrol returned safely. Throughout the day notwithstanding the mines and exchanges of fire, only three casualties had been incurred.

The night of 19 August had passed quietly, but with daylight enemy shelling increased both in volume and accuracy. In the early afternoon the Battalion was put on four hours' notice to move to Le Plein and then on towards Troarn. Lieutenant Colonel Carson was briefed by Brigade Headquarters and told that the Belgian Brigade Group would take over his positions. The Battalion began to prepare for its move and was extremely unlucky to receive a direct hit from an enemy artillery piece that knocked out a 6-pounder anti-tank gun crew. Other casualties were described as light.

By 2400hrs, the Battalion was concentrated at Le Plein and was then moved by troop carrier to Troarn. From here they marched to their lying-up area at Ste Richer, all done in the pouring rain in a temperature that left men as wet on the inside as on the outside. On arrival in their area fires were lit and the men began to dry out, but it was to be a brief respite. After the evening meal Lieutenant Colonel Carson was summoned to Brigade Headquarters and issued with new orders to move to another lying-up area at Lieu St Laurent, which the Battalion reached at 2130hrs with only one detour being necessary along the way.

By 0600hrs on 20 August Lieutenant O'Hara Murray and a rifleman had carried out a reconnaissance patrol, but were forced back by heavy rifle and automatic fire. It was obvious that the enemy were holding the bridges over the River Dives. In the early afternoon the Battalion was put on four hours' notice to move to Le Plein. Throughout the day enemy artillery fire fell at the rate of two rounds per minute, although only six enemy guns were involved – any more and the Battalion would have found the position untenable. The Belgians were due to take over that evening and the Battalion began ferrying out food, blankets and other equipment, the move being made more difficult by the loss of three Bren gun carriers and two trailers to enemy shellfire, this from an already inadequate number. The Belgian Group arrived earlier than expected and as their advance units drove into the Battalion position one of their Bren gun carriers detonated a Teller mine. To add insult to injury it was at exactly the same spot that the Battalion had lost their water cart and tank support. German Teller mines were proving resolute to all forms of detection – other than driving over them. Two of the Battalion's medical orderlies performed distinguished service in rescuing those Belgian soldiers who had been aboard the carrier. One of these men, Rifleman Johnston, was later awarded the George Medal. The injured men, their uniforms burnt from the explosion, were all carried to safety. The changeover was complete by 2200hrs, casualties within the Battalion on this day being five, including Rifleman George Walker.

As darkness fell on 21 August, the Battalion moved through torrential rain to a lying-up point at Lieu St Laurent. In the early hours of the following morning Lieutenant Colonel Carson received orders to put the Battalion on thirty minutes' notice to move.

At 1130hrs that morning the Battalion advanced through the Devons and the Ox and Bucks on its way to take up new positions on a spur close to Vauville. As it was en route, orders were received to continue and take Deauville and the hill behind it. Initial reports were that the town was clear of enemy and the Battalion Intelligence Officer was sent forward to confirm this. As Lieutenant Burke entered Deauville he was received as a most welcome liberator by the citizens and it was only with the utmost difficulty he was able to return to the Battalion to report that all was clear. Although the citizens were friendly, the enemy were not, had blown all the bridges over the River Touques and were still occupying Trouville.

At this point Lieutenant Colonel Carson received orders from Brigade to proceed as far as possible and to seize the central bridge, which they assured him was still intact. The Battalion was then to cross the river and establish a bridgehead on the far bank. On entering the town without meeting any resistance, Battalion Headquarters was established in the former German commander's residence, with elements of a Belgian Brigade to the Battalion's eastern and southern flanks. B Company was sent to the area of

Vieux Deauville, while on going to where it was directed D Company found itself in full view of the enemy and was quickly relocated. A Company, detailed to occupy Touques railway station, did not have an easy time of it due to the actions of the Belgian company already in residence. By not digging in properly the Belgians exposed themselves to the enemy and brought down artillery and machine-gun fire.

C Company came under artillery fire at 1930hrs as it was deploying and Major 'Killer' Johnston, the Company Commander, was killed. Lieutenant Laird, one of his platoon commanders was wounded, as were the CSM, two radio operators and several riflemen. With the second in command absent on a reconnaissance, Sergeant Redpath quickly took over and saw to the successful evacuation of the wounded, some nearby French civilians volunteering to act as stretcher-bearers.

As day broke the next morning an assault boat slowly nosed its way through the mist towards the enemy-held bank of the River Touques. On their return the patrol confirmed that the enemy was still present, so Lieutenant Colonel Carson decided that any assault across the river would have to be carried out further upstream and a spot opposite the village of Bonneville sur Touques was selected. Once again packs were lifted onto tired shoulders and the Battalion slipped away from Deauville and upriver to the area of La Poterie. As the Battalion withdrew they attracted the attention of the enemy and A Company suffered several casualties leaving the railway station, including Lieutenant Daniel McGrath wounded and Corporal Ernest Southam from Belfast, killed.

That afternoon another assault boat crossed the river and a patrol, supplied and led by Lieutenant O'Hara Murray of 10 Platoon, made its way to the church at Bonneville sur Touques. As the patrol neared the church it came under heavy machine-gun fire from the direction of the railway line and beat a hasty withdrawal. Subsequent intelligence revealed that this railway line was the main line of enemy resistance and was garrisoned by between one and two thousand men – obviously another place where a crossing would be inadvisable. The Battalion was withdrawn to an area between Glatigny and La Poterie. This was out of German mortar range and would allow a degree of rest before the river assault, which was inevitable. That night four separate reconnaissance patrols were sent across the river, all four succeeding in penetrating the enemy-held area for a depth of some 1,000 yards.

The morning of 24 August followed a quiet, if very wet night. The patrols that had been sent out during the hours of darkness had penetrated the enemy lines to a depth of 1,000 yards and three of the four had encountered the enemy. Only one casualty was reported – Rifleman Charles Feeney, who had been awarded the Military Medal in Normandy, drowned while crossing a river. Battalion Headquarters was informed that 2nd Ox and Bucks had successfully crossed the river and that the Belgian Brigade had occupied Trouville. Lieutenant Colonel Carson was then ordered to bring his Battalion across the river immediately and to occupy Bonneville sur Touques and Ste Philibert. By 1200hrs the Battalion had successfully crossed the river and had occupied its first objective; by 1615hrs the Battalion had reached the second, Ste Philibert, without meeting any opposition. Here the FFI proved to be most helpful in finding billets, and supplying information on enemy movements and their next line of defence. This information was duly passed back to Brigade Headquarters, but due to the fact that they were on the move, was unable to be acted on.

The following morning the Battalion was placed on two hours' notice to move. At 1100hrs they moved out, following the line of advance of the Ox and Bucks. They in turn moved forward until stopped just before their objective, Manneville le Raoult, where the Ox and Bucks fought a hard battle while the Battalion waited in reserve. There was no action during the day and the only moment of excitement came when a shell narrowly missed Lieutenant Colonel Carson and his command group. That evening D Company was attached to the Ox and Bucks as a 'counter-attack reserve'.

At 2050hrs a German prisoner was brought in to the Battalion position. He proved to be a NCO from the 630 Assault Gun Battery and when questioned supplied the Intelligence Platoon with quite a lot of useful information. Directly to the front of the Battalion were some 500 infantry, 120 of whom were German regular troops, equipped with two 50mm anti-tank guns, two 20mm flak guns dug in for ground use, fifteen heavy and five light machine

1. Men of the 2nd Battalion crew a French 25mm anti-tank gun in the St Pol area during the time known as the 'Phoney War'. *(RUR Museum)*

2. Men of the 2nd Battalion resting in an unnamed town during the withdrawal to Dunkirk. *(RUR Museum)*

3. Waiting on one of the 'lorry'
   piers on the beach at
   Dunkirk. *From front to rear:*
   Captain Garnett, Rifleman
   Weir, Lieutenant J. A. St.
   Maur Shiel, Lieutenant
   Sturgeon, Lieutenant
   Colonel Knox, Lieutenant
   Carberry.
   (RUR Museum)

4. The majority of the
   Battalion came back
   from France aboard
   HMS *Icarus*.
   (RUR Museum)

5. Lieutenant Colonel 'Ghandi' Knox, from Whitehead, County Antrim, receives a Bar to his DSO from HM King George VI, on his return from Dunkirk.

St Patrick's Day 1944, General Bernard presenting the shamrock to Major de Longueuil. On the Major's right is Lieutenant Jim Campbell; on the Major's left, Captain Watson, Lieutenant Diserens and Lieutenant Rand.

(RUR Museum)

7. RSM Sam Fleming talking to Montgomery prior to Normandy. 'Tommy' Harris is in the background. Fleming would be awarded the Military Cross for his actions in Normandy. *(RUR Museum)*

8. Major Donlea MC, Montgomery and 'Tomm Harris prior to D-Day. *(RUR Museum)*

9. Montgomery talking to Rifleman 'Sticky' Ryan MM. Ryan had been awarded his medal for his action at Ypres in 1940 and was one of those responsible for the safe arrival of the 2nd Battalion on the beach on D-Day.   *(RUR Museum)*

. Rifleman McCracken showing Lieutenant Colonel Harris, Major Tighe-Wood and Montgomery the load he would have to carry when landing on Queen Red. To this would be added one of the dreaded folding bicycles.
(RUR Museum)

11. 'Canloan' officers, who served with both the 1st and 2nd Battalions. It is believed that eight such officers served with 1st Battalion and at least one with the 2nd.
(*RUR Museum*)

12. Men of the 2nd Battalion on Sword Beach on the afternoon of 6 June 1944.
(*RUR Museum*)

13. A Company, 2nd Battalion, inland from Queen Red. Extreme right is Rifleman McNaul from County Antrim. *(RUR Museum)*

14. This section of riflemen has successfully unloaded the jeep and trailer after landing in Normandy. Also on board are the pilot and co-pilot of the Horsa, recognized by their rucksacks as opposed to the infantrymen's web equipment. *(RUR Museum)*

15. The view towards Cambes from Anisy. A long shallow slope over open ground, which although covered in waist-high corn in June 1944, offered no cover from bullets or shrapnel. *(D. McGurk)*

16. The remains of the stone walls around Cambes. In 1944 they were approximately 10 ft high.

17. Lieutenant Rand and Sergeant Rainey MM, C Company, 2nd Battalion in Caen, July 1944. *(RUR Museum)*

18. The Memorial to the 2nd Battalion commemorating their attack on the village of Cambes-en-Plaine on 9 June 1944, and all the lives lost by thhe Battalion from D-Day until 16 Septemberr 1944. *(D. McGurk)*

19. Corporal Ed Harvey, 1st (Airborne) Battalion, from Chadolly St, Belfast. He was wounded in Normandy and on his return home was presented with a wallet of notes from his neighbours. *(Airborne Battle Study Group)*

20. Lieutenant Robin Rigby and a section of Riflemen beside a Hotspur glider. They sport the Pegasus flash, but retain the pre-airborne helmet. All are armed with the newly issued Sten gun, of which more than two million would be produced in the Second World War. *(RUR Museum)*

21. German PoWs taken on Operation Varsity. They are seated in front of a 1st Battalion Horsa glider, one of the few to land without damage during the Rhine crossing. *(RUR Museum)*

22 & 23. The Reconnaissance Platoon, 1st (Airborne) Battalion, on patrol in the Ardennes in December 1944. These photographs were posed for *Picture Post*, which also supplied the snowsuits.

24. Digging in on the east bank of the Ijssel on 24 March 1945. These men are from D Company, 1st (Airborne) Battalion.

25. German frogmen captured by Major Ronnie Wilson's A Company as they attempted to blow up a bridge in the 1st Battalion area.

26. Officers of the 1st Battalion in Germany. Robin Crockett, Robin Rigby, Huw Wheldon and Ronnie Wilson. The house in the background was used as the Officers' Mess. The former owner, a German general, was under house arrest with his family and they lived in some of the upstairs rooms. One afternoon the General came down, bought all the officers a drink, thanking them for their kindness and good behaviour, returned to his family and shot them all before turning the pistol on himself.

27. The Royal Ulster Rifles meet the Russians. A few days later the situation had changed as the front-line Soviet troops were withdrawn and replaced by more 'political' soldiers.

28. Major Norman Wheeler
commanded Support Company of
the 2nd Battalion in Normandy. He
had previously served in Albania
with SOE. He was wounded on the
crossing of the Escaut Canal in
September 1944.

29. Riflemen Billy Martin and
'Yank' Keenan from Belfast.
Both served in the 1st
Battalion. Martin lost a leg in
Normandy to a tank shell.
Keenan got his nickname
because of his resemblance to
the American actor Alan Ladd.

30. Corporal John 'Doggy' Gilliland from Newtownards, County Down. He was awarded the MM for his actions in Normandy with the 1st Battalion. He had previously served on the North-West Frontier and in Palestine prior to landing in Normandy on D-Day with D Company.

31. Rifleman John Ryan was recalled to the Colours in December 1940. Deemed too old to serve with the Battalion, he was seconded as a machine-gunner aboard various merchant ships, seeing action in the Atlantic, Mediterranean, Indian and Pacific Oceans. He is one of the few Riflemen to be awarded the Pacific Star.

33. Rifleman George Griffith served with the Malay Regiment post-war.

32. Major General J. C. 'Tommy' Harris, CB CBE DSO, who led the 2nd Battalion from Normandy to the Ardennes. *(RUR Museum)*

34. 'In a class of his own', Master Patrick McCutcheon at a regimental fancy dress competition. He was the son of WOII McCutcheon of Herefordshire, who was killed on Operation Varsity.

guns. For artillery support the Germans had a 75mm infantry gun and eight 81mm mortars dug in close to the village. The NCO also stated that all officers had gone missing after the order to withdraw had been given. The exact time was unknown, this being issued at the last moment. He said that the men, some of whom were raw recruits, were afraid to surrender.

In view of this Lieutenant Colonel Carson decided to push on to the next objective, the village of Berville-sur-Mer. The Ox and Bucks would follow up after clearing Manneville. The Devons already had one platoon across the Seine close to the coast and would advance on Berville from that direction. After midnight the Battalion was informed that the Ox and Bucks had cleared Manneville and Lieutenant Colonel Carson ordered the riflemen to pass through their positions and on to Berville. There was no enemy action, the only delay being a part of the road cratered about a mile and a half from the village. On the outskirts of Berville the leading platoon of C Company captured a further three Germans, along with their horse which was immediately named Pegasus and used by Major Hynds in lieu of his airborne bicycle. At 0930hrs, the Battalion entered Berville. Operation Paddle was over.

In the village, the local residents had been celebrating their liberation for some time. Calvados, the local spirit, was flowing and an angry crowd had gathered at a café, threatening to lynch the proprietress, who was accused of being a collaborator. It took the intervention of Lieutenant Burke, the Intelligence Officer, and a rifleman with fixed bayonet to persuade the crowd to take their accusation to Battalion Headquarters, where the matter was put into the hands of the Field Security Police. The next few days were spent in resting and cleaning weapons and equipment. Word was received at Battalion Headquarters that the Military Cross had been awarded to Major Hynds and Captain Huw Wheldon for their gallantry on Hill 30 during the attack on Ste Honorine.

Normandy had cost the Battalion 6 officers and 45 other ranks killed; 1 officer and 33 other ranks missing, and 18 officers and 385 other ranks wounded or evacuated through illness. On the evening of D-Day, 47 officers and 817 other ranks had landed in France.

Home – September–December 1944

On 1 September 1944, the Battalion returned to England, its campaign in Normandy over. Although it was assumed that there would then be a lengthy period in which the Battalion would rest, retrain and re-equip for the next major airborne operation, this was not to be.

The remainder of the month was spent in taking on strength not only reinforcements, but also those members of the Battalion who had been wounded during the fighting in Normandy. These included Lieutenants Alan Malcolm, D Company, 'Tim' Dooley, Signals Platoon and CSM William McCutcheon of C Company, who had since been awarded the Military Medal. At the same time the Battalion had some valued officers posted out. Captain Bob Sheridan went to the 2nd Parachute Battalion, as did Lieutenants Lloyd Bizzell and Maurice Duhault, Canadian loan (Canloan) officers, who were assigned to the 1st Parachute Brigade, to make up for losses suffered at Arnhem the previous September.

During October and November the Battalion underwent a hard and extensive period of training, including an 'air course', managed by Major Gerald Rickcord, OC B Company. This was carried out at Netheravon airfield, where many of the new replacements got their feet off the ground for the first time.

At the beginning of December the entire Battalion was sent on seven days' leave, which made the return to barracks at Bulford just before Christmas difficult for many men, especially those with young families. Nevertheless, once back in camp a valiant effort was made to prepare for the festive season. There was also the feeling that the Battalion would not be seeing action before the spring and an improvement in the weather.

The run-up to Christmas brought some good cheer when Rifleman Tommy Cully held a wedding reception in a small village in Berkshire. The Battalion had been stationed here after its return from India and many old friends were present. One of the star turns of the night was Sergeant 'Bunny', a man whose voice could charm the birds out of the trees. Back at camp in Bulford the remainder of the Battalion made preparations for the festive season, the dining rooms and various messes were decorated, and the cooks worked long hours on the many puddings. But it was a Christmas dinner none in the Battalion would enjoy.

The Ardennes (Belgium, Winter 1944/45)

On the evening of 20 December, Robin Rigby was enjoying a long hot soak in his bath, prior to what he hoped was going to be a good dinner and a few drinks. The sudden banging on the bathroom door by his batman quickly put an end to such thoughts. On reporting to Brigade Headquarters he was informed that on 16 December the Germans had attacked American forces in the Ardennes along a 60-mile front, most of it held by newly arrived green troops. The German forces were organized on a three-Army front using a total of twenty-five Divisions, of which eleven were armoured.

The 6th Airborne Division was to move to its port of embarkation at Folkestone on 22 December and make best possible speed to the front to assist in stemming the advancing German forces. An advance party of the Battalion under the command of Major John Drummond left on 21 December. The main party left Bulford the following day at 1730hrs, being escorted through a thick London fog by the Metropolitan Police, arriving at the transit camp at Dagenham by 2200hrs where they settled down for a short rest. From Dagenham the Battalion moved to Folkstone and was loaded on to Landing Ships Tank 362A and 364A, arriving in Ostend at 0900hrs on Christmas Eve. There was then a period of some confusion.

At the port they were loaded into lorries of the RASC and driven to Waregem where they were supposed to meet the advance party. After a wait of some six hours Lieutenant Colonel Carson was informed that the advance party had gone on to Dinant. Furthermore, the Battalion should not have been at Waregem at all, but back in Ostend, where the Battalion transport was waiting for them. After some difficulties a message was passed ordering the transport to come up with all possible speed to rendezvous with the Battalion at Berchem. Here the Battalion had been allocated billets for the night, thanks mainly to the efforts of the Quartermaster, Lieutenant Tom Smith, from

Newtownards, County Down and the magnificent hospitality of the local inhabitants.

The move of the Battalion transport party was eventful to say the least. Under the command of Major Warner, OC HQ Company, and Captain Steadman, Motor Transport Officer, they had embarked at Gravesend on 23 December, having lost only one vehicle out of a hundred in a road accident as they drove through London. Tom Warner had enlisted as a Rifleman and was eventually promoted to Company Sergeant Major, before being granted a commission on 17 June 1940. As a Captain he had commanded B Company and was wounded when a hand grenade exploded in company lines on 1 June 1944. He had returned to the Battalion the previous September and been given command of HQ Company. Dean Steadman was a Canloan officer, one of those seconded from the Canadian Army, which found itself with more officers than it required in 1944. The Royal Ulster Rifles were lucky in that they had such men serving with both battalions. The transport arrived in Calais at 0200hrs on 24 December and after much confusion and an all-night drive arrived at Berchem at 0400hrs on Christmas Day. Drivers and passengers were a sorry sight, almost frozen in their seats and very hungry. There was barely time to thaw out and get a cup of tea before the now complete Battalion received new orders at 0730hrs. Their destination was Charleroi, where they arrived at 1800hrs, once again frozen to the bone and hungry. Here the vehicles were met by a guide from Divisional HQ, who took them to Dinant where the advance party was waiting. In the town the companies were dispersed to their billets, not an easy task due to narrow and congested streets. Eventually a hot meal was prepared for all ranks, the first in nearly twenty hours.

Prior to the Battalion's arrival a German reconnaissance unit from Kampfgruppe von Bohm had moved against the bridge over the Meuse at Dinant. Shermans of the 3rd Royal Tank Regiment had held them off and while the main body of tanks had withdrawn back across the Meuse, a few Shermans held a tight bridgehead on the east bank. On Boxing Day the Battalion was tasked with guarding the bridge against any further German attacks. Major Tony Dyball's D Company was responsible for the bridge itself, while the remainder of the Battalion took up positions on the high ground beyond. Here they remained, with all companies dug in across open countryside and in arctic conditions. On 27 December a section of 17-pounder anti-tank guns was attached to the Battalion. These guns were more than capable of dealing with any German tanks, including the Tigers.

While still very cold the sky had cleared and Allied aircraft made successive strikes against German positions and supply routes, practically grinding the attack to a standstill. On 30 December the Battalion, in concert with the remainder of the 6th Airlanding Brigade, was ordered to prepare to move south. At 0900hrs an order was received at Battalion Headquarters directing Major John Drummond to proceed immediately to take command of 2nd Battalion Royal Ulster Rifles. This led to a reorganization of command within the Battalion: Gerald Rickcord became second in command, Major Ken Donnelly took command of B Company, while Captain Frederick Gann became second in command of D Company.

New Year's Day dawned at Dinant after a quiet night and by 1400hrs the Battalion had reached Ciergnon. No casualties were reported and the weather had deteriorated with the temperature well below freezing. Two days later a mid-morning patrol discovered the presence of enemy anti-tank mines at Lissoir, which turned out to be four German Teller mines. At 1500hrs, a reconnaissance patrol reported Havenne, Wanlin, Vignee and Villers-Surlesse unoccupied by the enemy. At 2300hrs, it began to snow.

The Battalion was established at Ave-et-Auffe on 5 January. The duty officer recorded that at 1359hrs more snow fell, setting a picturesque scene worthy of a Christmas card, although from the transport point of view and for foot patrols it proved to be a totally different matter. The following day at 1300hrs, the Battalion was established in the village of Wavreille, having taken over the positions of the 7th Parachute Battalion. At 1415hrs, six artillery shells fell in the Battalion area, presumably from enemy guns.

At 2000hrs, an 'O' Group was called. 53rd Reconnaissance Regiment was sent to Haguemont and 7th Parachute Battalion moved to the Battalion's right flank in the Rochefort area. The Battalion suffered one casualty in A Company on this date when Rifleman McConkey was wounded while in position at the junction of the Wavreille–Forrières Road.

Visibility decreased as fog set in and the temperature dropped well below freezing point. Through the gloom tanks were seen milling about in the immediate front of the Battalion and were presumed to be enemy. A patrol from the Reconnaissance Platoon, under the command of Captain Harry Croft, went halfway to Forrières-St-Martin and discovered that the road was mined. Light Armoured Reconnaissance units plied the Wavreille–Rochefort area, but found no sign of the enemy. The Battalion had a squadron of tanks under command to act as immediate fire support, artillery and mortar tasks were allocated and local night patrols sent out.

On 7 January at 1800hrs an 'O' Group was called and the Battalion was told to expect an attack. There was also an added problem concerning identification for it had been discovered that German units wearing American uniforms were operating in the Brigade area and elsewhere.

Four machine-gun teams from the Armoured Reconnaissance Regiment reinforced the Battalion's positions, while the Pioneer Platoon laid mines at potential weak points and along the front of D Company, which was particularly exposed. That night patrols were again sent out to attempt to contact the enemy and establish the identity of anyone wearing an American uniform. At 2359hrs, the Battalion area was shelled with six shells landing in the immediate area for the fifth time that day. There was more snow, with an inch falling in a very short time, no casualties were reported and it remained very cold. In later years when anyone in County Armagh mentioned to a certain solicitor about how cold it was they received the reply, 'You should have been in the Ardennes, that was cold!'

As 8 January dawned it was still very cold. There had been intermittent enemy artillery fire from self-propelled guns during the hours of darkness and patrols reported Lesterny occupied by the enemy but that the bridge appeared to be intact. Patrols also reported Forrières occupied, although enemy tanks were seen leaving the village. When questioned the local civilian population reported approximately 200 German troops in the village.

At 1300hrs, patrols reported mines and trip wires in the vicinity. Later in the afternoon the Reconnaissance Platoon came under fire and Sergeant Bill Wright from Londonderry was killed. In the same incident Captain Harry Croft and Rifleman Scott were wounded, the latter, from Belfast, having only recently recovered from wounds received in Normandy. As a result of this incident command of the Platoon devolved to Captain Milliken.

At 1420hrs, the Armoured Reconnaissance unit entered Forrières and reported no opposition. A deserter from the 9th Panzer Division was taken and reported that he had arrived at Forrières on 6 January along with ninety reinforcements. The following day at 2000hrs, the reconnaissance unit of 9th Panzer had withdrawn, being relieved by a battalion of infantry, which had now obviously left. There was further intermittent shelling for the remainder of the day, which caused a few casualties, but none fatal. As the Battalion settled down for the night it was obvious to all that an advance into the village would be made the following day and tactical plans were drawn up.

An entry in the Battalion War Diary for 9 January reported that the intermittent shelling had continued throughout the night. 6th Airlanding Brigade ordered the Battalion to advance towards the village and if little resistance was met, to advance into the village and hold the high ground surrounding it. By 0800hrs, reconnaissance patrols reported that enemy troops were evacuating the village and there was the sound of demolitions. On reaching the bridge the patrol found that an attempt had been made to blow it, but only those charges situated at two of the corners had exploded and the bridge was still serviceable. At 1600hrs A Company, led by Major Charles Vickery crossed the bridge supported by a squadron of Sherman and Honey tanks of the 29th Armoured Brigade, commanded by Major Wigan. This squadron had been of enormous assistance to the Battalion during their time at Wavreille, where they had shown the utmost co-operation and willingness to go anywhere, despite abundant minefields and near impassable tracks, sometimes two to three feet deep in snow.

As darkness fell in the late afternoon the road ahead was seen to be blocked by both a large number of felled trees and numerous booby traps. The Battalion Pioneer Platoon, under the command of Lieutenant J.P. Archer, with the assistance of some Royal Engineers, was sent forward to deal with the obstacles. The first hurdle was a roadblock consisting of approximately fifty felled trees stretching over a distance of 150 yards. Once these had been cleared there remained several suspicious objects, such as farm carts and crates, which had to be checked for booby traps. Finally the road itself had to be swept for mines. By late evening the task was complete and the Battalion transport could be brought forward, with all ranks enjoying a hot meal to finish the day.

Following a relatively quiet 10th January night the Battalion received orders to push on to Nassogne on foot, with the exception of four jeeps of the Mortar Platoon, under the command of Captain Robert Martin. Support was provided by a troop of Sherman tanks of 29th Armoured Brigade. A and D Companies advanced with B Company out on the left flank, while Major Huw Wheldon's C Company remained in Forrières to provide a firm base. As A Company reached the top of the hill leading out of the village they came under mortar fire from Nassogne, the men immediately went to ground and no casualties were suffered. The Shermans attempted to come forward but a combination of extensive mine-fields and rough ground forced them to a standstill.

As arrangements were made for a set-piece battalion attack a reconnaissance patrol was sent forward but no discernible enemy could be found and by 1500hrs the Battalion had occupied the village. A search uncovered some enemy who had been hiding in the houses and were more than willing to surrender; A Company captured seventeen, while B Company found four hiding in a cellar. The prisoners revealed that the main body of enemy had left approximately an hour previously with eight or nine tanks, their destination Champion.

With enemy resistance being so negligible Lieutenant Colonel Carson decided to push on towards Grune, the next village on the line of advance. The Battalion's Mortar Platoon and transport were still stuck in Forrières due to the minefields, but Carson was confident that Lieutenant Archer and his Platoon would soon have them cleared. The Battalion arrived in Grune at 1730hrs, to see a lone self-propelled gun retiring at great speed, pausing only to fire a few ineffectual shots in their direction. A Company took more prisoners; the Battalion War Diary states fifteen and again they were more than willing to surrender. The transport arrived at 1900hrs, having had as much trouble from almost a foot of hard-packed snow as from enemy mines.

After another quiet night the Reconnaissance Platoon was sent out and made contact with elements of the 1st Canadian Parachute

Battalion in Bande at 1300hrs. A report received by Battalion HQ an hour later caused a degree of disquiet. The Reconnaissance Platoon had been shown the bodies of thirty-four Belgian civilians close to the village; all were male and had been shot in the head. The 9th Parachute Battalion had discovered these bodies when two patrols, one led by Sergeant Garrett, the other by Sergeant Daniels, had met just outside the village and Daniels could smell something strange. Jumping down into a deep hole almost filled with fresh snow, he discovered the murdered villagers. A little later the village curate and a survivor came out and met Lieutenant Alan Jefferson of the 9th Battalion, telling him just what had happened.

Subsequent investigations revealed that an SD unit operating in the wake of 2nd Panzer Division had arrived in the village on 24 December 1944. They were looking for resistance fighters who were responsible for killing REX members (REX was a Belgian political movement co-operating with the Germans, the head of which was Leon Degrelle, probably the most notorious collaborator of the War). All the men had been brought to the sawmill in the Grand Rue of Bande, where the SD men interrogated them. A little later all men older than thirty-five were given permission to go, but the remainder were brought to the Café de la Poste where they were executed one by one, each with a gunshot in the neck. Only one man, Leon Praille, managed to escape – he had lashed out at his guard and fled into the nearby woods. With the knowledge that Allied troops were close by the SD unit had made no serious attempt to follow him into the forest. Members of the 7th Parachute Battalion later took responsibility for the burial of the bodies.

In the early hours of the morning Lieutenant Tom Smith, Battalion Quartermaster, was doing his rounds when his jeep hit a mine, both he and his driver were injured by shrapnel in the subsequent explosion and the jeep was completely destroyed. A Battalion newspaper 'The Shamrock Leaf' began to be circulated on a daily basis and did much to raise morale.

The Battalion was informed that the 6th Airborne Division had completed its task in Belgium and the following two weeks were to be spent in training and recreation, while waiting to be shipped back to the United Kingdom. Daily foot patrols were sent out into the surrounding tracts of forest, which stretched for many miles.

These were usually carried out by the Reconnaissance Platoon, who also provided men for a photo opportunity. This was for the benefit of the magazine *Picture Post* and the men were issued with snowsuits for the patrol – when the photographer departed so did the snowsuits!

All ranks remember the hospitality of the people of Belgium with fondness and it was with a degree of regret that they left for duty in Holland.

The Battalion was sent to the town of Sevenum in Holland, close to the River Maas, arriving on 24 January. Here the Battalion relieved the Argyll and Sutherland Highlanders and took under its command a company of recently raised Dutch troops, who made up in enthusiasm for what they lacked in experience. To alleviate the language difficulty Captain Milliken was permanently attached to this company and thereafter pestered the life out of the Adjutant with applications for interpreter's pay!

Throughout the night of 25–26 January there were numerous alarms. At 0223hrs, the Dutch company reported a patrol of twelve enemy crossing the river towards their position and the Battalion mortars and machine guns opened fire as B Company stood to, there was no enemy reaction. At 0810hrs a trip flare was set off on the right of the Battalion area, but again nothing was seen. During the hours of daylight patrols scoured the surrounding countryside with no result, except the odd shot from the far bank. Just before midnight the Devons, on the flank of the Battalion, were fired at by German heavy machine guns.

While in position in Holland the Battalion formed a 'boating club' with Lieutenant O'Hara as commodore. All voyages were taken at night and the frequent trips to the far bank of the Maas were made for the purpose of collecting information on enemy positions and the landing of agents and saboteurs. On one occasion a patrol led by Lieutenants Malcolm and England went across with the intention of capturing several Germans who were believed to be manning a wireless post. Unfortunately the patrol encountered a minefield and Lieutenant England, Lance Corporal Bell and Rifleman Cochrane were wounded, who were all successfully evacuated to safety. Sporadic enemy shelling continued and on Saturday, 27 January Lieutenant Maurice Fogt was killed while liaising with the Dutch company; he was twenty-four years old and the last casualty suffered by the Battalion before its return to England.

Despite their contributions to the action popularly known as the Battle of the Bulge the Battalion was disappointingly not granted a battle honour.

England

Tuesday, 20 March, 1945, East Anglia, England. The Battalion moved to its transit camp and for the next two days was briefed for its role in Operations Varsity and Plunder, the crossing of the Rhine.

Operation Varsity, 24 March 1945
– 'A mass of splintered gliders . . .'

In AD 9, the Rhine, flowing at 8 metres per second, was the boundary of the civilized world. Here the legions of Rome had reached as far as they could go. Near here the Roman Army under Quintilius Varus was attacked while on the march and encumbered by their heavy baggage train. The German tribes under Arminius had attacked from the flanks and rear over a period of some three days, and the Romans were completely destroyed; Varus committed suicide in the field to avoid falling into enemy hands. Mere 'barbarians' had humbled the best soldiers of the Roman Empire.

The consequent failure of Operation Market Garden, Montgomery's attempt to 'bounce' the Rhine in Holland and hope-fully end the War by Christmas 1944, brought an immediate end to strategic Allied airborne plans for that year. The following spring saw a renaissance in such thinking and what followed was one of the most successful, if unnecessary, airborne actions of the Second World War – Operation Varsity in March 1945.

As winter gave way to spring and the failure of Hitler's last counter-offensive, the Battle of the Bulge, three huge Allied army groups were poised for the invasion of the Fatherland. General Henry Crerar's First Canadian Army had advanced from the

Netherlands to the Rhine in Operation Veritable, beginning on 9 February 1945. The US Ninth Army, under the code name Grenade, had captured the city of Cologne and reached the river on 5 March. General George Patton's Third Army had reached the Rhine on 22 March, having attacked through the Eifel, inflicting heavy casualties and achieving a surprise crossing at Oppenheim on 23 March. The main allied assault code-named Plunder was to be commanded by Field Marshal Montgomery, a set-piece battle preceded by a two-week air bombardment.

The major geographical obstacle was the Rhine itself, a wide, swift-flowing river, defended by forces of unknown quality, but soldiers now ready to fight for their homeland. An assault across the Rhine was the inevitable prelude to ending the War in the West. For this to be a success a combination of ground and air assault was the only option if casualties were to be kept to a minimum. It was therefore proposed that the airborne forces would be dropped between the River and those enemy forces attempting to move up for any counter-attack. The operation was to be called 'Varsity' and in complete reverse to earlier airborne operations the airborne forces would be dropped following the arrival of the ground forces – it was hoped that this would bring a certain amount of confusion to the German troops. The force allocated for Varsity was the XVIII Airborne Corps, under the command of Major General Matthew B. Ridgeway. This in turn consisted of the British 6th Airborne Division, commanded by Major General Eric Bols and the American 17th Airborne Division under Major General William Miley. The 17th were making their first combat jump, although they had fought as infantry in the Battle of the Bulge. The drop was to be made in front of the British Second Army, part of Montgomery's 21st Army Group.

Across the Rhine was the German First Parachute Army supported by adequate anti-aircraft guns. While most of the German unit strengths were down to about 30 per cent, few had ever completed a parachute jump; but they were defending their homeland. For the 1st (Airborne) Battalion Royal Ulster Rifles, the large number of 20mm anti-aircraft guns would prove deadly.

Varsity

The river assault was due to start at 1130hrs on Friday, 23 March. Crossings were to be made at several places, with a considerable airborne element dropping and landing the following morning in an area some 7 miles to the north-east of Wesel, a town that by the end of the battle would see 97 per cent of its buildings destroyed.

The principal task of the airborne force was to prevent the movement of enemy reserves arriving from the east and moving against the Allied bridgehead. It was intended to land the force in as short a time as possible in order to swamp what was expected to be considerable enemy resistance. Intelligence sources had warned that enemy artillery and infantry units occupied the landing and drop zones; elements of a panzer unit were also being held in reserve some miles to the east. As the successful outcome of this operation would make it impossible for the enemy to hold the river line a fierce and rapid reaction was expected.

The Battalion was tasked with three objectives: the seizing of the bridge over the River Ijssel to the east of Hamminkeln; the capture of the level crossing and station situated approximately halfway between the town and the river; and the prevention of any enemy penetration into the Divisional area from the south-east.

Major Tony Dyball's D Company was to land on LZ U1 and was to seize the river bridge by a coup-de-main action. Major Charles Vickery's A Company was to land on LZ U2 and was to occupy the level crossing and railway station area. The remainder of the Battalion was to land on LZ U3 and would concentrate at a group of houses to the east of the landing zone. From here they would move across country and complete the allocated defensive perimeter of the Battalion, taking in those objectives previously seized by D and A Companies. The landing of the Brigade was scheduled for 1020hrs, with the US 513 Parachute Infantry Regiment landing at the same time on their right flank. Both artillery and air support was to be available on a considerable scale, with particular attention being paid to those enemy anti-aircraft positions defending the landing zones.

On Saturday, 24 March the Battalion, in company with other elements of the 6th Airlanding Brigade, travelled from their transit camps to the airfields. The Ulster Rifles went to Rivenhall near

Colchester, arriving at 0500hrs. With take-off not for another two hours the men removed their equipment, drank tea and in C Company kicked a football about to keep warm. Rifleman Paddy Devlin from County Galway had been trained as a sniper, but on this occasion thought a Bren gun might be of more use. Devlin had collected the weapon from the armoury along with seventeen magazines – as many as he thought he could carry – each one filled with twenty-eight rounds of ammunition and stuffed into every conceivable pouch and pocket.

Take-off began at 0700hrs with a flight time of more than three hours to look forward to. As the air armada approached the Rhine smoke from the previous day's bombardment had obscured much. Crossing the river German anti-aircraft fire became heavy and many gliders were hit, resulting in lost equipment and dead men. A post-battle report stated that of the 400 gliders used in the operation only one in five landed undamaged.

Support Company Headquarters had taken off from Rivenhall. The Dakota towed the Horsa off the ground with ease and all on board settled down for the flight to the Rhine. The glider load consisted of Major Liddle and six others from the Company, their jeep fitted with a trailer and a motorcycle. In the cockpit of the Horsa, Pilot Officer Rushworth and Flight Sergeant Gillate, RAF personnel attached to the Glider Pilot Regiment, flew with both skill and relaxed informality in equal measure. Cruising height for the journey was 2,500 feet and as they neared the target area they found the landing zones obscured by a thick haze and smoke from the recent bombing.

As the Horsa carrying 18 Platoon of Major Huw Wheldon's C Company bounced along in the wake of the tug, Sergeant George Redpath from Belfast looked around at the men who would be his responsibility in the coming battle. Among them were Rifleman Russell, also from Belfast, who had grown up in an orphanage and now saw the Battalion as his home. Next to him was Rifleman Herbie Tattle from London, deep in conversation with Bertie Birchall from Birmingham. Lance Corporal John Lucy and Rifleman Charlie McCrea formed a Bren gun team. Lance Corporal George Gibbs sat alongside Rifleman Paddy Devlin, the fact that they came from either side of the Irish border making no difference at this time.

The drop zone of the 3rd Parachute Brigade appeared plainly marked by the myriad of coloured parachutes strewn about it and the glider made its approach through German anti-aircraft fire that was described as 'considerable'. As the Horsa circled, gradually losing height, there was still no sign of the landing zone, it was not until the glider flew across the railway line that the pilot got his bearings. By then they were too low to make the LZ and were forced to come down on the zone intended for the Ox and Bucks, approximately one mile to the north of their target. As the glider touched down on German soil the starboard wheel collapsed and the wing was ripped from the glider. Thankfully no casualties were caused, but the awkward angle ensured that a good twenty-five minutes were taken up with unloading the jeep, trailer and motor-cycle. This was achieved despite interference in the shape of some not very accurate fire from an enemy 20mm cannon in a field on the other side of the railway line. Although there were no casual-ties caused, both glider and jeep were hit several times.

Considering the circumstances, reduced visibility and heavy flak, it was no surprise that the landings were anything but accurate. In the area used by the Ulster Rifles the Germans deployed twelve single-barrel 20mm and an equal number of triple-barrelled anti-aircraft guns. The gliders came down over a wide area and collisions on the landing zones were common, with German machine-gun and mortar fire resulting in further damage and casu-alties. While the enemy was certainly shocked by the landings, his reaction was both fast and deadly. Streams of machine-gun fire, anti-aircraft shells and mortar bombs peppered the zones and both armoured cars and self-propelled guns made early appearances.

Major Liddle gathered his small force together and moved south along the railway line. Although the Devons had previously cleared this area it was still under fire from 20mm cannon, albeit firing from some distance away. Using what cover was provided by stationary goods wagons and some store dumps the party made its way south until making contact with Lieutenant Ellis and his two Vickers machine guns situated on the railway some 300 yards north of the Battalion objective. The Vickers were trading bursts with the 20mm and giving as good as they got. A little further along Major Liddle found Lieutenant Laird at the level crossing, where he had under his command two platoons of A Company and a platoon of the Devons. The Lieutenant informed Major Liddle that some men of D Company were holding the Ijssel bridge.

Major Dyball's glider had come in to LZ U1 at 1025hrs and skidded to a stop some 150 yards from its intended target, the bridge over the River Ijssel. Within a matter of seconds two more gliders came down in the same area and all three disgorged their loads in double quick time. Those men sitting in the front of the Major's glider made an unexpected egress via the cockpit window, those in the rear managing to get out through the side door. As this was happening German machine gun bullets were punching their way through the flimsy plywood shell of the glider and one man was killed while three others received various wounds. The dead man was the Company signaller and a quick examination showed that his radio had also taken a number of bullets so any hope of contacting the other parts of the Company was severely reduced.

When prisoners were taken later in the battle these men would be found to be from a company of an 'Ear Battalion', so called because all men suffered from hearing difficulties, which must have been handy during the previous air bombardment. Their commanding officer was a young Lieutenant just out of training, so the bridge guard was both his first and last command.

As the enemy machine gun continued to search out new targets the men sought whatever cover was available. The glider itself offered little, but its starboard wing had gouged a shallow trench in the earth on landing and this was quickly deepened with entrenching tools and occupied. A Bren gun was brought into action and began to reply to the enemy machine gun. While the Bren gun's 500 rounds per minute did not begin to compare with the German MG42's 1,200, its inherent accuracy in the hands of a trained rifleman quickly silenced the enemy gun. Almost immediately another machine gun opened up from close to the same position and Major Dyball realised it would be unwise to remain in this position any longer. Consequently he decided to make a dash across the open ground to the woods and see if any friendly forces could be found. Under covering fire from the Bren gun he ran into the woods and met two Glider Pilots, two men from the Ox and Bucks and several Royal Engineers. The men in the woods had a good firing position overlooking the house containing one of the German machine guns. The remainder of D Company

Headquarters was moved into the wood and went into action against two more Germans found there who were swiftly dealt with. From the wood a trench ran towards both the house and bridge. The German garrison was still in the building, but some could be seen making their way to the rear. When one of Dyball's men saw a party of Germans advancing towards the wood along the trench, one of the riflemen primed a hand grenade and waited for the group to get closer. With the Germans only 20 yards away the grenade was thrown, unfortunately exploding on the lip of the trench and not inside it. Nevertheless, almost as one man the group put their hands in the air and were promptly taken prisoner. Dyball then took the two Glider Pilots plus two riflemen and ran down the trench towards the house. As they got to it they met Lieutenant Bryant and his No. 21 Platoon, who had advanced from the north, capturing both house and occupants. The haul so far was twenty-five prisoners, with another twenty-five taken shortly afterwards.

Dyball then crossed the bridge and found Sergeant Joe 'Bash on' McCrory in command. The commander of 22 Platoon, Lieutenant John Robertson, a Londoner, had been severely wounded both in the air and shortly after landing; he would later die of his wounds. Sergeant McCrory, despite being wounded in four places, had taken command and done a good job in clearing the enemy from the eastern bank of the river. Dyball then set about taking up all-round defence against any possible counter-attack. This consisted of his Company Headquarters, two understrength platoons, some men from the Glider Pilot Regiment and Ox and Bucks and a few anti-tank gunners without guns, some fifty men in all. Later in the day five self-propelled guns came down the road on the east bank towards the bridge. A PIAT was fired at the leading vehicle from a range of 25 yards, hitting it on the side. Although not seriously damaged all five vehicles speedily moved out of range and sight.

One of C Company's gliders made a bad landing, including Lieutenant 'Tony' Vöhswinkel's Horsa which came to a standstill in a cloud of dust and ended up at an awkward angle. As the Platoon disembarked Rifleman Hamill saw that the Lieutenant was trapped by a piece of seating. Returning to the glider, which was under fire from several locations, the Rifleman used his bayonet and the on-board axe to cut the wounded officer from the wreckage. For his actions Hamill was later awarded the Military Medal.

Only two of A Company's gliders had landed in the correct place. Major Ronnie Wilson's glider was hit by anti-aircraft fire as it came in to land and exploded shortly after coming to a standstill. Only the co-pilot had failed to escape, but there was no time to unload any of the equipment. The gliders carrying Lieutenant Fred Laird's No. 7 Platoon and Lieutenant John Stewart's No. 10 Platoon were the two that landed where they should and the two subalterns immediately set off for their objectives. While enemy infantry were few and far between there was a considerable amount of 20mm fire coming from the direction of Hamminkeln. A hundred yards to the west of the railway line they met a platoon from the Devons who had discovered fifty German soldiers sitting in a barn waiting to be captured. Laird being the senior rank organized all three platoons into defensive positions around the area of the level crossing. A short time later Major 'Paddy' Liddle of Support Company arrived complete with two Vickers machine guns and crews, who were quickly slotted into the defences.

No counter-attack developed, but three self-propelled guns came roaring out of Hamminkeln, drove towards the position and rattled over the level crossing and the river bridge. As A Company had no 6-pounder anti-tank guns, a PIAT did manage to fire one round, which caused some damage, but the Germans were not intent on fighting and continued on without any retaliation.

Lieutenant Colonel Carson's glider came in for a hard landing and split in two. Carson was severely injured and Gerald Rickcord immediately assumed command. When the glider carrying Charles Vickery crash-landed and Vickery was killed, Ronnie Wilson was told by Rickcord to take command of A Company. Later Wilson was hit in the head and taken to the RAP situated in a house close to the railway line. The medics in residence were from 195 Airlanding Field Ambulance, as well as 'Doc' Rees, the Battalion MO. The MO cleaned up the wound and discovered that a combination of swollen eyes and dried blood had stuck Ronnie Wilson's eyelids shut having feared the wound had blinded him.

Captain Robin Rigby, the Battalion Adjutant, landed at 1030hrs, skidding to a halt some 80 yards from an enemy position. The landing had been hard and the Horsa was badly damaged, making it impossible to unload the jeep and trailer. Another C Company glider had crash-landed between Rigby and the houses, and was

164

burning fiercely, the on-board ammunition exploding at regular intervals. A few minutes later half a platoon from C Company arrived from the direction of the houses and reported that their glider had also caught fire with about two-thirds of the platoon getting out alive. They had attempted to take possession of the houses along the road, but had been driven off by superior numbers and firepower. Later still another platoon from C Company and one from B Company arrived with a batch of prisoners, men who had been captured in the houses on the western side of the road in an action that had cost the life of B Company's commander, Major Ken Donnelly. Donnelly had been born in Dublin, one of the many 'neutrals' to fight in the British Army, and just twenty-five years old. With no idea if any more of the Battalion were going to appear, Rigby placed a small group of Bren guns in the ditch and prepared to launch an attack through the orchard. As he was about to set off he saw Lieutenant Colin O'Hara Murray and his platoon beginning their advance through the apple orchard. With a swift change of plan Rigby ordered smoke from his 2-inch mortars to be brought down, while he led his assault against the houses in an attack at right angles to O'Hara Murray. For the next fifteen to twenty minutes the fighting was mostly with Sten guns and grenades, with the Germans mostly putting up a half-hearted attempt at defence and prisoners were plentiful. When the action was over the sixteen Glider Pilots present were put in charge of the hundred or so prisoners, while B and C Companies occupied their planned positions.

By now it was 1115hrs and wireless contact had been made with D Company, who declared the bridge in safe hands. There was still no word from A Company. With the arrival of the Liaison and Signals Officers and their No. 62 Set a link was made with Brigade Headquarters. For the next hour more men drifted into the area, including the Battalion medical staff who had been collecting wounded on the landing zone. At 1215hrs, Rigby decided to move all troops in his area along the original battalion route. Without the Reconnaissance Platoon, still somewhere on the LZ, the order of advance was as follows: one platoon of C Company acted as flank guard, while another acted as rearguard; the two 6-pounders moved in alternate bounds on the left flank, the right was now secure as American gliders could be seen landing on the immediate right during the move. During this time Lieutenant John Wright arrived, having crossed the Rhine as part of the seaborne tail and having somehow found the Battalion in the midst of the battle. Later two platoons of the Ox and Bucks joined the column and all arrived with A Company at the railway level crossing.

Sergeant George Redpath's platoon had come in on the far side of a ploughed field from their objective, a T-junction south-east of the village. There was sporadic machine-gun fire all around as the Sergeant led his men towards the road junction. By now Paddy Devlin had been in action with his Bren gun for some time as there was no shortage of targets. Sergeant Redpath ordered the Platoon forward and Devlin followed, picking up his empty magazines as he went. Experience in Normandy on D-Day had taught the men to pick up discarded Bren and Sten gun magazines – spare ammunition could always be brought up to the front line and magazines recharged.

As Sergeant Redpath's platoon made their way towards the east, Paddy Devlin was having problems with his empty magazines. Since he was carrying the Bren gun on his own initiative he was not accompanied by a No. 2, so that responsibility for the ammunition was all his. When he dropped some of the magazines he stopped to retrieve them and soon found himself alone. A German machine gun, firing from the wood to the east of the road, began to find his range and bullets fell around him. As Devlin ran for cover the machine gun suddenly stopped and he saw that the crew were reloading with a fresh belt of ammunition. A ditch appeared some 20 yards ahead and he ran full tilt towards it. With only feet to go the Germans fired again and a bullet clipped his right arm just below the elbow breaking the arm, and gouging along his side and back.

As Devlin lay in the open, fearful that the Germans would begin to bring down mortar fire on the area, he spotted Rifleman Birchall looking in his direction from the nearby ditch. Having attracted his attention Birchall, accompanied by Charlie McCrea, dragged the wounded Bren gunner into shelter. Devlin complained that he was bleeding profusely from his back, but when McCrea examined him he found that the bullet had penetrated two tins of condensed milk in the Rifleman's pack. What was more important was that the bullet had missed the anti-tank mine also in the pack, which would have ended things instantly for the Galway man. As the two men struggled to carry Devlin towards the RAP some 200 yards away, they approached a Horsa that had crashed across the road, blocking it completely. As the three men reached the glider there was a cry of 'Tanks!' and Devlin found himself lying by the side of the road as the other two found cover close by.

The 'tanks', which were in fact eight-wheeled armoured cars, were driving along the road towards Hamminkeln. The leading vehicle increased speed and attempted to drive through the wooden glider, but the driver lost control and the car skidded into the ditch. As the commander climbed from his turret he was hit in the head by a burst of fire. The second vehicle also tried to crash through the wreckage, but by now two 6-pdr anti-tank guns had come into action, as had some Bren guns, and both armoured cars and glider went up in flames.

Three Germans survived the ambush unscathed and were quickly taken prisoner. Rifleman Devlin was also recovered from his position in the ditch and taken to the RAP where Captain Rees attended to his injuries and ensured he received a mug of hot sweet tea. For Paddy Devlin Operation Varsity was over and he spent the remainder of the day wrapped in a blanket until he was transported to the Field Hospital before being then flown back to England.

Enemy infantry continued to hold houses to the east of the bridge while German armoured elements were reported moving in the area of Ringenburg and in a nearby wood. Prisoners of war were still being collected from various locations and by nightfall some 650 were held in the Brigade 'cage'; many of these had been taken by the Battalion and all were now guarded by men of the Glider Pilot Regiment. That night there was little enemy activity on the Battalion's front, but elsewhere things were different. At 0230hrs, a group of enemy attempted to rush the northern bridge from the direction of Ringenburg. The 2nd Battalion Ox and Bucks held this part of the line and within ten minutes they were forced to blow the bridge to prevent it falling into enemy hands. Another attack was launched on the western side of the perimeter, this time by a force of approximately 100 enemy who attempted to break through to the Brigade area, but were stopped by the men of the Devons and suffered severe casualties.

Despite the horrendous flak as the glider force came in to land the Battalion experienced very little enemy artillery during the day. The presence of three German self-propelled guns that appeared on the Battalion's front was quickly dealt with by Typhoons called down from their waiting 'cab rank'.

Liberator bombers flying as low as 80 feet made free-fall resupply drops, causing friend and foe alike to run for their lives as the bundles fell and bounced across the drop zones. On Landing Zone P, the local farmer and his family sheltered under a large chestnut tree beside their farmhouse as heavy wicker baskets and metal containers plummeted to the ground, some bouncing into the air, while others embedded themselves in the fields. These containers were used for carrying both reserve weapons and ammunition. Those used by machine gun platoons weighed 300lbs and held four boxes of ammunition for the Vickers, with the remaining space taken up by Bren gun magazines, carton-packed .303 rounds, 2-inch mortar smoke bombs, type 36 and Hawkins grenades. The container was marked with white squares measuring 5 x 5 inches with the letter 'M' painted on each side. Containers for other units were similarly packed.

With Battalion Headquarters established in a wood to the southeast of the railway crossing, B and C Companies dug in at their allotted positions, while A Company moved down to cover the exit from the village of Hamminkeln. Their position was taken by Major Peter Jackson and men of the Glider Pilot Regiment who had flown them to Germany. On the evening of 24 March the casualty roll of the Battalion was stated to be sixteen officers and 243 other ranks.

The RAMC Main Dressing Station (MDS) for the Brigade was situated in some cow byres and for the following twenty-four hours it was filled to capacity with the wounded. These included Lieutenant Colonel 'Hank' Carson and Lieutenant Maidment. Among those killed was Rifleman David Stothers of C Company, who came from Heatherbell Street, Belfast.

Earlier, CSM 'Bill' McCutcheon had been killed while escorting a group of German POWs, hit in the head by a single shot from a sniper. The CSM was twenty-eight years old, came from Herefordshire, and was married to Vera Amy, who lived in Belfast.

At 0730hrs on Sunday 25 March, the men of the Brigade were preparing a meagre breakfast in the early morning darkness.

Suddenly the roar of diesel engines shattered the silence and two Panther tanks complete with Panzergrenadiers riding on them emerged out of the gloom. The 40-tonne vehicles, storming along at their full road speed of 30 miles per hour, raced towards the bridge, but the Anti-Tank Platoon was not to be panicked. A carefully aimed shell from a 6-pounder stopped the leading tank literally in its tracks and it began to burn, the Panzergrenadiers scattering for cover. A second shot inflicted damage to the following Panther and it withdrew out of range. Deprived of their armoured support the Panzergrenadiers quickly lost their appetite for a fight and also retired. The appetite of the riflemen had not been diminished in the slightest and with soaring morale they settled down to finish their breakfast. By 0930hrs, the Battalion was able to report the perimeter free of enemy. Able support was available in the shape of succeeding 'cab ranks' of Typhoons that circled overhead and were on immediate call. As reconnaissance patrols were sent out into the surrounding area and reported only scant enemy movement, wireless messages informed Brigade that they were to be relieved by the 52nd (Lowland) Division.

At 1045hrs, a squadron of DD Sherman tanks and self-propelled anti-tank guns arrived, having successfully crossed the Rhine. At 1530hrs, the sound of enemy tanks was heard from the surrounding area, the Battalion stood to, but no enemy vehicles were sighted.

At 0600hrs, on Monday, 26 March the Rifles were relieved by the Highland Light Infantry of the 52nd (Lowland) Division and prepared to move forward. At 0930hrs, a swift advance commenced with the Devons on the right flank and the Rifles on the left. The self-propelled anti-tank guns provided support and while their main armament was not required, their machine guns were most welcome.

The Rifles' objective was a high ridge overlooking the town of Brunen. As the Battalion deployed for the attack they came under fire from German mortars and self-propelled guns situated on the ridge. Closing on the objective small-arms fire also began to be felt from supporting enemy infantry. As the Battalion reached the bottom of the ridge it had to cross a vast expanse of open ground, so smoke was called for from the supporting guns of the Yeomanry Battery. RAF Typhoons also provided cover, firing salvoes of rockets into the rear area of the defenders, their targets marked by orange smoke, again provided by the supporting guns. By the end of the day the Battalion had suffered few casualties and the objective had been attained with the capture of 180 prisoners taken in total by the Brigade. Post-battle Intelligence reports showed that the enemy had consisted of KG Karste/426 Regiment, KG Becker and 184 Erz Battalion Hutz.

With nightfall came the rain, a cold penetrating rain. A reconnaissance patrol was sent forward into Brunen, reporting that the town was in ruins and seemed deserted apart from the two prisoners brought back.

The US 17th Airborne Division had advanced forward on the Battalion's right flank and contact was established in the vicinity of the town.

With daybreak on Tuesday, 27 March the Battalion shook itself awake and began to dry out from the previous night's rainfall. There was no movement forward that day and much effort was put into cleaning weapons and getting a hot meal. During the day a party of reinforcements arrived and these were detailed off to the various companies.

Wednesday proved to be another wet day and the Battalion marched to Rhade in the pouring rain. Here they took up defensive positions and for a change were able to avail themselves of good, warm, dry billets in which to spend off-duty periods during the night.

At midnight an 'O' Group was called and orders were issued for them to continue on to the town of Coesfeld the following day, together with the 2nd Squadron, 4th (Armoured) Battalion, Grenadier Guards, under the command of Major G.E. Pike. Major Ronnie Wilson's A Company was selected to ride on the tanks and would advance with a modicum of comfort provided by the warmth of the Sherman's engine decking. The remainder of the Battalion would continue on foot.

Again high ground had to be taken. A Company were forced from their mounts by air-bursts delivered from enemy flak guns deployed in the ground role and there was some strong resistance in the shape of five 88mm anti-tank guns assembled in and around the railway station. The Battalion suffered casualties in this attack including Major Huw Wheldon of C Company. Despite this the

Battalion was able to send forward patrols and later occupied the town. Coesfeld, in keeping with most other German towns, had received more than its fair share of attention from Bomber Command. By now both infantrymen and tank crews had realized that this bombing quite often did more to impede the advance than assist it, as cratered roads and collapsed buildings hindered Allied tanks and gave excellent cover to German infantry and snipers.

The 'bag' of prisoners taken after this action consisted of 200 soldiers and approximately 140 Todt Organisation workers, men from Poland, Russia, France and Yugoslavia.

Thursday, 29 March was a quiet day for the Battalion. The 3rd Parachute Brigade moved through their positions while the riflemen were able to relax for a time and take care of outstanding maintenance and administrative problems.

On Saturday, 31 March the Battalion set out for Greven, following in the footsteps of the 3rd Parachute Brigade. Approaching the town in the dark, the riflemen passed through the paratroopers' positions and moved further on.

The Dortmund Ems Canal had previously been spanned with a Class 9 Bailey bridge and the Rifles crossed with dry feet on Sunday, 1 April, albeit in a great hurry as the bridge was the prime target area for German 88mms and shells could and did fall without warning. Major Dyball with D Company was in the van and was nearing their objective when the forward scouts found themselves almost on top of a German flak position, a battery of twelve 105mm anti-aircraft guns deployed in the ground role. The enemy was not slow in responding. Within a few seconds the air was alive with the scream of shells and the flash of air-bursts and tracer. D Company immediately went to ground and began to crawl towards the enemy guns. A PIAT team got close enough to try a shot and a bomb was lobbed into the Battery position. With a massive detonation the ammunition erupted, the noise of exploding shells adding to the vast crescendo of noise. As the Battalion dug in and held its ground, a call went out for supporting artillery and this soon arrived in the form of counter-battery fire, which forced the enemy to withdraw, having destroyed any guns they were unable to take with them. By dawn reconnaissance patrols confirmed the German retreat and A Company advanced into the Battery position and occupied it. In this action several men were wounded and Rifleman Percy Conyers from Birmingham was killed.

On Monday, 2 April, the Battalion was again ordered to advance and capture the town of Lengerich. When local civilians were questioned conflicting and unconfirmed reports made it impossible to establish the strength of the defenders, it was decided to employ a method that would become known in later days as 'reconnaissance by fire'. All available artillery, anti-tank guns, machine guns and mortars fired for ten minutes into the town. The result of this was that several houses were set on fire and some casualties caused among the defenders. C Company, now led by Major Robin Crockett, advanced into the town and experienced a degree of opposition from small-arms fire. Despite this the centre of the town was reached and the Company, along with the remainder of the Battalion, fanned out to begin clearing the individual buildings. C Company was later in the area of the railway station when the Germans put in a most determined counter-attack. The Company suffered casualties, but managed to hold its ground and the attack was driven off. Examination of the dead and wounded of the attacking force showed that among them were NCOs from a training school in Hanover, men very experienced in combat.

On the right flank of the Battalion the Ox and Bucks had been delayed and had yet to reach their objective, as a result of which the Battalion was ordered to detach a force to seize this objective. Despite being almost fully occupied with various tasks in and around the town, Captain Colin O'Hara Murray and B Company were detailed to carry this out. For support he had the tanks of the Grenadier Guards, who had once again come up to join them. This attack, although successful, cost the Battalion casualties and the Grenadiers two tanks.

To meet the expected German counter-attack a platoon of anti-tank guns under the command of Lieutenant L.J. Robillard, a Canloan officer, was sent to reinforce them. As the platoon made its way towards the railway station it was ambushed and the entire platoon, complete with vehicles, was captured. Later in the day a German hospital was 'liberated' and two of the patients turned out to be Sergeant Shorthouse and Rifleman Walker. In the meantime the Devons were having their turn with the NCOs from Hanover, finding them just as tough as the riflemen had. It took a determined effort to prevent this battle group from retaking the town again that night. As the evening quietened down the men of Battalion Headquarters settled down for a much-needed meal. An enemy shell that arrived through the window interrupted this and although the meal was totally ruined, no casualties were reported.

The following day the Battalion carried out an uneventful move to the south-west of Osnabruck, and were able to rest for a few hours before the Brigade was ordered to move again the following day. This time the Battalion was in the van and supported by the tanks of the Grenadiers. A report from a reconnaissance unit of 6th Airborne Division reported the presence of enemy ahead. Those troops who were riding on the back of the Grenadiers' tanks dismounted and battle was joined, with A Company being deployed on the right of the road, the axis of advance, and D Company on the left. B and C Companies were retained in the centre and to the rear. The attack entailed an advance across open country against a well-concealed and dug-in enemy. Every house, garden and crossroads was a strongpoint and considerable support from artillery, mortars and fire from the Grenadiers' tanks was needed. As the attack continued two intervening villages were 'burnt up' by the Battalion and numerous enemy killed, captured or driven off. The action lasted three hours during which the Rifles suffered thirty casualties, of which eight were killed. These included Rifleman David Grissam from County Londonderry and Rifleman Cecil Johncock from Gloucestershire. Major Dyball was wounded in the leg and Lieutenants Rycroft, Mills and Burke, the Battalion Intelligence Officer, were also wounded. The Grenadiers lost another tank.

When this particular part of the advance passed, the remaining villages ceased to cause any trouble. The village of Buer, bedecked with the white flags of surrender was duly handed over by the Burgomaster. There was no opposition and eighty dejected prisoners were taken.

The day ended with the Battalion liberating Stalag XIC, a camp that held some 3,000 men, mostly French, Russians, Poles, Greeks and Yugoslavs. Surprisingly the camp staff were still in attendance and were promptly put under arrest. The joy of those released was tremendous to say the least and their insistence of giving flowers and wanting to shake the hand of every man that passed made it difficult to keep the advance moving. The night was spent at the town of Blasheim.

On Thursday, 5 April the Battalion became the reserve battalion of the Brigade, which did not necessarily mean that things were quiet. At 0900hrs, a start was made and the Brigade set off for the town of Petershagen on the River Weser. Those tanks operating in advance of the Brigade were coming up against determined opposition, with small parties of German tank-hunters, armed with both Panzerfaust and Panzerschreck, covering all approaches to the river. The Battalion was ordered to attack and capture the town and as they advanced were met by a group of civilians who stated they had the power to surrender the town to the Allies.

Due to the inherent distrust of the enemy it was decided that the offer would be refused and an artillery 'shoot' was called for. The guns of 212 Battery of the Yeomanry, under the command of Major Bill Anderson, combined with the Battalion's own mortars and machine guns proved most effective and the Rifles entered the town without meeting any opposition; forty prisoners were taken and no losses were reported. As night fell the Battalion settled down in the town for some well-deserved rest. Those town buildings fronting the river bank proved ideal for observation posts for the Royal Engineers who were tasked with spanning the river with a Class 40 Bailey bridge in the shortest time possible.

In the early hours of the morning of Friday, 6 April the Rifles received orders to cross the river in assault boats. The Ox and Bucks and Devons had previously crossed downstream and were now meeting strong opposition. The crossing went ahead without incident, it being carried out in what was described as a 'Bank Holiday' spirit. Morale was high and the Battalion was in the mood for a fight. At 1345hrs, the entire Battalion had successfully crossed the river, less the Anti-tank Platoon as the Bailey Bridge was not yet complete.

While the Battalion deployed, reports of enemy armour on their right flank were received, but nothing was seen.

During the early part of the night the Engineers completed the bridge and the guns and remaining vehicles of the Battalion came across, only to promptly bog down in some unexpected soft ground. From Headquarters came the word to extend the bridgehead. Captain Reg Ellis, in temporary command of D Company, was so far away from the remainder of the Battalion that they practically fought their own private battle, but fortunately they were still within range of the Battalion Mortar Platoon and machine guns, which lent able support throughout the action. The enemy continued to try and infiltrate D Company for the remainder of the night, but was eventually driven off as daylight broke. The remainder of the Battalion received several alarming reports of SS troops in the nearby woods, but none were seen.

The Battalion's B Echelon transport crossed the river on Saturday, 7 April, the same day that 11th Armoured Division passed through the Brigade's positions. Subsequent reports identified the enemy as Battle Group L.E.X., which was said to consist of three companies each of 100 men, five Panther and three Tiger tanks, three 75mm anti-tank guns, possibly three 81mm mortars and an unknown number of 105mm artillery pieces – more than enough to cause problems for the 6th Airlanding Brigade. Nevertheless, by the end of the day the Brigade had collected some 200 prisoners, losing Rifleman Terence Rockall, a Londoner, killed in action.

As the Brigade moved towards Munchausen on Sunday, 8 April, there was little resistance, no casualties were reported and forty prisoners were taken. The following day was quiet, so the Battalion took the opportunity to rest and get some proper food. On Tuesday morning Sherman tanks of the Grenadier Guards arrived and the Battalion again became part mobile. The advance encountered little in the way of opposition and by midday had met up with an American tank destroyer battalion. With no new orders from Division the next three days were spent resting, such a change from the hectic days of Normandy and the Ardennes.

On the morning of Saturday, 14 April, Lieutenant Colonel Rickcord and Captain Rees, the Medical Officer, drove to Brunswick to look for the CO's brother, Captain M.B. Rickcord, Royal West Kents, who had been discovered in Oflag 79, by American troops on the afternoon of 11 April. Before leaving the MO donated a bottle of champagne, two packets of compo rations and packets of cigarettes to the recently released POWs. Later in the day, the Battalion, led by the second in command, Major Liddle, advanced on the main axis of 15th (Scottish) Division, passing through the town of Celle before being billeted in houses to the north-east of the town. The following day, Sunday, 15 April, the Battalion moved out at 1200hrs; the roads were in a treacherous condition and had been mined and cratered by the enemy. As the Battalion struggled over, around and through these craters they eventually made their way into the still burning village of Standensen and relieved a battalion of the Glasgow Highlanders. On Monday the Battalion moved again, this time towards Lehmke, with orders to effect its capture. The Reconnaissance Platoon discovered the village was defended and enemy movement could clearly be seen. A two-company attack in conjunction with the Grenadiers' Shermans was put in, but the defence was lacklustre and by the end of the day the Battalion had suffered a few wounded in exchange for fifty prisoners. Despite the onset of darkness the Battalion was ordered to push on towards the village of Hanstedt, so D Company climbed aboard the Shermans and acted as vanguard in the move towards the village. A surprise encounter with some German infantry in the village resulted in their rapid departure aboard half-tracks, pursued by the firepower of both riflemen and Shermans. The remainder of the Battalion then came up and all ensconced for the night. The Germans were unaware that the village had been occupied and in the hours of darkness a German convoy attempted to pass through heading for Uelzen. Unfortunately for the Germans part of C Company's defence line lay across the road and a combination of mines, machine-gun and mortar fire stopped them in their tracks. During this time men from A and B Companies carried out aggressive patrolling in which several enemy casualties were inflicted and prisoners taken.

Tuesday, 17 April saw the Battalion preparing for another move forward, and the following day C Company took the lead towards the village of Rosche. There were two skirmishes during the course of the morning, with several enemy being killed in exchange for no casualties to the Battalion. By midday the Devons on the left flank had already captured Rosche, so the Battalion was ordered on towards Teyendorf. Grenadier Shermans were again attached to the Battalion, with D Company riding on them. As the force closed in on the village the leading Sherman lost a track to a high-velocity anti-tank shell and the infantrymen quickly debussed to cover. As the remainder of the Battalion deployed for the attack a barrage of

Nebelwefer rounds came down. While the sound of these rounds in flight did little for morale, their explosive power should not be underestimated. The successful battle for the village of Teyendorf cost the Battalion casualties including Rifleman Frank Coombes from Nottingham, Corporal P. Headland and Rifleman Fred Robinson from Chorlton cum Hardy.

The following day saw the Battalion dug in around the village and fended off attacks by German Marines who had been brought down from garrisons on the Baltic coast in an attempt to stem attacks by both British and American troops.

On 21 April it was raining hard and the Battalion had a 50 per cent stand-to. The woods to the Battalion front were to be denied to the enemy by means of fighting patrols that would dominate the area during the hours of daylight. One such patrol in platoon strength and led by Lieutenant Stewart became engaged with an enemy patrol and in the following clash casualties occurred on both sides. It could have been a total disaster had it not been for the presence of Captain Brownlow-Rea, a Gunner from the Yeomanry, accompanying the patrol as an FOO.* 'Alamein Joe', as he was known due to previous service in North Africa, was wounded in the face by a burst from an enemy machine pistol, but continued to operate his No. 68 wireless set, bringing down supporting artillery fire. This lasted as long as his wireless, which was actually shot off his back by the enemy. Undaunted, he picked up the rifle belonging to a wounded man and, firing with commendable accuracy for a Gunner he helped to withdraw the patrol from what seemed like an untenable position. For his action on that day he was awarded the Military Cross. The price to the riflemen was particularly heavy – in addition to nearly a dozen wounded, Rifleman Maurice Drilsma was killed. The following day another patrol was sent into the woods to recover his body and the Rifleman was buried where he fell with all due ceremony.

Little else happened for the remainder of the month. When Major General 'Windy' Gale visited the Battalion and told them what a good job they had done since Operation Varsity, the

* The Captain belonged to the 51st Light Regiment (Worcestershire Yeomanry) and was a Forward Observation Officer.

officers were most grateful but the men just wanted to go home.

On 29 April the Battalion moved from its position at Allenbostel, being relieved by units from the US XVIII Airborne Corps, and marched the 24 miles to Thomasburg. The next day was another long route march and the Battalion crossed the Elbe in darkness at Lauenburg, unopposed. They continued to move throughout the hours of darkness, crossing the Elbe–Traue Canal before moving on to Sweedorf. It was about here that members of Major Ronnie Wilson's A Company saw suspicious movement in the water and after several bursts of fire and a few hand grenades thrown into the canal brought a number of German frogmen to the surface. They were dressed in rubber suits and were equipped with explosives with which they hoped to disrupt the crossing. After having their photograph taken they were removed to the POW cage.

At 0130hrs on 1 May, the Battalion was ordered to advance on the town of Gresse, to the south-east of Hamburg. No opposition was encountered and the following day the Battalion prepared for the final advance to the River Elbe. The 3rd Parachute Brigade acted as spearhead for the Division and in an almost unopposed advance had captured about a thousand prisoners by the end of the morning. It was apparently obvious that a complete German military collapse was imminent so that afternoon the Battalion was ordered onto every available vehicle and proceeded post haste for Wismar. As they drove along they passed crowds of released POWs – infantry, RAF and airborne. Among the crowd were spotted two despondent and dirty figures, instantly recognized as Sergeant Torr and Corporal Doherty, both of whom had been captured shortly after Operation Varsity had begun.

By nightfall they had reached Barnekow where some fifty American ex-POWs were found. Donating some of their captured transport, the Americans were sent back towards Divisional Headquarters where they were redirected towards their own lines.

The problem of released POWs and refugees fleeing in terror from the advancing Russians was beginning to cause a major headache. Major Robin Crockett and C Company were ordered to open a refugee camp near Niendorf and within a few hours had amassed 5,000 people; without any rations to feed them, they had only the Company medics for the treatment of injuries, disease and pregnant women. Thankfully both Crockett and C Company were relieved of their responsibility and returned to Battalion duties.

It was now evident that the riflemen were to stay in the area for the foreseeable future. Russian troops were close by and several official visits were arranged, with cordial exchanges of watches, headgear and anything else that could serve as a souvenir.

Major Ronnie Wilson arranged a party for a company of Russian troops and A Company put on quite a spread of food, wine and entertainment. A good time was had by all and a reciprocal invitation was issued for A Company to visit the Russians a few days later. As the Company prepared for the party Rifleman Dawson, Ronnie Wilson's batman, heated house bricks in the fire to press his officer's battledress. Approaching the Russian camp they were met with a warning burst of machine-gun fire and told in no uncertain terms to go away – apparently the combat troops had been removed and their place taken by political troops.

So ended the War for the 1st (Airborne) Battalion, the Royal Ulster Rifles. The summer of 1945 was warm and bright and all ranks enjoyed their remaining time in Germany despite rumours of being sent to the Far East to fight the Japanese. They say that the battle is won when an infantryman stands on contested ground. The Battalion had contested Normandy, the Ardennes and the Rhine – here they stood and here they would stay until ordered elsewhere.

Roll of Honour
The Royal Ulster Rifles
1939–1945

Introduction

At the beginning of this research we were unable to find a nominal roll for either battalion in any of the campaigns. Information on the 2nd Battalion in France 1940 was particularly sparse. By referring to the Commonwealth War Graves Commission web site we were able to trace many of those who were either killed in action or died of their wounds between 1939 and 1945. There exists in the regimental museum a copy of the register kept by Company Sergeant Major Drumgoole of all those men of the 2nd Battalion who were admitted to the Regimental Aid Post from D-Day until November 1944. In Volume III of the regimental history written by Charles Graves, there is a list of those killed while serving with both the 1st and 2nd Battalions along with those who served with the London Irish Rifles, although the list does contain some errors. For all other information on the men who served with both battalions I am indebted to the archives of the Royal Ulster Rifles Museum, Belfast, Airborne Forces Museum, Aldershot and the memories of those riflemen and others who survived to tell the tale. The local Northern Ireland wartime newspapers provide a tremendous amount of information on those men who were wounded, missing and killed, but must be treated with caution. Those papers published in Eire, as the Republic of Ireland was then known, did not provide any details on Irishmen serving in the British Army, nor were they allowed to carry death notices of such men. In June 1944, Mr J. Dillon, Independent member for County Monaghan, made a plea to Mr de Valera to relax the censorship regulations under which families in Eire could not refer to the rank or give other details of fathers, sons and brothers killed in the War in obituary notices. Mr de Valera declined to agree to any relaxation of the said censorship.

We have listed all sources in the appropriate section and if there are any omissions they are ours alone.

1st (Airborne) Battalion

Allen, Charles Henry Belton, Lieutenant-Colonel, No. 36245
Died aged 37, 7 April 1943, whilst with Royal Inniskilling Fusiliers. Son of Maj. Henry George Allen, OBE, RAVC, and Rosamunde Elizabeth Allen; husband of Katharine Elizabeth Mary Allen, of Barnby Dun, Yorkshire. Buried Beja War Cemetery, grave 1.N.1.

Allen, J.A., Corporal, No. 7012090
Killed in a motorcycle accident in Birmingham on 24 July 1941, this was before the Battalion had been designated as an airborne unit.

Anderson, Daniel, Rifleman No. 14742454
From Edinburgh, he was killed on 24 March 1945 and is buried in Venray War Cemetery, grave 8.E.12.

Araow, J., Rifleman, No. 7014039
Killed in action, no mention on the CWGC website as of 6 July 2005; he is listed in Volume III of the regimental history by Charles Graves.

Archdale, Michael Mervyn, Lyon 'Mickey', Lieutenant, No. 105616
The son of Colonel F.A. and Mrs M. Archdale of Southbourne, Bournemouth, Hampshire. He served with Corran Purdon during his time at the Depot at Armagh (Gough Barracks). They would go out shooting in the summer evenings and bring home something for the 'pot' in the Officers' Mess kitchens. Killed in action as a Lieutenant in Normandy on Sunday, 25 June 1944, while commanding 12 Platoon, B Company, he has no known grave and is commemorated on the Bayeux Memorial, Calvados, France, panel 17, column 3; he was 23 years old.

Archer, John Philip, Lieutenant, No. 320388
The son of George Israel and Sarah Archer, he commanded the Pioneer Platoon in the Ardennes. Mortally wounded on 24 March 1945 on Operation Varsity; buried in Reichswald Forest War Cemetery, grave

38.F.9; he was 23 years old. (On attachment from the Warwickshire Regiment.)

Ayres, Richard John, Sergeant, No. 7012633
Born on the Isle of Anglesey, he resided in County Armagh. Received the C-in-C's Certificate for his actions in Normandy and was i/c the company snipers. Killed in action on 24 March 1945 on Operation Varsity. Buried in Reichswald Forest War Cemetery, grave 40.E.4.

Bain, David, Rifleman, No. 3129907
Born in Nairnshire, Scotland, he was the son of Alexander and Jane Bain and resided in Inverness prior to enlisting. Killed on 24 March 1945, aged 25 and buried in Reichswald Forest War Cemetery, grave 40.C.10.

Barr, John, Corporal, No. 3135123
The son of John and Jessie K. Barr of Kilwinning, Ayrshire, he was killed on 27 March 1945, aged 27, and is buried in Reichswald Forest War Cemetery, grave 34.C.2.

Barry, Patrick Edmund, Lance Corporal, No. 7020645
The son of Jeremiah and Ada Barry and the husband of Ida Margaret of Charlton, London. He was killed on 7 June 1944, aged 32, and is buried in Ranville War Cemetery, grave 1A.H.17.

Barry, Terence, Lieutenant, No. 228664
Attached to 1st Battalion, the London Irish Rifles. Died 5 December 1943, aged 22. The son of Patrick and Margaret Barry, of Sittingbourne, Kent. Buried Cassino War Cemetery, grave III.C.13.

Beechey, Edward Henry Evison, Lieutenant, No. 193885
On secondment to the 2nd Battalion the London Irish Rifles. Died 21 January 1943, aged 32. The son of the Revd. J.W. Beechey and of Emily Georgina Beechey (née Clements); husband of Lucy Eleanor Beechey (née Fairbrass), of Hove, Sussex. Buried in Medjez-El-Bab War Cemetery, grave 5.C.11.

Bell, George William, Rifleman, No. 7046436
From Rathfriland Street, Banbridge, County Down, he was the son of George William and Mary Jane Bell. Served in Normandy and the Ardennes. He was killed during Operation Varsity on 24 March 1945, age 23 years. Buried in Reichswald Forest Cemetery, Germany, grave 39.D.9.

Bennett, William A., Rifleman, No. 14795542
Born in Kent, he was killed on 5 April 1945. Listed in the Army Roll of Honour, but not listed on the CWGC website as of 6 July 2005.

Black, Peter Gresham, Captain, No. 162687
Attached to 1st Battalion, Royal Irish Fusiliers. Died 18 February 1943.
Commemorated on the Medjez-El-Bab Memorial, Face 30.

Blount, Ronald, Rifleman, No. 7016818
The son of Ernest and Winifred Rosa Blount of Tooting, Surrey, he served
in the Signals Platoon. Killed on Monday, 10 July 1944 in Normandy and
is buried in La Delivrande War Cemetery, grave VIII.L.2; he was 24 years
old. His brother Kenneth Robert was also killed while on active service.

Blythe, John, Rifleman, No. 7019887
Born in Ayrshire, Scotland, he was the husband of Mrs Blythe of Coldagh,
Ballymoney, County Antrim. Pre-war he was well known in the Ballymoney
summer league football competitions. Killed on 10 July 1944, buried in
Ranville War Cemetery, grave IVA.B.19.

Bond, George William, Rifleman, No. 5347523
The son of Samuel Sidney and Ellen Bond of West Norwood, London,
he died on 17 April 1945, aged 28. Buried in Berlin War Cemetery,
grave 11.Z.14.

Bonham-Carter, Mervyn Charles Brian, Captain, No. 100641
Attached to 1st Battalion, the London Irish Rifles. Died 3 March 1944,
aged 26. The son of Lt Col Brian Hulbert Bonham-Carter, 14th Punjab
Regt., Indian Army, and Dorothy Bonham-Carter, of Ilton, Somerset. His
brother Basil Edgar also fell. Buried Beach Head War Cemetery, Anzio,
grave XIV.E.12.

Boustead, John Derek Athling, 'Geezil', Lieutenant, No. 155053
The son of Cedric and Joyce Boustead and the husband of Lalergie Nugent
Boustead of Bridport, Dorsetshire. Killed in action on 7 June 1944, at Ste
Honorine, Normandy. Buried in Ranville War Cemetery, grave IVA.L.8;
he was 26 years old. His party song in the Mess was 'One Meat Ball'.

Boyd, Norman, Rifleman, No. 7022506
The son of Francis and Margaret Boyd of 29 Upper Charleville Street,
Belfast, he had joined the Battalion in May 1943. Mortally wounded
during Operation Varsity on 24 March 1945. He has no known grave and
is commemorated on the Groesbeek Memorial, Holland, panel 8. He was
21 years old.

Brun, Victor George, Rifleman, No. 7016711
From Kensington, London, he was killed in 24 March 1945, buried in
Venray War Cemetery, grave 8.F.5. He was 25 years old. (Normally those
killed in action during Varsity were buried in Reichswald Forest War

Cemetery. The fact that Brun is buried here in Venray would indicate that he had originally been wounded on the battlefield and brought to the military hospital at Venray, later dying of his wounds.)

Brunton, James Joseph, Corporal, No. 6410153
Born in Eire, he resided in Belfast prior to enlisting. Served in A Company, he was killed on 24 March 1945 on Operation Varsity. Buried in Reichswald Forest War Cemetery, grave 34.C.3.

Bryans, Robert Charles, 'Shots', Rifleman, No. 7012754
From Barrack Hill, County Armagh, he served in B Company and was killed on 24 March 1945, during Operation Varsity. Buried in Reichswald Forest War Cemetery, grave 38.C.3. He was the uncle of the current Regimental Secretary, Major R.J. Walker MBE.

Bryant, Sydney, Lieutenant, No. 180715
Died 1 February 1945. Buried Taukkyan War Cemetery, Burma, grave 10.H.6.

Bryce, Charles, Lance Corporal, No. 2888733
Born in Dundee, Scotland, he was killed on 24 March 1945; buried in Reichswald Forest War Cemetery, grave 40.F.4.

Bryson, Michael, Sergeant, No. 7010791
Born in Londonderry, he died on 6 July 1942; commemorated on the Brookwood Memorial, panel 14, column 3.

Bulloch, Alexander Armour, Rifleman, No. 2985831
Born in Glasgow, Scotland, killed on 26 March 1945, aged 26. Buried in Reichswald Forest War Cemetery, grave 48.D.4.

Burbidge, S.R.E.R., Lieutenant, No. 304907
On attachment from the Royal Sussex Regiment, he served in C Company and was killed on 31 March 1945. Buried in Reichswald Forest War Cemetery, grave 33.D.8.

Burns, Hugh, Rifleman, No. 14742171
Killed in action on 2 April 1945; buried in Reichswald Forest War Cemetery, grave 34.D.7.

Burns, P., Rifleman, No. 14468417
The son of William and Mary Ann Burns of Manorhamilton, County Leitrim, Eire, he died of wounds on 1 June 1947, aged 20. Buried in Hamburg War Cemetery, grave 9A.K.2.

Calveley, Donald, Rifleman, No. 3774116
From Liverpool, he was killed on 28 March 1945 and is buried in Venray War Cemetery, grave 1.E.2; he was 26 years old.

Chambers, Thomas, Lance Corporal, No. 7013649
Served in 20 Platoon, D Company, he was killed while leading the 5th Camerons to the forming-up point prior to the attack on Ste Honorine on 13 June 1944 at Longueval. He was the third son of Mr Thomas Chambers and the late Mrs Chambers of Tullymore, Broughshane, County Antrim, he was 25 years old and had seven years' service. His wife Sylvia and baby son resided in Swansea, Wales. Buried in Ranville War Cemetery, grave IIIA.L.4.

Charles, Allen, Lance Sergeant, No. 7019670
Served in Support Company, he was killed on 8 June 1944 in Normandy by 'friendly fire'. The son of Mr and Mrs Robert Charles of Londonderry and the husband of Mavis of Weston-super-Mare, Somerset, he is buried in Ranville, grave IVA.E.2; he was 23 years old.

Chesson, Stanley Reginald Gordon, Rifleman, No. 1788333
Died 23 December 1943, aged 32. The son of Ernest and Jessie Chesson, of Tottenham; husband of Gertrude M. Chesson. Buried Tottenham and Wood Green Cemetery, grave 17.

Clements, John McMillan, Warrant Officer 3rd Class (PSM), No. 7008349
Born in Belfast, the son of John and Agnes Jean Clements. Husband of Margaret Clements, of Belfast. Died at sea on 19 October 1939, aged 38. Commemorated on the Brookwood Memorial, panel 14, column 3.

Connolly, Alexander L., Lance Corporal, No. 14737740
Born in Eire, he resided in Coventry prior to enlisting. Served in B Company and was killed on 24 March 1945, on Operation Varsity. Buried in Reichswald War Cemetery, grave 40.D.3.

Connolly, James, Rifleman, No. 7046879
Born in County Down. Served in C Company, killed in action on 2 April 1945. Buried in Reichswald Forest Cemetery, grave 34.D.9.

Conyers, Percy Roy, Rifleman, No. 14672037
Died 1 April 1945, aged 19. Son of George Henry Conyers, and of Maud Beatrice Conyers, of Smethwick, Staffordshire. Buried in Reichswald Forest War Cemetery, grave 32.A.4.

Coombes, Frank, Rifleman, No. 14299431
Born in Nottingham, he was killed on 19 April 1945; buried in Hanover War Cemetery, grave 7.H.11.

Cooper, John, Rifleman, No. 3458149

Born in Manchester, he served with C Company in Normandy, the Ardennes and on Operation Varsity. Killed on 2 April 1945 and is buried in Reichswald Forest War Cemetery, grave 34.D.8.

Cousins, Charles Joseph H., Rifleman, No. 7014912

The son of Charles H. and Ellen H. Cousins and husband of Kate R., of Hammersmith, London, he was killed on 13 June 1944, aged 28. Buried in Hermanville War Cemetery, grave 1.L.1.

Coyle, John, Sergeant, No. 7010276

From Ballyscullion, County Londonderry, he was the husband of Greta and resided in Belfast. Served in A Company and landed on DZ N at Ranville at 2100 hrs on 6 June 1944. Believed killed at Ste Honorine the following morning. Buried in Ranville Cemetery, grave IVA.N.8; he was 34 years old.

Cranston, Andrew Stewart, Lieutenant, No. 235669

The son of Andrew Cranston MA and Effie S. Cranston, he was on attachment from the Bedfordshire Regiment. Joined the Battalion as a Lieutenant at 1400hrs, 6 July from the Beach Sub-Area as a replacement, being assigned to A Company and was killed on 10 July 1944, buried in Ranville on 12 July 1944, grave IVA.B.21.

Crawford, Wilnor, Rifleman, No. 7019461

The son of John and Elizabeth Crawford of Ballymena, County Antrim, he had enlisted in the RUR in 1943. Served in 21 Platoon D Company and landed at Ranville on DZ N on 6 June. Killed in action during the fighting around Breville on 14 June. Buried in Ranville Cemetery, grave IV.AG.17, he was 21 years old.

Creaney, William John, Rifleman, No. 7019654

The son of Mr William Creaney of Coolfin Street, Belfast. Reported as 'missing in action' in the *Belfast Telegraph* of July 1944, he had four and a half years' service and was 22 years old. Served as a Private in the Special Air Service Regiment, AAC, died on 17 June 1944, commemorated on the Bayeux Memorial, panel 18, column 2. Prior to enlisting he had been employed by Mr William Biggs Mineral Water Factory, Lisburn Road, Belfast.

Croft, Henry Leonard 'Harry', Captain, No. 204475

Born in London, he was the son of William and Ethel Croft and the husband of Susan Theresa. He was second in command of B Company in August 1944 and took command of the Reconnaissance Platoon when Captain Rigby became Adjutant. Wounded on 8 January 1945 at

Wavreville, while commanding the Reconnaissance Platoon. Killed in action on 24 March 1945 on Operation Varsity. Buried in Reichswald Forest War Cemetery, grave 40.E.5.

Dempster, Edward, Corporal, No. 7012285
Born in Belfast, he was the son of James and Byers Dempster and the husband of Betty of Westfields, Hereford. Remembered as a fine footballer. A member of 19 Platoon D Company, he was one of those riflemen who were parachute trained. Killed on 7 July 1944 and buried in Hermanville War Cemetery, grave 2.A.3.

Dillon, Edward Charles, Rifleman, No. 14403337
Born in London, he was the son of Peter Christopher and Edith Mabel Dillon, husband of Margaret of Willesden, Middlesex. Served in D Company, he was killed on 6 August 1944, aged 20. Buried in La Delivrande War Cemetery, grave IV.B.10.

Donald, Thomas, Rifleman, No. 6983243
An ex-Royal Inniskilling Fusilier, he was the son of William and Martha Donald of 12 Utility Street, Belfast. (His residence was in Britannic Street.) Reported as missing in action on 25 March 1945, during Operation Varsity. He is known to have landed on LZ U and was believed to have been killed on this date. No known grave and is commemorated on panel 8 of the Groesbeek memorial in Holland; he was 22 years old.

Donaldson, Lumsden, Rifleman, No. 14720141
The son of William Wilson and Annabella Hay Donaldson of Pollockshawe, Glasgow, he was killed on 2 April 1945, aged 28. Buried in Reichswald Forest Cemetery, grave 33.C.4.

Donnelly, Kenneth Herbert, Major, No. 85695
The son of John H. and Gertrude Mabel Donnelly of Rathgar, Dublin, Eire. Second in command of D Company in August 1944. Commanded B Company from 1 January 1945 and was killed by a sniper on 24 March 1945, during Operation Varsity. Buried in Reichswald Forest War Cemetery, grave 38.C.7; he was 25 years old.

Donovan, Michael, Corporal, No. 7020302
Born in Eire, he served in the Mortar Group (23 Platoon) of Support Company. He was a well-known and popular singer. Shot as the Group rendezvoused on the landing zone during Operation Varsity on Saturday, 24 March 1945; he was 28 years old. Buried in Reichswald Forest War Cemetery, grave 38.F.6.

Dowling, Michael Joseph, 'Mike', Lieutenant, No. 237706
Left the Battalion with Terence Otway to serve in the 9th Parachute Battalion. Killed during the attack on the Merville Battery on D-Day; he was 34 years old. The son of William and Mary Dowling of Rednal, Worcestershire, he has no known grave and is commemorated on the Bayeux Memorial, panel 18, column 1.

Drilsma, Maurice, Rifleman, No. 14832403
Born in Liverpool, he was the son of Isaac and Adelaide Drilsma. Killed on 21 April 1945 and buried in Hanover War Cemetery, grave 7.H.10.

Dwyer, John, Sergeant, No. 7013702
Born in Eire. He was killed instantly when a No. 75 grenade (Hawkins Anti-tank Mine) exploded in B Company lines on Thursday, 1 June 1944. He was the son of George Andrew and Mary Ann Dwyer; he was 31 years old. Buried in St Mary's Churchyard, Burton Abbots, Oxfordshire.

Dwyer, Stephen, Rifleman, No. 6104911
Born in Eire, he was the son of John and Christina Dwyer of Dublin. Killed on 11 November 1944 in the United Kingdom. Buried in St Bridget's Sec., grave V.K.3075. Commemorated at the Screen Wall, panel 1, Glasnevin/Prospect Cemetery, Dublin.

Edge, Willoughby, Rifleman, No. 14695860
Served in the Mortar Group of Support Company, he was shot in the stomach and later died of his wounds on Monday, 2 April 1945, he was 34 years old. He was the son of Albert and Alice Edge and the husband of Gwennie Mary Edge of Wardle, Cheshire. Buried in Reichswald Forest Cemetery, grave 37.F.6.

Edmonds, George, Rifleman, No. 5681989
Born in London, he was the son of Mr and Mrs G.F. Edmonds of Edgeware, Middlesex. Killed in action on 12 July 1944, buried in La Delivrande War Cemetery, grave IV.B.4.

Elkin, John, Rifleman, No. 6985544
Born in County Tyrone, he was the son of Thomas and Sarah Jane Elkin of Drumquin, County Tyrone, Northern Ireland. Killed on 23 March 1945 and buried in Reichswald Forest Cemetery, grave 34.C.9.

Farrell, Patrick, Rifleman, No. 14400077
Born in Eire, he served in C Company and was killed on 24 March 1945 during Operation Varsity. He has no known grave and is commemorated on the Groesbeek Memorial, panel 8; he was 21 years old.

Feeney, Charles, Rifleman, No. 6984231, MM
Served in B Company, awarded the Military Medal for bravery under fire at Ste Honorine on 7 June 1944. During the attack, Rifleman Feeney's Platoon became pinned down on the edge of a wood close to the objective. Feeney and the Platoon Commander had moved some 50 yards into the wood when they were in turn pinned down by enemy snipers. Exposing himself to enemy fire Rifleman Feeney threw 77 Grenades (smoke) towards the enemy, therefore enabling the Platoon Commander to organize a flank attack on the position. As this happened, Rifleman Feeney remained behind and assisted a wounded man to the rear, carrying him some 400 yards under enemy mortar fire across open country. His coolness and courage were an inspiration to all concerned during the operation. Killed while on patrol on 24 August 1944, buried in Trouville Communal Cemetery, Divn. 23, Row 5, grave 18, he was 22 years old.

Fogt, Maurice Peter, Lieutenant, No. 253984
The son of George and Vera Louise Fogt (née Bryans) of Chelsea, London. Commissioned into the RUR on 7 March 1943, he served in Headquarters Company and was the 'loading officer' for Normandy. He was killed on Saturday, 27 January 1945 in the Maas sector of the front, while engaged on liaison duties, he was 24 years old. Buried in Venray War Cemetery, Limburg, Netherlands, grave III.E.12.

Frost, Edgar Charles, Corporal, No. 7016838
Born in London and served in the Mortar Group of Support Company, he was killed on 24 March 1945 on Operation Varsity. Buried in Reichswald Forest War Cemetery, grave VII.K.6.

Gann, Frederick Dow, Captain, No. 130172
Born in Kent, served in Normandy and the Ardennes and commanded 18 Platoon C Company on D-Day. He was second in command of the Company in the Ardennes. Killed when his glider was raked by machine-gun fire as it landed on 24 March 1945 on Operation Varsity. He was the son of Frederick and Amelia Robertson Gann and the husband of Dorothy Violet of London. Buried in Reichswald Forest War Cemetery, grave 39.D.10; he was 37 years old.

Gardiner, Arthur, Rifleman, No. 7020506
From The Bridge, Monkstown, County Antrim, he had seen four years service prior to his death on 2 April 1945. Buried in Reichswald Forest Cemetery, Germany, grave 34.D.6.

Glass, Samuel, Rifleman, No. 70200302

The son of John and Agnes Glass of Belfast and husband of Sarah of Grimsby, Lincolnshire, he was an ex-member of the Young Soldiers Battalion (Devonport). Landed at Ranville as part of A Company at 2100hrs on 6 June 1944. Killed in action the following day and buried in Ranville Cemetery, grave 1A.A.1.

Godsave, Percy Alexander, Rifleman, No. 7045689

The son of Charles and Gertrude Godsave of London, he served in either A or B Company. Killed on 7 June 1944 and buried in Ranville Churchyard, grave 31.

Gourlay, William Miller, Rifleman, No. 14698590

Died 4 April 1945, aged 19. Son of James and Jane Gourlay. Buried in Reichswald Forest War Cemetery, grave 33.D.11.

Gover, Derek Owen, Rifleman, No. 1440138

The son of John and Kate Gover of Moordown, Bournemouth, Hampshire, he was killed on 2 April 1945; buried in Reichswald Forest War Cemetery, grave 33.C.3.

Grady, Francis Joseph, Rifleman, No. 14616868

Served in Support Company, he was killed on Operation Varsity on 24 March 1945. He was the son of Annie Grady and the stepson of Tom Bosco of Warrington, Lancashire. Buried in Reichswald Forest War Cemetery, grave 40.E.8; he was 19 years old.

Greer, Henry, Lance Corporal, No. 6985178

Died 8 June 1944, aged 21. Buried Ranville War Cemetery, grave IVA.G.2.

Griffiths, Alewyn, Rifleman, No. 1651787

The son of David John and Margretta Griffiths and husband of Megan of Llanelly, Carmarthenshire. He was killed on 24 March 1945 and is buried in Reichswald Forest War Cemetery, grave 34.C.1.

Grissam, David, Rifleman, No. 14449287

From Ardreagh, Aghadowey, County Londonderry. He died of wounds on Wednesday, 4 April 1945; he was 21 years old. Buried in Reichswald Forest War Cemetery, grave 55.G.3.

Gualdi, Charles Joseph, Lance Corporal, No. 7017133

The son of Enrico and Teresa Gualdi of London and the husband of May of Ilfracombe, Devon, he was killed, aged 27, on 16 June 1944; buried in Hermanville War Cemetery, grave IVA.D.17.

Halfpenny, George William, Lance Corporal, No. 14413054
The son of Walter Everard and Annie Halfpenny of Sutton-in-Ashfield, Nottinghamshire. He was on attachment from the Northamptonshire Regiment when he was killed on 25 March 1945, aged 20; buried in Reichswald Forest War Cemetery, grave 34.B.3.

Halvey, Joseph Patrick, Rifleman, No. 14409065
Born in Eire, he was resident in London prior to enlistment. Killed on 7 June 1944, aged 19 and buried in Bayeux War Cemetery, grave X.M.7. He was the foster son of James and Margaret O'Connor of Kentish Town, London.

Hampson, Thomas Sidwell, Rifleman, No. 14786938
The son of William James and Leonora Hampson of Liverpool, he was killed on 24 March 1945, aged 18. Buried in Rheinberg War Cemetery, grave 13.A.10.

Hampstead, William George, Lance Corporal, No. 7022436
The son of Alice Jane Hampstead of South Woodford, London, he was wounded in the chest by shrapnel on 9 June 1944. Returned to the United Kingdom, he died on 14 June 1944 and is buried in City of London Cemetery, Square 20, grave 104124.

Hankey, Thomas, Rifleman, No. 6409930
The son of Mrs. C. Hankey of Stella Gardens, Irishtown, Dublin, he had originally served in the Royal Sussex Regiment. Landed on LZ N at Ranville at 2100 hrs on 6 June. Killed in action on 7 June as the Battalion attacked Ste Honorine, he was 26 years old. Buried in Ranville War Cemetery, grave IIA.N.6.

Harding, Albert Edward, Lance Corporal, No. D/27709
Served in C Company, he was killed on Thursday, 16 August 1944. He was the son of William and Ellen Harding and the husband of Rose Gertrude of Hammersmith, London. Buried in Hammersmith New Cemetery, Surrey, plot 16, section C, grave 6.

Harding, James Clarence, Private, No. 7367653
Royal Army Medical Corps attached to the 1st Battalion. He was killed on 19 April 1945, aged 26. Buried in Hanover War Cemetery, grave 7.H.12.

Harman, John, Rifleman, No. 5990060
The son of John William and Violet Mary Harman of King's Langley, Hampshire, he died on 10 August 1943 in the United Kingdom. Buried in King's Langley (All Saints) Churchyard.

Harvey, Clarence, Rifleman, No. 14677429

Born in Staffordshire, he was killed on 25 March 1945, aged 19. He has no known grave and is commemorated on the Groesbeek Memorial, panel 8.

Headland, Peter, Corporal, No. 5960503

Born in Norwich, he was the son of Ernest James and Mabel Headland of Bedford. Killed on 19 April 1945, aged 19. Buried in Hanover War Cemetery, grave 7.H.8.

Hegan, William James, Rifleman, No. 7046474

The son of William and Jane Hegan of Tormore, Newry, County Down, he landed on LZ N at Ranville on 6 June. Killed in action on 23 June, the first day of Operation Epsom. Buried in Ranville Cemetery, grave III.A.B.4. His brother and three sisters also served and survived the War. There is a memorial to him in Downshire Road Presbyterian Church, Newry.

Helme, Samuel, Lance Corporal, No. 1086450

Born in Lancashire, he was the son of Richard and Alice Helme of Morecambe, Lancashire. Killed on 20 June 1944, buried in Reichswald Forest War Cemetery, grave 59.F.2.

Henry, Hugh, Rifleman, No. 7013163

The son of Hugh and Mary Henry of Crumlin, County Antrim and the husband of Margaret of Paisley, Scotland. Served in C Company in Normandy and the Ardennes. He landed by glider on LZ U at 1000hrs on 24 March at Hamminkeln during Operation Varsity, the crossing of the Rhine. Believed killed shortly after landing, he has no known grave. Commemorated on the Groesbeek Memorial, panel 8, aged 29.

Hilton, Francis, Rifleman, No. 7019976

He had completed five years' service when he was killed on 31 March 1945, aged 30. Buried in Reichswald Forest War Cemetery, grave 33.B.6. He was the son of Frederick and Agnes Hilton of Garfield Place, Ballymena, County Antrim.

Hoey, Robert (Bob), Private, No. 7012466

Army Catering Corps, attached to 1st (A) Battalion. From Carnalea, County Down, he was the son of Robert and Elizabeth Hoey and husband of Elizabeth Hoey. He was the company cook in C Company. Killed by enemy mortar fire on 9 July 1944, while cooking food for the Company in a barn. The building was hit by a mortar bomb, he was not wearing his helmet at the time and was killed instantly by shrapnel. Buried in Ranville War Cemetery, Calvados, France, grave IVA.C.19; he was 28 years old. Killed on the day his twin sons were born.

Holmes, James, Rifleman, No. 3598771
Born in Blackburn, Lancashire, he was the son of John and Sarah Holmes.
Served in A Company and was killed on 24 March 1945; he was 24 years
old. Buried in Reichswald War Cemetery, grave 40.A.1. His brother John
also died on active service.

Howard, Walter Chadwick, Rifleman, No. 1492783
Born in Manchester he served in A Company and was mortally wounded
by gunshot in the face and left side on 19 July 1944 at Troarn. Buried in
Ranville War Cemetery, grave IVA.12 The son of John Chadwick
Howard and Mary Ann Howard of Gorton, Manchester, he was 27 years
old.

Howe, David, Rifleman, No. 14731768
The son of Thomas and Barbara Armstrong Howe of Paisley, Scotland,
he was killed on 24 March 1945, aged 23. Buried in Reichswald Forest
War Cemetery, grave 34.B.7.

Hughes, Christopher, Rifleman, No. 14768203
Born in Guernsey, Channel Islands, he was killed on 24 March 1945,
buried in Reichswald Forest War Cemetery, grave 34.B.10.

Hunter, William Herbert, Captain, No. 224892
The son of Herbert Charles and Ellen Hunter of Belfast, Northern Ireland,
he died on 11 October 1945. Buried in Munster Heath War Cemetery,
grave 2.B.7.

Hyde, William Wright, Corporal, No. 7021059
The son of Jessie Hyde of Belfast, Northern Ireland, he was killed on 24
March 1945, aged 23. Buried in Reichswald Forest War Cemetery, grave
40.D.6.

Ingham, John, Rifleman, No. 14829484
The son of Ernest and Florence Ingham of Walshaw, Lancashire, he was
killed on 4 April 1945, aged 18. Buried in Reichswald Forest War
Cemetery, grave 33.B.2.

Jarman, Richard E., Rifleman, No. 14685407
The son of Charles and Ada Maria Jarman of Milton, Southsea,
Hampshire, he was killed on 18 August 1944. Buried in Ranville War
Cemetery, grave IIA.G.14. His brother William also died on active service.

Jefferson, Norman, Corporal, No. 7013019
The son of Thomas and Sara Jefferson of Lisburn, County Antrim, he
landed on LZ N at Ranville at 2100 hrs on 6 June. Died of wounds on 8
June during the attack on Ste Honorine. A total of six men were killed

and forty-seven missing on this date. He is interred at Ranville Cemetery, grave II A.C.5. He was 26 years old and had eight years' service. Three brothers also served.

Johncock, Cecil Henry, Rifleman, No. 557209
The son of Henry Cecil and Annie Elizabeth Johncock of Minchinhampton, Gloucestershire, he was killed on 4 April 1945, aged 23. Buried in Reichswald Forest War Cemetery, grave 33.C.2.

Johns, William Henry, Rifleman, No. 7022700
The son of Henry H.J. and Elizabeth M. Johns of Waddon, Croydon, Surrey, he was killed on 7 June 1944. Buried in Ranville War Cemetery, grave IA.L.17.

Johnston, Arthur Fraser, Lance Corporal, No. 7016889
Born in London. Killed in action on Saturday, 24 March 1945, aged 25. Buried in Reichswald Forest Cemetery, Kleve, grave AO.E.9.

Johnston, Eric Francis 'Killer', Major, No. 66181
The son of Mr and Mrs Frank Johnston of Ballagh Lodge, Newcastle, County Down. Educated at Campbell College, he attended Sandhurst, being commissioned into the RUR on 6 January 1937. He served in Palestine and the North-West Frontier prior to the War. Commanded C Company as of 8 July 1944 and was killed at 1930hrs on Tuesday, 22 August 1944 at Deauville by shrapnel; he was 29 years old. Buried in Tourgeville War Cemetery, grave 4.G.4.

Johnston, George, Rifleman, No. 7018396
The son of John James and Hannah of Bailieborough, County Cavan, he served in D Company as a Rifleman and was killed on Saturday, 24 March 1945, aged 25, during Operation Varsity. Buried in Reichswald Forest War Cemetery, grave 40.B.11.

Johnston, William (Curley), Rifleman, No. 7018189
Lived at Circular Road, Newtownards, County Down, husband of Joyce, his mother lived in Scotch Street, Downpatrick. A Rifleman in 19 Platoon of D Company, he landed by glider on LZ N at Ranville at 2100hrs on 6 June. Killed in action on 19 June at Breville. Buried in Ranville Cemetery, grave VA.Q.2. He was 22 years old. He had four years' previous service and had worked as a printer in Belfast before the War. His father served in the RIR in the First World War, his brother in North Africa and a cousin, an Irish Guardsman, was a prisoner in Germany.

Jones, Ian Russell Aylmer, Captain, No. 129585
The son of Felix Edward Aylmer and Cecily Minnie Jane Jones of Weybridge, Surrey, he was well known as an actor. Died on 20 February 1943, aged 26, in an accident. Buried in Clewer (St Andrews) Old Churchyard, NW corner.

Kelly, John Joseph, Lance Sergeant, No. 7019204
Born in London; served in the Signals Platoon, he was killed while in the same glider as Captain Martin on 24 March 1945 on Operation Varsity, he was 26 years old. Buried in Reichswald Forest War Cemetery, grave 42.E.6.

Keogh, Patrick Francis Bartle, Rifleman, No. 7014137
Killed in action on Monday, 19 June 1944, while serving as a Rifleman with the Signals Platoon. He was the son of Bartle Bernard and Anne Joyce Keogh, and the stepson and nephew of Bernice Keogh of Tangasseri, Quiton, India. Buried in Ranville Cemetery, grave IVA.E.17, he was 23 years old.

Kidman, William Henry, Lance Corporal, No. 7022031
The son of Bertie Edward and Rosina Isabella Kidman of Dalston. He was the husband of Grace and was killed on 21 June 1942 in the United Kingdom. Buried in Manor Park Cemetery, collective grave 7.

Lenihan, John, Rifleman, No. 6409951
Born in Eire, resident in Belfast, he was the son of Cornelius and Elizabeth Lenihan and husband of Margarete E. Lenihan of Weston-super-Mare, Somerset. Killed on 24 March 1945, he is buried in Venray War Cemetery, grave 8.E.9; he was 25 years old.

Lowe, Leonard, Rifleman, No. 14640325
Born in Birmingham, he was the son of Amos and Jane Lowe of Halesowen, Worcestershire. He served in B Company and was killed on 7 June 1944. Buried in Ranville War Cemetery, grave IA.L.13.

Lowndes, Harold, Rifleman, No. 7048064
The son of Ellison and Florence Lowndes of Hanley, Stoke-on-Trent, he died on 18 June 1945 in the United Kingdom, while attached to HQ 6th Airborne Division. Buried in Stoke-on-Trent (Hanley) Cemetery, grave 16054.

MacFadden, John Terence, Lieutenant, No. 105619
From Belfast, he was the son of Doctor and Mrs. A.W.J. McFadden CB. An ex-pupil of Campbell College, Belfast, he had played rugby for Northern Ireland. After leaving school he was employed by the Prudential

Insurance Service. Commissioned into the Artists Rifles and served as a Lieutenant with the Royal Ulster Rifles. Transferred to Airborne Forces, he had seen service in Sicily. Served at Arnhem and was taken prisoner. He died of illness in Camp XIB, Fallingbostel. Buried in Hanover War Cemetery, but not listed on the Commonwealth War Graves Register.

Magill, Nathaniel Morton, Rifleman, No. 14416538
From Belfast, he was the son of James and Mary Magill of Britannic Street, Belfast and the nephew of Mrs E. Hanna. Originally served in the General Service Corps. Served in 19 Platoon D Company and was killed at Longueval on Sunday, 11 June 1944, while clearing the orchard to the rear of Battalion HQ of snipers. He is buried in Ranville Cemetery, grave IIIA.F.4; he was 19 years old. Two brothers served in the 2nd Battalion and a third elsewhere.

Maginnis, George Alexander, Lieutenant, No. 203952
The son of Edward and Matilda Maginnis of Aughnacloy, County Tyrone, he was commissioned on 6 September 1941. Attended the Royal School, Armagh and played rugby for Ulster. He served in B Company as a Lieutenant and was killed by shrapnel from an enemy mortar shell at Breville on 18 July 1944, aged 33. (CWGC website says 19 June.) Interred in Ranville Cemetery on the following day, grave IVA.B.13.

Maguire, Patrick, Rifleman, No. 7047994
Served in D Company, he was killed on Wednesday, 7 June 1944, aged 30. The son of Mr and Mrs Thomas Maguire of Lisnageer, County Monaghan, he has no known grave and is commemorated on the Bayeux Memorial, panel 17, column 3.

Majurey, Thomas, Rifleman, No. 7013776
The son of Andrew and Dorothy Majurey of Belfast, he died on 3 June 1940 in the United Kingdom. Buried in Belfast City Cemetery, Glenalina, Extn. Sec S.J. G312.

Mallett, Jack, Rifleman, No. 7011055
The son of Jeremiah and Emma Mallett of Londonderry, he died on 19 April 1941 in the United Kingdom. Buried in Londonderry City Cemetery.

Markey, Tom, Rifleman, No. 14832464
The son of Stanley and Jane H. Markey of Waterfoot, Lancashire, he died on 31 March 1945. Buried in Reichswald Forest War Cemetery, grave 33.B.5.

Martin, Edward Charles, Rifleman, No. 14575975
The son of John Charles and Annie Elizabeth Martin of Morden, Surrey, he died on 26 April 1945, aged 21. Buried in Becklingen War Cemetery, grave 4.F.1B.

Martin, Robert Dickson, Lieutenant, No. 109577, MC
Born in London, a former member of the Artists Rifles. Commissioned on 3 June 1940, commanded the Reconnaissance Platoon in August 1944. Served in the Mortar Group of Support Company, hit while in the air on Operation Varsity, 24 March 1945. Died shortly after landing and buried in Reichswald Forest War Cemetery, grave 42.E.7.

Mathers, Ernerson, Rifleman, No. 7012008
Died 8 May 1940, aged 25. The husband of Susan Mathers, of Belfast. Buried in Karachi War Cemetery, grave 8.C.10.

Matthews, Gwilym George, Rifleman, No. 1817161
The son of Henry and Elizabeth Matthews of Caerphilly, Glamorgan, he died on 23 December 1943, aged 25. Buried in Omagh New Cemetery, Sec. A. Inner, grave 138.

McBurney, William Ashwood, Rifleman, No. 7046106
From Banbridge, County Down, the son of Joseph and Annie McBurney, he was killed in action on 12 June 1944, aged 23, in the area of Le Mesnil. Interred in Ranville War Cemetery, grave IIA.5.1.

McCarthy, Terence, Corporal, No. 7013745
The son of Terence and Selena McCarthy of Etna Drive, Belfast, he had transferred to the Battalion in May 1943. Served in 19 Platoon of D Company and was killed in action on 13 June 1944, buried in Ranville Cemetery, III.A.M.4, aged 29. His father had served in the First World War.

McCayna, George, Corporal, No. 7015140
The son of Martin Joseph and Elizabeth McCayna of Bethnal Green London, he served as a Corporal in C Company and was killed on Wednesday, 7 June 1944 at Ranville. Buried in Bayeux War Cemetery, Calvados, France, grave X.M.4. He was 24 years old.

McConnell, Charles, Rifleman, No. 7012767
The son of James and Elizabeth McConnell; husband of Catherine Jane McConnell, of Belfast. Died 11 September 1944. Buried Oscott College Cemetery, Birmingham, Section A, grave 306. He was 28 years old.

McCoo, John, Rifleman, No. 6985059
Served in 19 Platoon of D Company, he was killed while on a patrol
sweeping the woods to the rear of Battalion HQ on 13 June. He is buried
in Ranville, grave IIIA. K.4, and was 21 years old. From Richhill, County
Armagh, his three brothers also served, Samuel with the RUR, Cecil in the
RAF and William in the Royal Inniskilling Fusiliers.

McCool, Francis, Rifleman, No. 3526964
Born in Eire, died on 19 December 1941, he has no known grave and is
commemorated on the Brookwood Memorial, panel 14, column 3.

McCullough, Joseph, Rifleman, No. 14442976
From Clandeboye Place, Bangor, County Down, joined the Battalion in
1943. Served as a Rifleman and took part in Operation Varsity, died of
wounds received on Sunday, 25 March 1945. Buried in Reichswald Forest
War Cemetery, grave 40.F.3; he was 19 years old. His brother Samuel
served with the 1st Airborne Division and was taken prisoner after
Operation Market Garden.

McCutcheon, William James, WOII, No. 7012822, MM
Served in C Company as a WOII, he was awarded the Military Medal in
August 1944. He was killed on 24 March 1945, on Operation Varsity,
the crossing of the Rhine. Buried in Reichswald Forest War Cemetery,
grave 38.C.6; he was 28 years old. He was the son of Hugh and Rose Ann
of Harpenden, Hertfordshire; his widow, Vera Amy, lived at 18 Wadham
Street, Belfast.

McFarland, Norman, Rifleman, No. 6983599
Killed in action on Wednesday, 7 June 1944, he was the son of Robert
and Letitia McFarland of Culvahullion, Gortin, County Tyrone and the
husband of Doreen Edith McFarland of Ilfracombe, Devon; he was 21
years old. Buried in Ranville War Cemetery, grave IA.J.17.

McFaul, John George, Lieutenant, No. 137934
The son of Robert John and Achsah Louise McFaul of County Monaghan,
Eire, he was killed in a motorcycle accident in 1941, aged 26. Buried in
Hereford Cemetery, plot A (C of E) grave 5560. His Mess song was
'Father O'Flynn'.

McGonigal, Eoin Christopher, Lieutenant, No. 97290
Killed in action, aged 20, while serving with the Special Air Service on 18
November 1941. The son of Mr Justice McGonigal, KC, and of Margaret
McGonigal, of Dun Laoghaire, Co. Dublin. His widowed mother lived at
Kingstown, Dublin. Commemorated on the Alamein Memorial, column
71. He was the brother of Sir Ambrose McGonigal MC (RUR, 12

Commando and SAS) and of Mrs Letty Carson, wife of Colonel R.J.H. Carson OBE.

McGrath, Daniel, Lieutenant, No. 288791
An 'old boy' of Coleraine Academical Institution, he came from Mountsandal, Coleraine, County Londonderry. Commissioned into the Royal Irish Fusiliers on 1 March 1944. Served as a Lieutenant in 8 Platoon A Company, he was killed on 26 March 1945 and is buried in Venray War Cemetery, grave 8.E.11. An older brother, Captain William McGrath, DSO, No 74563, was killed in North Africa on 19 February 1942, while serving with the Royal Engineers.

McGuire, Nicholas, Rifleman, No. 7014413
The son of Nicholas and Mary McGuire of Grange, County Waterford. He joined the Battalion in May 1943, and was killed on 19 June 1944 in the area of Le Plein/Bois de Bures. Buried in Ranville Cemetery, grave VA.2.6.

McIlroy, James, Rifleman, No. 7012990
From Belfast, joined the Battalion in May 1943. He was mortally wounded while serving in D Company at Longueval on 9 June 1944; buried in Ranville Cemetery, grave IA.D.3, he was 30 years old. The son of Henry and Sarah McIlroy and husband of Nancy McIlroy of Belfast.

McMillan, Malcolm, Rifleman, No. 3196800
Killed in action on 4 April 1945; buried in Reichswald Forest War Cemetery, grave 33.D.10.

McQuillan, Robert Harper, Rifleman, No. 6985348
Born in County Antrim, killed on Wednesday, 7 June 1944, aged 21. Buried in Bayeux War Cemetery, grave X.M.2.

Mearns, Herbert, Corporal, No. 14412609
From Coleraine, County Londonderry, he had originally served in the General Service Corps. He was the son of Margaret Mearns. He was killed in action during enemy attacks on the Battalion on 9 June 1944 at Longueval. Interred in Ranville Cemetery, grave IIA.H.5; he was 19 years old.

Merrell, Walter Richard, Rifleman, No. 6104465
Born in London, he was killed on 7 June 1944; buried in Ranville War Cemetery, grave III.B.25.

Millar, Thomas Hugh, Rifleman, No. 7012135
Died on 18 May 1943. Buried in Carnmoney Cemetery, Sec. A.G., grave 44.

Mills, Wilfrid Arnold, Lieutenant, No. CAN
The son of Wilfrid and Lily Mills of Merritton, Ontario, Canada and husband of Luella. A Canloan officer he was on attachment from the Royal Hamilton Light Infantry, RCIC. Killed in action at Lendrick on 16 April 1945 and buried in Holten Canadian War Cemetery, grave V.A.5.

Miskimmin, Robert James, Rifleman, No. 7019396
The son of Matthew John and Mary Miskimmon and husband of Florence Violet of Ramsbury, Wiltshire, he was killed on 24 March 1945, aged 23. Buried in Venray War Cemetery, grave VIII.E.2.

Mitchell, Harrison, Lance Corporal, No. 7369966
RAMC attached to the Battalion. The son of Harrison Mitchell, and of Mary Elizabeth Mitchell of Workington, Cumberland, he died on 24 March 1945, aged 28. Buried in Reichswald Forest War Cemetery, grave 40.F.7.

Moffett, James Campbell, Rifleman, No. 7012388
The son of Mr W.J. Moffet of Drumahall, Montalto, Ballynahinch, he died of wounds on 13 July 1944, in Normandy. He had ten years' service. Buried in Ryes War Cemetery, Bazenville, grave IV.J.5.

Moore, James, Rifleman, No. 7017079
The son of John and Annie Moore of Wigton Street, Belfast and the husband of Annie, he was killed on Saturday, 24 March 1945, he was 30 years old. He has no known grave and is commemorated on the Groesbeek Memorial panel 8.

Moore, William James, Lance Corporal, No. 14219689
Born in County Down, he was killed on Wednesday, 20 June 1944 in Normandy, aged 20. Buried in Ranville War Cemetery, grave IA.L.12.

Morgan, Reginald Norman 'Reggie', Lieutenant, No. 176458
Commissioned on 1 March 1941, War Substantive Lieutenant as of 1 September 1942, Temporary Captain as of 15 March 1943. Listed as missing in action as of 7 June 1944. He was last seen leaving Ste Honorine with his platoon after the withdrawal had been ordered. Body found on 11 July when the Battalion re-entered the town. The son of Richard and Emily Morgan of Belfast, brother of Harry R. and also a cricketer; buried in Bayeux, grave X.M.6.

Morrison, Robert, Rifleman, No. 7013673
Born in Belfast, the foster son of Rosina Reid, of Monkstown. He died on 2 March 1941, aged 25. Buried in Carnmoney (Holy Evangelists) Church of Ireland churchyard extension.

Mullins, Patrick James, Rifleman, No. 7019652
The son of Mary Mullins, he came from Lisburn, County Antrim. Served in the Anti-tank Platoon. Believed to have been killed by 'friendly fire' on 8 June as a result of an artillery barrage from the guns of 3rd Division's artillery support. Interred in Ranville Cemetery, grave IVA.D.2; he was 20 years old.

Muston, Harold, Rifleman, No. 14688128
Served in Support Company, he was killed on Operation Varsity, 24 March 1945. Buried in Reichswald Forest War Cemetery, grave 40.C.1; he was 19 years old and the son of Joseph and Gertrude Muston of Fareham, Hampshire.

Nelson, John Henry, Rifleman, No. 6985185
Born in Londonderry, he was killed on 7 June 1944, aged 22 and is buried in Ranville War Cemetery, grave IA.L.7.

Nolan, George, Colour Sergeant, No. 7011654
Born in County Antrim, he served in Support Company and was killed on Operation Varsity, 24 March 1945. Buried in Reichswald Forest War Cemetery, grave 40.F.5; he was the husband of Elizabeth Jane Nolan of Carmarthen.

O'Brien, Charles, Lance Corporal, No. 5125850
Born in Eire and resided in Belfast, he was initially listed in the local press as missing in action in Normandy in June 1944. Died on 7 June 1944 and has no known grave. Listed on the Bayeux Memorial, panel 17, column 3.

O'Connor, Patrick Joseph, Lance Corporal, No. 6409738
The son of John Joseph and Pruedentia Mary O'Connor of Drimnagh, Eire, he resided in Belfast prior to enlistment. Served in A Company and was killed in action on 7 June 1944. Buried in Bayeux War Cemetery, grave X.M.5.

O'Connor, Timothy, 'Wee Stiffy', Rifleman, No. 7019287
The son of John and Mary O'Connor, he came from Annascaul, County Kerry. Served in D Company; he was killed on 19 June 1944, aged 32, at Breville. Buried in Ranville War Cemetery, grave VA.Q.3.

O'Flanagan, Peter, Rifleman, No. 14411473
Served in 19 Platoon D Company, he was killed in action on 6 July 1944 and is buried in La Delivrande War Cemetery, grave VIII.K.4.

Oliver, John Chapman, Rifleman, No. 7012565
Killed on Wednesday, 7 June, aged 38. He was the son of Henry and Sarah Oliver of Church Street, Bangor, County Down and husband of Francis Nest Oliver of Abergwili, Carmarthenshire. He had served for almost twelve years in the regiment, seeing duty in India and China. Buried in Ranville War Cemetery, grave IVA.O.8. His father had served for twenty-one years in the Royal Navy.

O'Reilly, Michael, 7047510, Rifleman, DCM
The son of John and Mary O'Reilly from Dublin, he had originally enlisted in the Royal Irish Fusiliers. Killed on 7 June 1944, during the attack on Ste Honorine. Buried in Ranville Cemetery, grave IA.K.17, he was 21 years old.

O'Shea, Michael James, Rifleman, No. 7016308
Born in Eire and resided in London, he was killed on 24 March 1945, buried in Reichswald Forest War Cemetery, grave 40.D.4.

O'Sullivan, Robert Deyos, Lieutenant, No. 214657
Born in Hampshire, he died on 10 April 1943 while on attachment to No. 12 Commando. Buried in Lerwick New Cemetery, Terrace 7B, grave 9.

Owen, John Edward, Sergeant, No. 7022873
The son of George and Susan Owen and husband of Florence Maud of Bethnel Green, London, he died on 31 March 1946, aged 38; buried in Manor Park Cemetery, joint grave 30.

Parrott, Thomas Alfred, Corporal, No. 7019824
Killed in action on Friday, 23 June 1944, aged 24, while serving in the Signals Platoon. He was the son of John William and Maud Parrot of Tottenham, Middlesex, and the husband of Violet Alice. Buried in Hermanville War Cemetery, Calvados, France, grave 1.E.21.

Payne, Edward Daniel, Rifleman, No. 7016562
Served in the Signals Platoon as a Rifleman, he was killed on Thursday, 8 June 1944 in Normandy. Buried in Ranville War Cemetery, grave IVA.H.2; he was 24 years old and the son of Percy and Florence Payne of Surrey and the husband of Doreen Payne of Redruth, Cornwall.

Pellatt, Ronald Frederick, Rifleman, No. 7016860
The son of Francis William and Rose Winifred Mabel Pellat of London, he died on 18 September 1940, aged 20. Greenwich Cemetery, Sec. G, collective grave 69, SW panel 4.

Peters, Harold, Rifleman, No. 14735640
Born in Warrington, he died on 25 March 1945, aged 20. Buried in Reichswald Forest War Cemetery, grave 40.F.6.

Pett, Cyril Jesse, Rifleman, No. 7018649
Born in London, he died on 28 April 1941. Buried in Abney Park Cemetery, Sec. M5, joint grave RN57128.

Phillips, Henry, WOI, No. 7006718
Born in Eire, he resided in London. Died on 16 April 1941 in the United Kingdom. Buried in Belfast City Cemetery, Glenlina, Extn. Sec. AS Gr93.

Phillips, Isaac, Corporal, No. 7013175
The son of Alfred and Patience Phillips of Kingston-on-Thames. Previously employed as a salesman, he attested at London on 11 January 1937, joining the Battalion on 6 August 1937. Served in A Company, he was killed on Saturday, 24 March 1945 on Operation Varsity. Buried in Reichswald Forest War Cemetery, grave 40.C.5.

Prosser, Reginald Henry James, Rifleman, No. 7020918
The son of Henry and Florence Prosser of Southall, Middlesex, he served in 21 Platoon D Company. Killed in action on 9 June 1944, he has no known grave and is commemorated on the Bayeux War Memorial, panel 17, column 3.

Prouting, Philip James, Lance Corporal, No. 7016927
The son of Thomas and Eva Minnie Prouting of London, he died on 24 March 1945, aged 25. Buried in Reichswald Forest War Cemetery, grave 40.C.11.

Quinn, Richard, 'Dicky', Lieutenant, No. 90695
The son of Henry and Clara Quinn of Dulwich, London, he was a good friend of both Huw Wheldon and Ronnie Wilson, as barmen in Dublin would testify to. Commissioned on 6 November 1943. He commanded the Anti-tank Platoon in Normandy, killed by a sniper while inspecting his platoon's positions at 1015 hrs, on 16 June 1944; he was 34 years old. Buried in Ranville War Cemetery, grave IVA.F.17.

Raynham, Stuart Rex, Corporal, No. 7045517
The foster son of Walter and Lilian Hammond and husband of Alice Florence of Cranford, Hounslow, Middlesex, he served in Support Company; killed in action on 8 June 1944; buried in Ranville War Cemetery, grave IVA.K.8.

Reading, Geoffrey Emar Dawson, Rifleman, No. 14786387
The son of Harry and Amy Haynes of Banbury, Oxfordshire, he died on 4 April 1945, aged 19. Buried in Reichswald Forest War Cemetery, grave 33.B.3.

Redmond, Herbert Thomas, 'Bert', Sergeant, No. 7012576
Served in 20 Platoon, D Company, he was later promoted to Lance Sergeant and served in D Company. He was killed on 24 March 1945 on Operation Varsity; he was 25 years old. The son of William Joseph and Catherine Redmond of Whetstone, Middlesex, he is buried in Reichswald Forest War Cemetery, grave 40.E.7

Regis, Ernest George, Rifleman, No. 7014476
Born in Merthyr Tydfil, he died on 24 March 1945; buried in Reichswald Forest War Cemetery, grave 40.D.7.

Reilly, James Joseph Victor, 'Vic', Rifleman, No. 7012816
The son of Mr J. Reilly of Glasslough Street, Monaghan and Mrs Reilly, assistant teacher, Kilbarron National School, Ballyshannon. His wife and baby resided in Leeds. Killed on 7 June 1944 and buried in Ranville War Cemetery, grave IVA.J.8.

Riley, Robert, Corporal, No. 7017332
Killed on Monday, 19 June 1944 in Normandy, he was the son of Patrick and Mary Jane of Kimblesworth, County Durham and the husband of Rhoda. He was 28 years old. Buried in Ranville War Cemetery, grave IVA.H.17.

Robertson, John Weedon, Lieutenant, No. 293506
The son of Major Harold John Robertson and Vera of Wootton, Oxfordshire. Commissioned on 23 January 1944, he served in 22 Platoon D Company as a Lieutenant. Served in Normandy, the Ardennes and on Operation Varsity, where he was wounded while still in the air and again after the glider had landed. Unable to lead his platoon in the assault, he handed over command to Sergeant McCrory who was also wounded later in the action. Died of his wounds on 24 March 1945, buried in Reichswald Forest War Cemetery, grave 40.D.5.

Robinson, Frederick, Rifleman, No. 3443869
Killed on Thursday, 19 April 1945, he was the son of Mr and Mrs Alfred Robinson and the husband of Hilda, of Chorlton-cum-Hardy. Buried in Hanover War Cemetery, grave 7.H.9.

Rockall, Terence Lionel, Rifleman, No. 14615698

The son of William John and Ellen Rockall of Tufnell Park, London, he died on 7 April 1945 and is buried in Hanover War Cemetery, grave 15.J.3.

Sawyer, Albert Charles James, Rifleman, No. 6920834

Died 12 June 1944, aged 22. Son of Albert Edward Sawyer, and of Rebecca Sawyer, of Enfield Highway, Middlesex. Buried in Ranville War Cemetery, grave IA.K.1.

Scanlon, Brendon John, Rifleman, No. 14216134

Born in Eire and resided in Middlesex. Served in the 70th (Young Soldiers) Battalion, London Irish Rifles. He served in C Company in Normandy and was killed by shrapnel on 22 August 1944 at Deauville; he was 20 years old. He was the batman of Major Johnson, the Company Commander. He is buried in Tourgeville Military Cemetery, grave 4.G.3.

Seale, 'Theo' John, Lieutenant, No. 26895

Royal Irish Fusiliers, he was attached to B Company as a Second Lieutenant as of 18 May 1943. Fatally wounded when a hand grenade exploded in the Company lines on 1 June 1944, he was 23 years old. Commemorated on a plaque at St Mark's Church, Portadown. He was the son of Mr and Mrs William Pilkington Seale of Belfast Bank House, Portadown. Heavyweight boxing champion of the Battalion and a former leader of the Portadown College Boy Scout Troop, his brother, Squadron Leader T.C. (Terry) Seale, was killed in action in June 1941.

Seymour, Thomas John Leslie, Lance Corporal, No. 14688134

The son of Charles and Ethel Seymour of Newbury, Berkshire, he was killed on 8 February 1945, aged 19. Buried in Venray War Cemetery, grave III.E.12.

Shakespeare, Albert, Rifleman, No. 14591203

Born in Gloucestershire, he was the husband of Dorothy. Killed on 7 June 1944, aged 34 years, and buried in Bayeux War Cemetery, grave X.M.3.

Sheane, Hugh Macleod, Captain, No. 176459

Born in Nottinghamshire, he joined the Battalion in 1943. Died in hospital in Helmond on 27 November 1944. Buried in Mierlo War Cemetery, grave III.F.II. Received an MID.

Shore, Robert, Rifleman, No. 14216344

Born in Eire, resident in Gloucester, the son of Robert and Margaret of Queenhill, Worcestershire; died on 9 June 1944; buried in La Delivrande, IXJ 5-6, collective grave.

Sinclair, Donald Ian, Rifleman, No. 14676835
The son of Nicol Smith and Winifred Mary Sinclair of Gargrave, Yorkshire, he died on 24 March 1945 and is buried in Reichswald Forest War Cemetery, grave 40.E.11.

Smith, William Henry, Rifleman, No. 7013455
Killed on Tuesday, 20 June, aged 25. The son of William Henry and Mary Smith of 63 Weir Street, Belfast and husband of Mabel Beatrice Smith of Hereford; buried in Cambes-en-Plaine War Cemetery, row G 18. He had served for seven years in both Palestine and India.

Smyth, John Torbitt, Rifleman, No. 14411392
The son of William and Mary and husband of Gladys Rosie of Salisbury, he was killed on 25 August 1944, aged 19. Buried in Bayeux War Cemetery, grave III.I.2.

Southam, Ernest, Corporal, No. 7012844
The son of Mr and Mrs R. Southam of Northern Bank House, Belfast, he was killed on 23 August 1944, aged 24. His wife resided in Tredegar, South Wales. Three brothers also served and their father had previously served in the First World War. Buried in Tourgeville Military Cemetery, grave 7.G.5.

Spence, David Topping, Rifleman, No. 7018486
From Coniston Street, Belfast, he died of wounds received on Operation Varsity, 25 March 1945; he was 26 years old. Buried in Reichswald Forest War Cemetery, grave 48.D.3. His father served in the First World War.

Stanley, Reginald Henry, Rifleman, No. 11052761
Born in Oxfordshire, he was killed on 24 March 1945, aged 23. Buried in Reichswald Forest War Cemetery, grave 40.F.2.

Starr, Arthur Lionel, Rifleman, No. 7021234
Born in London, he was the husband of Kezia Starr of Tottenham, Middlesex. Died on 8 June 1944, aged 21. Buried in Ranville War Cemetery, grave IVA.F.2.

Stevenson, Robert James, Rifleman, No. 7019933
Reported as missing in action as of Wednesday, 7 June 1944. He has no known grave and is commemorated on the Bayeux War Memorial, panel 17, column 3. He was the son of Mr and Mrs Andrew Stevenson of Church Road, Carnmoney, County Antrim. He had four years' service and was 21 years old. Before the War he had worked for W.A. Ross & Sons, mineral water manufacturers.

Stogdale, John, Corporal, No. 3386927
Born in County Tyrone, he died on 10 June 1944, aged 22. The son of George and Phoebe Stogdale of Blackburn, Lancashire, he is buried in Hermanville War Cemetery, grave 3.B.3.

Stothers, David, Rifleman, No. 7013676
From Heatherbell Street, Belfast, the son of Sara Stothers. Served in C Company. He had eight years' service when he was killed on Saturday, 24 March 1945, aged 25. He has no known grave and is commemorated on the Groesbeek Memorial, panel 8.

Stubbs, Thomas, Rifleman, No. 7342471
Born in Manchester, died on 24 March 1945, buried in Reichswald Forest War Cemetery, grave 40.C.4.

Swaine, Alexander, Sergeant, No. 7011939
Served in 11 Platoon B Company, he was shot and killed two hours after landing on Operation Varsity, 24 March 1945. Buried in Reichswald Forest War Cemetery, grave 38.C.1; he was 31 years old.

Swift, Gerald Charles, Sergeant, No. 7012169
Served in C Company. He was killed on 24 March 1945 during Operation Varsity and is buried in Reichswald Forest War Cemetery, grave 34.B.6. The son of William and Mary and the husband of Emma Irene of Battersea, London, he was 30 years old.

Swingler, Eric Ronald, Rifleman, No. 1656465
The husband of Sylvia Swingler of Birmingham, he died on 2 April 1945. Buried in Reichswald Forest War Cemetery, grave 33.C.1.

Terry, Arthur Thomas, Rifleman, No. 1649728
Killed on 10 February 1945, he is buried in Venray War Cemetery, grave VIA.13; he was 32 years old.

Testro, Leslie George, Rifleman, No. 14672347
The son of William and Lily Testro of Waltham Cross, Hertfordshire, he was killed on 7 June 1944 and buried in Ranville War Cemetery, grave IA.M.7.

Thomas, David, Lance Corporal, No. 14641872
Born in Birkenhead, he died on 24 March 1945. Buried in Reichswald Forest War Cemetery, grave 34.B.9.

Thompson, Michael, Rifleman, No. 6409871
Born in Eire. Killed on 27 March 1945; buried in Venray War Cemetery, grave 1.E.3; he was 27 years old.

Thompson, Samuel, Rifleman, No. 14412439
The son of William and Agnes Thompson of Belfast, Northern Ireland, he was killed on 24 March 1945. Buried in Reichswald Forest War Cemetery, grave 40.E.10.

Topping, Samuel, Rifleman, No. 7017020
Killed in action on 17 August 1944, age 39, after three years' service. His home was at Millbrook Road, Lisburn, County Antrim; he was married with three children. His father had served with the Royal Irish Rifles in the First World War, being killed in August 1916. Samuel is buried in Ranville War Cemetery, grave IVA.J.2.

Trotter, James Wesley, Rifleman, No. 7047440
From Grangemore, Armagh, he was the son of Mrs F. Trotter. He was wounded in action and missing in action reported killed, aged 20, while serving with the 5th Parachute Battalion, AAC. He has no known grave and is commemorated on the Bayeux War Memorial, panel 18.

Turner, Wilfred, Rifleman, No. 7044822
The son of Charles and Annie Turner and husband of Victoria of Catford, London. Killed on 7 June 1944; buried in Ranville War Cemetery, grave IIA.D.3.

Turrell, Henry George, Rifleman, No. 7022592
The son of Henry and Alice Florence Turrell of Walthamstow, Essex, he died on 13 June 1944 and is buried in Ranville War Cemetery, grave IIIA.E.4.

Vickery, Charles Edward, Major, No. 126069
Born in Kent. Enlisted as a Rifleman and was quickly promoted to Company Sergeant Major. Later commissioned and served in Normandy in B Company. He was killed in action on 24 March 1945, while commanding A Company during Operation Varsity, buried in Reichswald Forest War Cemetery, grave 40.C.8.

Walker, George Joseph, Rifleman, No. 4207893
The son of James and H. Ellen Walker of Walsall, Staffordshire, he died on 20 August 1944 and is buried in La Delivrande War Cemetery, grave I.C.6.

Walsh, Philip, Rifleman, No. 6104907
Born in Belfast; died on 24 March 1945. Buried in Reichswald Forest War Cemetery, grave 40.F.1.

Waring, Samuel, Rifleman, No. 7021324
The son of Samuel and Elizabeth Waring of Downing Street, Belfast, he was reported as missing in action on the Rhine in the *Belfast Telegraph* of 17 September 1945. He had been killed on 24 March on Operation Varsity. Buried in Venray War Cemetery, grave 8.F.12; he was 22 years old.

Williams, Frederick James, Lance Corporal, No. 7016522
The son of Alexander Richard and Georgina Francis of East Ham, Essex, he died on 24 March 1945. Buried in Reichswald Forest War Cemetery, grave 39.D.11.

Williams, Pryce Wilson, Rifleman, No. 4201794
Born in Merioneth, he was the son of David Morris and Catherine Williams of Llanbadarn, Cardiganshire. He died on 5 July 1943 and is buried in Staylittle Baptist Chapel yard on the west side of the church.

Willis, Norman, Rifleman, No. 7017941
From Belfast, he was the son of James and Elizabeth Willis. Joined the Battalion in May 1943 and was killed on 9 June 1944 at Longueval while serving in 21 Platoon D Company. Interred in Ranville War Cemetery, grave V.B.23; he was 23 years old.

Wilson, Richard, Rifleman, No. 7013415
The son of Elizabeth Hogg of Belfast, he died as a result of shock following injuries caused by a bomb explosion on 26 February 1942, buried in Belfast City Cemetery, Glenalina Extn. Sec. R.1. grave 266.

Winfield, William, Lance Corporal, No. 4927999
The son of Joseph and Amy Sarah Winfield of Coton, Staffordshire, he was killed on 7 June 1944, aged 22 and is buried in Ranville War Cemetery, grave IVA.F.20.

Woodburn, John, Rifleman, No. 14663448
Killed on 6 June 1944 in Normandy, he has no known grave and is commemorated on the Bayeux War Memorial, panel 17, column 3; he was 19 years old. The son of Thomas and Mary Ann Woodburn of Manchester.

Wray, Thomas, Lance Corporal, No. 4462353
The son of Thomas William and Irene Wray of West Hartlepool, County Durham, he was killed on 7 June 1944 and is buried in Ranville Churchyard, grave 5.

Wright, William, Sergeant, No. 7011101
Served in the Reconnaissance Platoon and was killed by enemy mortar fire on Monday, 8 January 1945, at Wavreville he was 33 years old. The son of Mr and Mrs Robert Wright of Londonderry and the husband of Kathleen, he is buried in Hotton War Cemetery, Hotton, Luxembourg, grave V.D.1.

Young, William Pearson, Private, No. 7018947
From 'Coldagh' Ballymoney. Served with Special Air Service Regiment, AAC. Died 9 August 1944, aged 22. Buried in Marissel French National Cemetery, Coll. grave 326-329.

2nd Battalion

Abberley, Samuel, Rifleman, No. 6985634
From Hanbury in Staffordshire, he served in B Company and was treated in the RAP at Flers on 21 August 1944 (NYD stomach). He was later killed on 7 May 1945, aged 21 years (CWGC 5 May) and is buried in Venray War Cemetery, grave 7.G.10. The son of Francis Henry and Eva of Hanbury, Staffordshire.

Aldworth, John Richard St Ledger, Major, No. 117163
The son of a County Cork family; he was the son of Major J.C.O. and Mrs L.S.C. Aldworth and husband of Margaret Jean. He joined the Battalion as a Second Lieutenant when it was reformed after Dunkirk in June 1940. Described as a man of exceptional intellect, great charm and a superb sense of humour, he served for a time as Intelligence Officer; promoted to Captain he was appointed to command D Company in October 1942. In the summer of 1943 he became seriously ill with infantile paralysis. By various means, which could not quite be described as 'devious', he was retained on the Battalion strength despite his long absence in hospital. It was the opinion of the Commanding Officer that he was too fine an officer to lose and he returned to duty just after Christmas. A result of his illness was the legacy of a slight limp due to a permanent weakness of the muscles in his leg. Nevertheless, this did not deter him in any of his duties within his company. On 7 June, D Company was engaged in the bitter fighting at Cambes Wood. Due to greater than expected enemy resistance the Company was forced to withdraw leaving behind many casualties, including Aldworth, who had been killed by a gunshot wound. Buried in La Delivrande War Cemetery, grave IX.D.2.

Allen, John Maybin, Corporal, No. 7012090
From County Antrim, he was killed in a motorcycle accident in Birmingham on 24 July 1941; buried in Gravesend Cemetery, plot B.13, grave 1427.

Allen, Matthew Taylor, Rifleman, No. 7011561
The son of James and Agnes Jane Allen from Belfast and husband of Mary Elizabeth Allen of Darlington, County Durham, he died of wounds received on 3 June 1940 in France. Buried in Dover (St James's) Cemetery, row F, grave 2.

Allwood, Ronald, Rifleman, No. 14810311
Killed on Friday, 6 April 1945. The son of Oswald and Amelia Allwood of Hinckley, Leicestershire; he was 18 years old. Interred in Sage War Cemetery, Oldenburg, Niedersachsen, Germany, grave 6.B.9.

Anderson, George Frederick, Rifleman, No. 14691427
(Possibly Rifleman Anderson, A Company, attended RAP on 31 October at Venray suffering from diarrhoea and on 11 November at St Anthonis suffering with gastric flu.) On 18 September he was treated at the RAP at Petit Bogurg for a bruised back. The son of W.J. Anderson of Customs House, Essex, he was killed on 29 November 1944, aged 19 years. Buried in Venray War Cemetery, grave VI.B.7.

Armstrong, Bernard, Rifleman, No. 14220974
Born in Manchester, the son of Edward and Elizabeth Armstrong. Served in B Company; he was killed by shrapnel at Troarn on 27 July 1944. Buried in Banneville-La-Campagne War Cemetery, grave 1.A.21.

Arrowsmith, Leslie George, Rifleman, No. 14203241
The son of Robert and Margaret Arrowsmith of Fairfield, Liverpool, he served in B Company and was admitted to the RAP at Venray on 25 October 1944, suffering from gastroenteritis. Killed on 28 November 1944, aged 21, and buried in Venray War Cemetery, grave VI.C.9.

Ashton, Philip John, Captain, 36247
Killed in a road accident on 7 January 1940, in France. The son of Percy and Eveleen M. Ashton of Chelsea, London, husband of Joan. Buried in Cite Bonjean Military Cemetery, Armentières, plot 11, row A, grave 1.

Aubne, John Young, Rifleman, No. 14730889
Killed on Friday, 1 December 1944, he was the son of John Young Aubne and Elsie of Billingham, County Durham. Buried in Mierlo War Cemetery, grave III.F.12.

Bailey, Edward Francis, Rifleman, No. 7016406
Born in Essex, he was the son of James and Florence Ann Bailey and husband of Mary Bell Bailey of Bonchester, Roxburghshire; he resided in London prior to enlistment. Served in B Company and was killed by shrapnel in the back at Cambes on 9 June 1944. Buried in Cambes-en-Plaine War Cemetery, row J.9.

Bailey, John, Rifleman, No. 7011531
Born in London, he was the husband of Constance Violet Bailey of Enfield, Middlesex. Killed in France sometime between 30 May and 2 June 1940, he has no known grave and is commemorated on the Dunkirk Memorial, column 129.

Baker, Thomas Joseph, Corporal, No. 7016387
Served in C Company, he was killed by shrapnel on Saturday, 9 July 1944. He was the son of Thomas and Ada Baker of Rotherhithe, London. Buried in Ranville War Cemetery, grave V.C.10; he was 25 years old.

Ball, George Henry, Rifleman, No. 7044397
Killed on Friday, 21 July 1944. He was the son of George Henry Thomas and Georgina Mary Ball, and husband of Martha of Baddesley, Ensor, Warwickshire. Buried in Banneville War Cemetery, grave 1.A.23; he was 25 years old.

Ball, John Henry, Rifleman, No. 7016624
Born in London, he served in Support Company and was killed by shrapnel on Sunday, 9 June 1944 at Cambes. Buried in La Delivrande, grave VII.9.2; he was 24 years old. (According to the regimental magazine *Quis Separabit*, he was driving a wounded RE officer to the RAP at Anisy when his Bren carrier was hit by a shell.)

Banton, Harold John, Rifleman, No. 14706469
From Burton-on-Trent, he was killed on 30 November 1944. Buried in Venray War Cemetery, grave 6.D.7; he was 18 years old.

Barry, Denis Michael Gavin, Captain, No. 95533
Joined the Battalion from the Royal Irish Fusiliers in July 1944, taking command of 12 Platoon B Company. In January 1945 he transferred to C Company. The son of Brigadier Francis Barry and Ethel Mary Barry of Kinsale, County Cork, he was killed in action during the bitter street fighting in Lingen on 6 April 1945. Buried in Rheinberg War Cemetery, grave 12.K.24.

Baxter, Thomas, Rifleman, No. 7014010
Born in Belfast, he resided in Birmingham prior to his enlistment. Killed on 2 October 1939. Buried in Wool Holy Rood Churchyard, grave 30.

Baxter, William, Rifleman, No. 7019617
Born in County Antrim, he resided in Belfast prior to his enlistment. The son of James and Sarah Baxter of Glenravel, Belfast, he was killed on 13 November 1940. Buried in Newtowncrommelin Presbyterian Churchyard.

Beattie, James, Rifleman, No. 7010762
The husband of Isobella Beattie of Aberdeen Street, Belfast and the son of James Beattie of Memel Street, Belfast. He had previously worked in the shipyard. Died on 15 May 1940 and buried in Kessel-Lo churchyard, plot 27, grave 1.

Beattie, James Wharton, Rifleman, No. 7022747
Killed on Sunday, 9 July 1944 and is buried in La Delivrande War Cemetery, Douvres, Calvados, France, grave VII.A.9; he was 20 years old.

Beck, John, Rifleman, No. 7019095
Born in Belfast, he served in the Carrier Platoon of Support Company. Killed Tuesday, 27 February 1945, aged 21. He was the son of John and Esther Beck and the husband of Dorothy of Bingley, Yorks. Buried in Rheinberg War Cemetery, Kamp Lintfort, Nordrhein-Westfalen, Germany, grave 12.G.17.

Bingham, Stanley Henry, Rifleman, No. 7044554
Served in the Anti-tank Platoon of Support Company. Killed on 9 June 1944 when his 6-pounder anti-tank gun received a direct hit from enemy artillery. The son of Walter George and Amy Bingham, of Wolverley, Worcestershire. Buried in La Delivrande War Cemetery, Douvres, grave VII.L.3.

Bird, Alan Curtis, 'Dicky', Major, No. 105617, MC
Born in Surrey, he was a former member of the Artists Rifles. Served in D Company, France, 1940. Served as 2ic of D Company in Normandy. Killed in action on 26 April 1945 as the result of a landmine explosion, aged 35. He was the son of Sidney Arthur and Norah Agnes Bird. Buried in Becklingen War Cemetery, grave 8.G.11. Received a Commendation Card.

Borza, Edward Benigies, Rifleman, No. 7012132
Born in County Down. Died aged 24 of carbon monoxide poisoning in his billet at Lezennes on 31 October 1939. Buried in St André Communal Cemetery, row B, grave 61.

Bowen, William John, Rifleman, No. 7022530
Born in Glamorgan, Wales. (Possibly, Rifleman William John Bowen, D Company, wounded by shrapnel in the back on 8 November 1944 at Overloon.) Killed Sunday, 15 April 1945; he was 21 years old. Buried in Becklingen War Cemetery, grave 1.J.12.

Boyd, Eric, Corporal, No. 7021619
Born in County Tyrone, he was the son of David and Eva Boyd of 36 Onslow Gardens, Belfast and the husband of Muriel Edith Boyd of Rosevale Street, Creagh, Belfast, Northern Ireland. Educated at RBAI, he had served an apprenticeship with Messrs John D. Thompson and Co., Incorporated Accountants & Auditors, Donegal Square, Belfast. He was well known in musical circles in several districts of the city. Served in the Anti-tank Platoon of Support Company and was wounded by shrapnel in the legs at Cambes on Friday, 9 June 1944, when his Bren carrier was hit by shellfire. The leg had to be amputated and he died of his wounds the following day; he was 26 years old. Buried in Hermanville War Cemetery, grave I.H.9.

Bradley, Arthur Desmond, Rifleman, No. 7021600
Killed on 17 June 1944. The son of William and Jane Bradley of Magherafelt, County Londonderry, he was 19 years old. Buried in La Delivrande War Cemetery, grave IV.F.10.

Bradley, Arthur Joseph, Rifleman, No. 7017126
Served in D Company, he was killed by a gunshot wound on Wednesday, 7 June 1944 while at 'Wood Gazelle'. He was the son of Richard and Hannah Bradley of South Harrow, Middlesex and was 24 years old. Buried in La Delivrande War Cemetery, grave VII.K.7.

Bradley, George, Lance Corporal, No. 7014121
From Belfast, County Antrim, he was the son of George and Susan Bradley and the husband of Brigid Bradley of Tassagh, County Armagh. He served in A Company and was killed on Sunday, 9 July 1944. Buried in Ranville War Cemetery, grave IV.A.7.

Brandon, Charles Michael, Sergeant, No. 7013493
Born in Kent, he resided in Belfast prior to his enlistment. Killed on 29 May 1940, while serving in France. Buried in Dozinghem Military Cemetery, grave XVII.B.23.

Brooks, Kenneth Samuel, Rifleman, No. 7017967
Born in London, died on 13 August 1940, buried in East London Cemetery, Plaistow, grave 18290.

Browning, Thomas Dennis, Rifleman, No. 14672025
The son of Thomas and Frida Browning of Birmingham and husband of Leah Elsie, he was killed on 1 December 1944. Buried in Venray War Cemetery, grave VI.C.10; he was 19 years old.

Burges, Brian Ravensdale, Second Lieutenant, No. 308423
Born in Warwickshire. Joined the Battalion in January 1944 when it was stationed at Hawick. Served as a Platoon Commander in A Company. Killed at Troarn on 19 July 1944 by a gunshot wound to the side. He was the son of Leslie Ravensdale and Kathleen Alice Burges of Yelvertoft, Leicestershire. Buried in Banneville-La-Campagne War Cemetery, grave I.B.28.

Burgess, William, Rifleman, No. 1607298
Born in Salford, Manchester. Killed on Wednesday, 19 July 1944. He was the son of Annie Burgess and the husband of Mary Ann Burgess of Huntley Brook, Bury, Lancashire. Buried in Banneville War Cemetery, grave I.8.23.

Bushell, Albert Victor, Rifleman, No. 6215937
Served in D and later Headquarters Company, he was mortally wounded by shrapnel to the back on 14/15 October 1944 at Overloon. He was the son of Albert and Daisy Bushell of Harlesden, Middlesex. Buried in Overloon War Cemetery, grave IV.D.10, he was 21 years old.

Byrne, Frank, Rifleman
From Dublin, he served in the MT Platoon, killed on the beach at Dunkirk in June 1940. (Despite a mention in the regimental magazine and several anecdotal stories there is no trace of this man on the Commonwealth War Graves website as of 6 July 2005.)

Cairns, James, Rifleman, No. 7015467
Served in Headquarters Company and came ashore from Landing Craft Infantry (L) on Queen Red on the afternoon of D-Day. He was wounded by shrapnel on 10 July 1944 at Caen. The son of Hugh and Sarah Cairns, Ligoneil, County Antrim and the husband of Agnes Cairns of 12 Legnavara Street, Belfast, he had five years' previous service. Three brothers and a sister also served, and his father served in the First World War. Killed in action on 25 October 1944; buried in Gent City Cemetery.

Cairns, John O., Rifleman, No. 7021078
Born in County Down, he was the son of Robert E. and Mary Jane Cairns of Ashfield. Killed on 12 April 1945 and buried in Donacloney Old Graveyard, grave 240.

Calder, Leonard, Rifleman, No. 7019561
Born in Belfast, he died on 10 August 1943 and is buried in Carnmoney Cemetery, Sec. AF, joint grave I 39.

Capell, Kenneth Herbert Edwin, Rifleman, No. 6921567
The son of Thomas and Daisy Capell of St Albans, Hertfordshire, he was killed on 30 November 1944. Buried in Venray War Cemetery, grave 6.C.6; he was 20 years old.

Carruthers, Thomas, Rifleman, No. 997514
Born in Glasgow, Scotland. Killed 13 April 1944, he was 24 years old. Buried in Becklingen War Cemetery, grave 4.H.7.

Clarke, John, Corporal, No. D/24423
Born in County Down, he was killed on 28 March 1940 and is buried in Dundonald Cemetery, Sec. F.6, grave 188.

Clarke, Samuel Walter, Rifleman, No. 7014285
The son of Mrs Mary and the late Hugh Clarke of Glenvarlock Street, Belfast, and husband of Violet Lilian Clarke of Southcourt, Aylesbury, Buckinghamshire, who served in the ATS in England. He had transferred to the 1st Battalion Durham Light Infantry and was killed on 14 August 1944, aged 31. Buried in Arezzo War Cemetery, grave II.E.5.

Close, Charles Edward, Sergeant, No. 7016415
Served in A Company, he was killed on Tuesday, 4 July 1944 at Cambes. He was the husband of Ellen Jennie Close of Upper Holloway, London. Buried in La Delivrande War Cemetery, grave 11.G.1; he was 24 years old.

Coddington, Hubert Geoffrey John, Flight Lieutenant, No. 45331
The son of Capt. Arthur Coddington and Dorothy Coddington; husband of Yvonne Mary Coddington, of Wraxall, Bristol. Served in the Anti-tank Platoon; killed 10 November 1943, aged 24, in a flying accident while piloting a Lysander from an Army Co-operation Squadron of the RAF. Commemorated on Runnymede Memorial, panel 119.

Connolly, John, Rifleman, No. 7010230
Born in Glasgow, he resided in County Armagh. Served in D Company and was killed by a gunshot wound on Wednesday, 7 June 1944, at 'Wood Gazelle'; he was 36 years old. The son of James and Annie Connolly,

217

husband of Teresa Connolly of Shepherd's Bush, London. Buried in La Delivrande War Cemetery, Douvres, Calvados, France, grave IX.H.10.

Connor, William, Rifleman, No. 14746215
Killed on Friday, 2 March 1945. The son of John Francis and Mary Connor of St Helens, Lancashire, he was 18 years old. Buried in Reichswald Forest War Cemetery, grave 48.C.18.

Cope, Arthur James, Rifleman, No. 14665226
Born in London. Killed on Wednesday, 28 February 1945. Buried in Reichswald Forest War Cemetery, grave 62.F.1; he was 20 years old.

Cousins, Charles Joseph H., Rifleman, No. 7014912
The son of Charles H. and Ellen H. Cousins and husband of Kate R., of Hammersmith, London, he was killed on 13 June 1944, aged 28. Buried in Hermanville War Cemetery, grave 1.L.1.

Coxon, James Edward, Rifleman, No. 11426530
Killed on Friday, 2 March 1945. He was the son of James and Alice Gwyne Coxon of Portsmouth and the husband of Dora Ellaine Coxon of Manselton, Swansea, Wales. Buried in Reichswald Forest War Cemetery, grave 48.C.19; he was 30 years old.

Coyle, Joseph, Rifleman, No. 7012201
Born in Belfast, he lived in County Armagh. Killed in action on 15 May 1940. The son of Joseph and Mary Coyle of Lislea, Co. Armagh. He has no known grave and is commemorated on the Dunkirk Memorial, column 129.

Craig, Alexander, Sergeant, No. D/25005
The son of Alexander and Elizabeth Craig and the husband of Kathleen Craig of Belfast. Died 1 June 1945, aged 57, and is buried in C of I Cemetery, Newtownbreda, Belfast.

Craig, James, Lieutenant, No. 115186
The son of Richard J. and Mary Craig and the husband of Kathleen, he was born in County Antrim, but lived in County Down. Died on active service 10 May 1941, aged 46. Buried in Belfast City Cemetery and commemorated at Queen's University, Belfast.

Craig, Samuel, Rifleman, No. 7011030
Born in County Antrim, he was killed between 28 May and 2 June 1940, aged 30. The son of Robert and Jane Craig, he has no known grave and is commemorated on the Dunkirk Memorial, column 129.

Crangle, Hugh, Rifleman, No. 7018782
Served in A Company and was mortally wounded by shrapnel to the head at Cambes on 23 June 1944. The son of Henry and Elizabeth Crangle of 35 Lonsdale Street, Belfast, Northern Ireland, he was 30 years old. Buried in La Delivrande War Cemetery, grave VII.K.4. A brother, Guardsman Gerald Murray, Irish Guards, was killed in London in 1940, the result of enemy action.

Crawford, Wilnor, Rifleman, No. 7019461
Killed in action on 14 June, the son of John and the late Elizabeth Crawford of Moat Road, Ballymena, County Antrim; he was 21 years old. Buried in Ranville War Cemetery, grave IVA.G.17. He had served for four years prior to his death.

Creasy, Basil William Sidney, Rifleman, No. 7015952
Served in B Company and killed by shrapnel on Friday, 9 June 1944 at Cambes; he was 25 years old. The son of Alfred Harold and Elsie Clementina Creasy of Southend-on-Sea, Essex, he is buried in Cambes, row G, 19.

Crompton, Walter George, Rifleman, No. 6405699
Served in the Carrier Platoon of Support Company and was killed on Wednesday, 19 July 1944. He was the son of Walter George and Esther Beatrice Crompton of Worthing, Sussex and was 21 years old. Buried in Banneville-La-Campagne War Cemetery, grave I.A.29.

Cronin, John Francis, Rifleman, No. 7016464
Born in Eire. (Possibly Rifleman Cronin who served in D Company and was wounded by shrapnel in the chest and hand on 21 July at Troarn.) Killed 30 July 1944, and buried in La Delivrande War Cemetery, grave IV.E.2.

Crowe, J., Rifleman, No. 7012355
He was D Company cook in France, 1940, wounded. A member of the Battalion football team. Later served with the Gordon Highlanders and was killed on 24 March 1945. Buried in Reichswald Forest War Cemetery, grave 40.C.3.

Crumbie, Ernest, Rifleman, No. 14548677
Served in the Anti-tank Platoon, of Support Company. He was mortally wounded in the back by shrapnel on Monday, 3 July 1944; died the following day. The son of Ernest and Edith Evelyn Crumbie, he was 19 years old. Buried in Hermanville War Cemetery, grave 2.A.15.

Cunningham, William John, RSM, No. 7011364
The elder son of Mr and Mrs Isaac Cunningham of Orchard Cottage, Warrenpoint, County Down. He was killed on 17 June 1944 while serving with the 9th Parachute Battalion. Buried in Ranville War Cemetery, grave IIA.B.12.

Curry, Victor, Rifleman, No. 3774020
(Possibly Rifleman Curry of A Company who on 19 September 1944 was wounded by shrapnel to the left back at the crossing of the Escaut Canal, and attended the RAP at Overloon on 17 November suffering from a sore throat, before being returned to unit.) Killed 7 April 1945. He was the son of Thomas and Grace Rose Curry of Liverpool. Buried in Rheinberg War Cemetery, grave 12.K.25.

Daly, Philip Kevin, Rifleman, No. 6984190
The son of Philip and Maud Daly of Londonderry, he died on 12 November 1945, aged 22. Buried in Londonderry City Cemetery, Sec. M. Class D.

Darby, John, Major, No. 186287
Died 28 May 1944, aged 28. Attached to 1st King George V's Own Gurkha Rifles (The Malaun Regiment). Son of Richard F. Darby and Gladys M.P. Darby, of Chipstead, Kent. Buried in Imphal War Cemetery, grave 1.F.21.

Davidson, John, Rifleman, No. D/24391
The son of George and Mary Jane Davidson of Saintfield, Northern Ireland, he died on 11 September 1940. Buried in Saintfield C of I Churchyard, Sec. J.15.

De Blaby, Reginald Edward, Lieutenant, No. 177897
Died 23 March 1943, while seconded to 6th Battalion, Durham Light Infantry. Son of Capt. G.T. de Blaby and Mrs de Blaby, of Dublin, Eire. Commemorated on the Medjez-El-Bab Memorial, face 30.

Dennehy, Thomas, Rifleman, No. 7017238
Died 16 July 1940, aged 20. Son of Daniel and Margaret Dennehy, of Fairhill, Cork. Buried in Cork (St Joseph's) Cemetery, St James, grave 18.

Devine, Edward, Lance Corporal, No. 7010080
Born in Belfast, he was killed on 30 May 1940 in France, aged 34. The only death suffered by the Battalion that day. Nevertheless, he has no known grave and is commemorated on the Dunkirk Memorial, column 128.

Dick, James Martin, Rifleman, No. 14730903
From North, County Durham, he was killed on 30 November 1944, aged 18. Buried in Venray War Cemetery, grave 6.D.4.

Dickens, Frank Newbolt, Colour Sergeant, No. 7018002
Served in the Anti-tank Platoon of Support Company and was wounded by shrapnel in the right leg while at 'Farm Gazelle' on 7 June 1944. Killed in action on Friday, 6 April 1945 at Lingen; buried in Rheinberg War Cemetery, grave 12.L.8. He was the son of Horace Sidney and Elizabeth Dickens and the husband of Doris Annie Dickens of Cricklewood, Middlesex.

Dickson, Thomas, Lance Corporal, No. 7019627
The son of James and Eileen Dickson of Bangor, County Down, he died on 25 September 1943 in the United Kingdom and is buried in Bangor Cemetery, Sec.5.W, grave 79.

Diserens, Robert Charles, 'Bobby', Lieutenant, No. 264682
Joined the Battalion in March 1943 and was appointed to 14 Platoon C Company. He was fatally wounded by a shrapnel wound to the head on Friday, 9 June 1944 at Cambes; he was 21 years old. He was the son of Robert and Regine Julienne Diserens of Cricklewood, Middlesex. Buried in La Delivrande War Cemetery, grave IX.D.4.

Doyle, Charles, Rifleman, No. 7011327
Born in Belfast; died 15 May 1940, France; buried in Kessel-Lo Churchyard, plot 27, grave 3.

Driscoll, Charles Edward, Rifleman, No. 7020519
Born in London, he was killed on 20 July 1941; buried in Belfast City Cemetery, Glenina Extn, Sec. AS Gr10.

Dunleavy, William James, Rifleman, No. 24588
The son of Nelson and Catherine and husband of Margaret Dunleavy of Belfast, he died on 10 April 1942 in the United Kingdom, aged 41. Buried in Belfast City Cemetery, Glenlina Extn. Sec T.1. grave 411.

Dysart, Robert, Rifleman, No. 14409550
Died of wounds received on 28 November 1944. Buried in Venray War Cemetery, grave 6.F.7. The youngest of three soldier sons of Mr and Mrs H. Dysart of Kyle's Brae, Coleraine; he was 20 years old.

Eastwood, Frederick Albert, Rifleman, No. 7010000
Born in London, he resided in Germany prior to the War. Killed on 1 December 1944 and is buried in Venray War Cemetery, grave 6.D.8; he was 34 years old.

Edwards, Henry E., Lance Corporal, No. 7019725
The son of Henry and Martha Edwards of London, he was killed on 13 October 1941, in the United Kingdom. Buried in Wandsworth Cemetery, block 12, grave 534, SW panel 2.

Erskine, Kenneth, Rifleman, No. 7020024
Served in Support Company and was killed by shrapnel on Saturday, 14 October 1944 at Overloon; he was 22 years old. He was the son of Hamilton and Sarah Freeburn Erskine and husband of Agnes Elizabeth, of Worth, Kent. Buried in Overloon War Cemetery, Noord-Brabant, Netherlands, grave IV.D.11. The brother of Mr Clements Erskine of Spencer Street, Belfast, he had four years' service at the time of his death. His wife resided in Northfleet, Kent.

Fitzgeorge, George Frederick, Corporal, No. 14200443
Killed on Friday, 13 April 1945, he was 22 years old. The son of Gertrude Fitzgeorge of Higham Hill, Essex, he is buried in Becklingen War Cemetery, grave 4.H.2.

Ford, William Patrick, Lance Corporal, No. 5884174
Born in India, he resided in Burma prior to enlisting. Killed 1 December 1944 and is buried in Venray War Cemetery, grave 6.D.10; he was 25 years old.

Fox, William, Rifleman, No. 7015254
The son of John and Charlotte Fox of Belfast and husband of Ada, he died on 31 December 1939 in the United Kingdom, aged 29. Buried in Belfast City Cemetery, Glenlina Extn Sec. U1, grave 214.

Frost, Sidney Evelyn, Lieutenant, No. 264684
The son of Geoffrey Meadows and Dorothy Louise Frost of Great Elm, Frome, Somerset. Commanded 10 Platoon B Company and was killed on 4 July 1944 by a landmine. Buried in La Delivrande War Cemetery, grave VII.K.6.

Fullerton, Andrew, Rifleman, No. 7013832
Born in Gilford, County Armagh, he was the son of Joseph and Mary Fullerton. Killed sometime between 29 May and 4 June 1940 in France. Buried in Bleuet Farm Cemetery, grave 1.AA.7. He was 21 years old.

Fulton, Robert, Rifleman, No. 7011706
The son of Archie and Rose Fulton of Dervock, County Antrim, he was killed on 15 May 1940, aged 33. Buried in Leuven Communal Cemetery, row A, grave 5.

Gale, John James, Rifleman, No. 3781053
The husband of Eva Maud Gale of Braddon, Isle of Man, he was killed on 30 November 1944 and is buried in Venray War Cemetery, grave VI.C.12; he was 36 years old.

Gallagher, John, Rifleman, No. 14431679
Served in B Company and was killed by shrapnel on 2 July 1944 at Cambes. The son of John and Jennie Gallagher of Eglinton, County Londonderry, he is buried in La Delivrande War Cemetery, grave 11.G.4; he was 19 years old.

Garstin, Patrick Bannister, Lieutenant, No. 95531, MC
From Dublin, he was the son of Richard Hart and Mary Amelia Garstin, and the husband of Susan Nicola of Canterbury. As a Lieutenant he was a platoon commander at Louvain, in May 1940. Awarded the Military Cross for his actions on 16/17 May 1940. Medal presented by Montgomery at Tourcoing on 26 May. Promoted to Captain in September 1943, he was attached to D Squadron 1st Special Air Service Regiment. He was one of a party of SAS men captured and later murdered by the SS on 9 August 1944. Buried in Marissel French National Cemetery, Oise, France, grave No. 325.

Gibbens, Jabez Edward, Corporal, No. 7010952
The son of Walter and Daisy Gibbens of Nottingham, he was 26 years old. Killed in action on 15 May 1940 at Leuven. Buried in Kessel-Lo churchyard, Leuven, Vlaams-Brabant, Belgium.

Giddings, Joseph Edwin, Rifleman, No. 13065047
From Clapham, London, he was the husband of Hanna Constance and was killed on 28 November 1944. Buried in Venray War Cemetery, grave 6.D.1; he was 31 years old.

Gilpin, John Robert, Rifleman, No. 7013792
Born in Eire, he was the stepson of Mary Gilpin of Cultra, County Down, Northern Ireland. Killed sometime between 1 and 2 June 1940, he has no known grave and is commemorated on the Dunkirk Memorial, column 19.

Girvan, Robert, Leslie, Rifleman, No. 7021405
The son of Mr and Mrs Arthur Girvan of Ballyardle, County Down, husband of Margaret J. Girvan of Lisnacree. He was killed on 5 June 1944, in the United Kingdom. Buried in 'old ground', Mourne Presbyterian Churchyard, Kilkeel, N. Ireland.

Goodrick, Alfred Reginald, 'Reggie', Craftsman, No. 2122409
The son of John and Minni Goodrick and husband of Ida Mary of Tadcaster, Yorkshire. He served in the REME and was attached to the Battalion. Killed by shrapnel on 12 June 1944 at Cambes and buried in La Delivrande War Cemetery, grave VII.K.9.

Gordon, James Calderwood, Rifleman, No. 7011740
The son of Joseph and Agnes Ann Gordon and the husband of Ann Gordon of Belfast, Northern Ireland, he was killed on Friday, 9 June 1944 at Cambes. Buried in La Delivrande War Cemetery, grave VII.L.2; he was 32 years old. His late father served in the Royal Navy in the Great War.

Gough, William Richard, Rifleman, No. 14787301
The son of Joseph and Nellie Gough of Runcorn, Cheshire, he was killed on Saturday, 14 April 1945. He was 18 years old. Buried in Becklingen War Cemetery, grave 2.H.11.

Gover, Derrick Owen, Rifleman, No. 14400138
The son of John and Kate Gover of Moordown, Bournemouth, Hampshire, he resided in Southampton prior to enlistment. Killed on 2 April 1945 and buried in Reichswald Forest War Cemetery, grave 33.C.3.

Gracey, William, Rifleman, No. 7012043
Served in D Company and was wounded by shrapnel in the head while at 'Wood Gazelle' on 7 June 1944. Killed in action on 10 June 1944, aged 30. He was the son of John and Elizabeth Gracey of Hill Street, Lurgan, County Armagh and the husband of Winnie (née Taylor) of Victoria Street Place, Lurgan. Buried in Ann's Hill Cemetery, Gosport, Hampshire, plot 190, G29.

Graham, Thomas George, Rifleman, No. 7018906
Born in Belfast, he served in A Company and was wounded by shrapnel in the left side on 7 July 1944 at La Bisey. Killed on 10 July 1944, aged 22, and buried in La Delivrande War Cemetery, grave VI.F.5.

Grant, Alexander, Rifleman, No. 7012111
The son of Robert George and Janet Grant of Gateshead, County Durham and husband of Dorothy Lilian of Gravesend, Kent, he resided in Belfast prior to enlistment. Killed between 28 and 30 May 1940 in France and buried in Dozinghem Military Cemetery, grave XVII.B.32.

Green, William, Rifleman, No. 7022557
Born in South Shields, County Durham, he served in C Company and was killed by shrapnel on 19/20 July 1944 at Troarn; he was 21 years old. He

has no known grave and is commemorated on the Bayeux Memorial, panel 17, column 3.

Greenwood, Henry George, Rifleman, No. 14200468
Served in B Company and was killed on 3 July 1944 at Cambes, aged 21. The son of Charles Edward and Mary Helen Greenwood of New Beakton, East Ham, Essex. Buried in La Delivrande War Cemetery, grave II.G.3.

Greer, Joseph, Rifleman, No. 7011223
The son of Joseph and Jane Greer of Belfast, he died in a military hospital in Northern Ireland on 10 June 1944. His funeral was held in the Belfast City Cemetery on 13 June and was attended by his brothers. Extn. Sec. D.1. grave 332.

Gregg, Thomas, Lance Corporal, No. 7012187
Born in County Antrim, Northern Ireland, he died at sea on 1 June 1940, aged 25. He has no known grave and is commemorated on the Dunkirk Memorial, column 129.

Grinrod, William Frederick, Rifleman, No. 3778633
From Bury, Lancashire, he was the husband of Lillian. He was killed on 30 November 1944; buried in Venray War Cemetery, grave 6.D.5; he was 25 years old.

Guy, Melvern Roy, Rifleman, No. 14691055
Served in D Company and was killed by an almost direct hit from a mortar bomb on 13 October 1944; he was 21 years old. The son of Melvern and Rachel Guy of Risca, Monmouthshire, he is buried in Overloon War Cemetery, grave IV.D.8.

Halfpenny, John James, Rifleman, No. 7015482
Killed on 9 June 1944, aged 27. The son of Frank and Annie Halfpenny of Ligoniel, County Antrim, he is buried in La Delivrande War Cemetery, grave VII.L.4.

Hall, George, Rifleman, No. 14334018
The son of James and Ethel Hall of Chesterfield, Derbyshire, he was killed on 10 August 1944, aged 20, and is buried in St Charles de Percy War Cemetery, grave VI.C.2.

Hall, Kenneth, Rifleman, No. 7044009
Served in A Company and was killed by shellfire on 9 July 1944 at Hill 60; he was 26 years old. The son of John Henry and Mary Hall of Hasbury, Worcestershire, he is buried in Ranville War Cemetery, grave III.C.2.

Hall, Robert Stewart, 'Ronnie', Lieutenant, No. 177406

Previously served with the Loyal Regiment, joining the Rifles as a Lieutenant in early January 1944 and given command of 8 Platoon A Company. Killed in action on 9 June 1944 by a shrapnel wound at Cambes; he was 26 years old. Prior to enlisting he had been employed as a junior staff officer in the Ministry of Agriculture at Stormont since 1937. He had been educated at Hilltown PES, Sligo Grammar School and the Mountjoy School, Dublin. A keen rugby player for the Civil Service. The son of Robert and Isabella (née Armstrong), husband of Helena Theresa (née Gunton) of Helford, Cornwall, he is buried in Cambes-en-Plaine War Cemetery, row G5.

Hall, William, Rifleman, No. 7019578

The son of William and Mary Hall of Glynn, County Antrim, he was killed on 10 August 1943, aged 21, in the United Kingdom. Buried in Gracehill Moravian Burial Ground.

Hamilton, Francis Cecil, 'Frank', Rifleman, No. 7019643

The son of Thomas and Grace Hamilton of Lurgan, County Armagh, he was resident in Belfast prior to enlistment. Killed on 15 February 1941, aged 21, in the United Kingdom. Buried in Lurgan New Cemetery, Sec. S. grave 385.

Hamilton, James, Rifleman, No. 7011031

Born in Belfast, he was killed between 30 May and 2 June 1940 in France. No known grave and commemorated on the Dunkirk Memorial, column 129.

Hamilton, William Harkness, Rifleman, No. 7015181

The son of Robert and Christine Hamilton of Belfast, Northern Ireland, he was killed on 16 May 1940 in Belgium, aged 20. Buried in Leuven Communal Cemetery, row B, grave 9.

Hamstead, William George, Lance Corporal, No. 7022436

The son of Alice Jane Hamstead of South Woodford Square, London. Died of wounds on 14 June 1944, aged 21. Buried in City of London Cemetery, square 20, grave 104124.

Hancock, Anthony Strangman, Lieutenant, No. 249763

From Lisburn, County Antrim, he was the son of Captain Dugal Strangman and Vivien Fearne Hancock. He was on attachment from the Royal West Kent Regiment (The Buffs) and commanded 16 Platoon C Company as of September 1944. He was killed at Bremen on 26 April 1945. Buried in Becklingen War Cemetery, grave 8.G.4.

Hanna, William, Captain, No. 112985
Died 2 August 1943, aged 22. Attached to 1st Battalion, Royal Irish Fusiliers. The son of Walker and Sue Hanna, of Armagh. Buried in Catania War Cemetery, Sicily, grave IV.F.9.

Harris, Leslie Charles, Lieutenant, No. 327957
The son of John Henry Harris and Mavis Harris of Beckenham, Kent. On attachment from the Notts and Derby Regiment (Sherwood Foresters) and joined 14 Platoon C Company on 7 March 1945. Killed near Harpstedt on 13 April 1945. Buried in Becklingen War Cemetery, grave 4.H.1.

Hartley, Peter, Rifleman, No. 3654396
Born in Bradford. Served in D Company as a Rifleman and was killed by a gunshot wound on 7 June 1944 at 'Wood Gazelle'; he was 19 years old. Buried in La Delivrande War Cemetery, grave IX.J.8.

Haslett, Samuel Quigley, Rifleman, No. 7011727
Born in Londonderry, he was killed on 29 May 1940 and buried in Woeston Churchyard, grave 6.

Haycock, William, Bugler, No. 7011437
Born in Belfast, he was killed on 18 May 1940 and buried in Heverlee War Cemetery, grave 12.D.7.

Hayes, Alfred, Private, No. D/24602
Born in County Tyrone, he was killed on 6 February 1940 and buried in Holywood Cemetery, County Down, Northern Ireland, grave 341.

Hefferlin, John, Rifleman, No. 7018196
Born in County Fermanagh, he was killed on 16 March 1941 in the United Kingdom. Buried in Milltown RC Cemetery, Sec. A.L.G., grave 37.

Holden, Stanley, Rifleman, No. 3782973
The son of Joseph and Margaret Holden and the husband of Elizabeth Holden of Blackburn, Lancashire. Killed on 19 July 1944, aged 20, and buried in Banneville War Cemetery, grave I.A.20.

Holmes, William Samuel, Lance Corporal, No. 7045707
Killed on 21 July 1944, he was 29 years old. The son of William J. and Sarah K. Holmes and the husband of Doris Ethel Holmes of Kingsbury, Middlesex, he is buried in Banneville War Cemetery, grave I.A.24. Formerly Royal Irish Fusiliers.

Holt, James Henry, Rifleman, No. D/25043
Born in Cheshire, he was killed on 10 June 1940 in the United Kingdom and buried in Belfast City Cemetery, Sec. P.2. grave 704.

Hood, William, Rifleman, No. 7015364
The son of William and Martha and husband of Robina Hood of Belfast, he was killed on 10 March 1941 and is buried in Belfast City Cemetery, Glenlina, Extn. Sec. D1, grave 96.

Hooper, Frederick Edward, Lance Corporal, No. 7012021
Born in London. Served in HQ Company and was mortally wounded by shrapnel at 'Wood Gazelle' on 18 June 1944, aged 27. The son of Frederick Charles and Alice Lily Hooper of Forest Hill, London, he is buried in La Delivrande War Cemetery, grave VIII.D.1

Horrocks, Robert, Rifleman, No. 14219374
The son of James and Annie Horrocks of Bolton, Lancashire, he was killed on Thursday, 26 April 1945, aged 21. Buried in Becklingen War Cemetery, grave 8.G.1.

Howson, Alwyn Bernard, Rifleman, No. 14655340
Served in A Company and was fatally wounded by shrapnel in the neck on 2 October 1944 at Cuy. He was the son of Bernard and Annie Elizabeth Howson of Beighton, Yorkshire; he was 19 years old. Interred in Uden War Cemetery, Noord-Brabant, Netherlands, grave 2.E.10.

Hughes, Andrew Donney, Rifleman, No. 7021551
The son of Edward and Elizabeth Hughes of Belfast, Northern Ireland and brother of Miss May Hughes of Spamount Street, Belfast. Enlisted in 1941 and subsequently transferred to the 9th Battalion Cameronians. Killed on 26 June 1944 and buried in St Manvieu War Cemetery, grave VI.H.19.

Hunter, Samuel, Rifleman, No. 7017055
The son of Isaac and Sarah and husband of Catherine Hunter of Belfast, County Antrim, he died on 26 January 1941 and is buried in Belfast City Cemetery, Glenlina, Extn. Sec. T1, grave 118.

Hursey, James, Rifleman, No. 7018479
Served in D Company and was killed by a gunshot on 7 June 1944 at 'Wood Gazelle', aged 22. The son of Arthur and Margaret Hursey of Killester, Dublin, Eire, he is buried in Cambes War Cemetery, row J4.

Ireland, Thomas, Driver, No. T/7007689
The husband of Mrs M. Ireland of Stanley Lane, Belfast, and the son of William and Ellen Ireland, also of Belfast, he transferred to the Royal

228

Army Service Corps and was killed on 11 August 1944. Buried in Bayeux War Cemetery, grave XII.C.11. He had served for a total of twelve years.

Irish, Henry, Rifleman, No. 14436258
Born in London. Served in B Company as a Rifleman and was killed by shrapnel on 7 August 1944 at Montisanger, aged 18. Buried in St Charles, grave IV.C.7.

Irvine, John, Rifleman, No. 14688534
The son of David and Agnes Irvine of Paddington, London. He was taken to the RAP on 13/14 October 1944 at Overloon and died of his wounds on 15 October, aged 19. Buried in Overloon War Cemetery, grave IV.D.12.

Irvine, John, 'Jack', Rifleman, No. 1647367
Born in Glasgow. Wounded by shrapnel in the back at Troarn on 20 July 1944. Killed on Sunday, 23 July 1944, aged 24. Buried in La Delivrande War Cemetery, grave III.E.1.

Jamieson, William Henry, Rifleman, No. 7018997
Born in Belfast, he died on 12 August 1943; buried in Carnmoney Cemetery, Sec. AF. joint grave I.39.

Johnson, Alan Cecil, Rifleman, No. 14423673
The son of Cecil and Gertrude Johnson of Catford, London, he was killed on Wednesday, 18 October 1944, aged 19. Buried in Mierlo War Cemetery, grave I.D.2.

Kane, David, Rifleman, No. 7043667
Born in Londonderry, he resided in County Tyrone. He was killed on Friday, 6 April 1945. The son of Samuel and Elizabeth Kane of Tobermore, County Londonderry, he is buried in Rheinberg War Cemetery, grave 12.J.22.

Kane, Derek Stanley, Rifleman, No. 7019200
The son of Edwin and Alice Amy Kane, and husband of Dorothy Edith Kane of Cricklewood, London, he died on 1 March 1943 and is buried in Willesden New Cemetery, Sec. P., grave 2171.

Kane, Thomas, Lance Corporal, No. 7011474
Born in Belfast, he served in D Company, he was killed by a gunshot wound on 7 June 1944 while in action at 'Wood Gazelle', Cambes. He was the son of Mr & Mrs James Kane of Belfast, and husband of Olive Hope Kane of Newport, Isle of Wight; buried in La Delivrande War Cemetery, collective grave IX.D.5-7.

Kane, William Henry, Rifleman, No. 7018769
Served in D Company and was killed by a gunshot wound on 7 June 1944 while at 'Wood Gazelle', Cambes; he was 22 years old. The son of Alexander and Isabella Kane of 32 Joseph Street, Belfast, he is buried in Cambes War Cemetery, row G 16. His brother Alexander was wounded in France and was in hospital in June 1944.

Kealy, Desmond Patrick, Corporal, No. 6711786
Born in Eire, he resided in London. Wounded by shrapnel in the back on 1 July 1944 at Cambes. At Teinray on 20 November 1944, he was killed by a gunshot wound to the side, the result of an accident. Buried in Venray War Cemetery, grave 2.D.3; he was 31 years old.

Keegan, Daniel, Rifleman, No. 7021986
Died 14 August 1942, aged 19. The son of Daniel and Annie Keegan of Bally Bough, Co. Dublin, Eire. Buried in Plymouth (Efford) Cemetery, RC Sec.C., grave 3437.

Keenan, James, Lance Corporal, No. 7012717
The son of James and Annie Keenan of Belfast and husband of Jessie Keenan of Troon, Scotland, he died on 19 August 1942. Buried in Dundonald (Troon) Cemetery, Sec. JI, grave 113.

Keenan, William, Lance Corporal, No. 7011506
Born in Eire, he served in B Company and was fatally wounded by shrapnel on 5 July 1944 at Cambes; he was 30 years old. The son of Hugh and Margaret Keenan of County Armagh, he is buried in La Delivrande War Cemetery, grave 11.G.6.

Kelly, Hugh Francis, Rifleman, No. 7023165
Killed on Sunday, 18 June 1944, aged 21. The son of Hugh and Sarah Ann Kelly of Jamaica Street, Belfast, Northern Ireland, he is buried in Bayeux War Cemetery, grave XI.F.20.

Kelso, Samuel, Rifleman, No. 7015487
Served in A Company, he was killed in action by a shrapnel wound to the head on Monday, 23 October 1944; he was 25 years old. The son of Robert James and Matilda, and husband of Edith Annie, of Yeovil, Somerset, he is buried in Venray War Cemetery, Limburg, Netherlands, grave 2.F.13; he left a baby son.

Kerr, Andrew, Rifleman, No. 7011071
Born in Belfast, he was killed on 29 May 1940, aged 31, and is buried in Boezinge Churchyard, grave 11.

Kerr, Robert, Lance Corporal, No. 24470
Born in Belfast, he was killed on 15 December 1940, aged 43. Buried in Belfast City Cemetery, Glenlina Extn. Sec. Q. grave 85.

Keys, Thomas, 'Tommy', Rifleman, No. 14431912
Served in A Company and was killed on Thursday, 20 July 1944, aged 19. This happened when a force of German tanks attacked the Company. The son of James and Agnes M. Keys of Belfast, he is buried in Ranville War Cemetery, grave IX.C.29. His brother served in the Irish Guards.

Kidd, John Kenneth, Major, No. 164756
Died 10 March 1945, aged 24. Attached to 8th Battalion, 12th Frontier Force Regiment. The son of Capt. William Ruddock Kidd and Evelyn Maud Kidd (née Garrett); husband of Constance Aileen Kidd (née Stevens). Buried in Taukkyan War Cemetery, Burma, grave 17.D.1.

King, Norman, Rifleman, No. 14729153
Born in Lancashire, he was killed on 27 February 1945 and is buried in Reichswald Forest War Cemetery, grave 48.A.10.

King, Thomas William, Rifleman, No. 841864
The son of Henry Dickson and Hilda King of Pembrokeshire, he was killed 9 July 1944, aged 30. Buried in Banneville War Cemetery, grave IX.B.24.

Kinnin, John Calvert, Corporal, No. 7012389
The son of Isaac and Emily of Belfast, he died on 17 February 1942 in the United Kingdom. Buried in Carnmoney Cemetery, Sec. B.B., grave 148.

Knox, Francis, Rifleman, No. D/24471
Born in County Antrim, he was the husband of E. Knox of Belfast. Died on 8 May 1940, aged 55, and is buried in Dundonald Cemetery, Sec. E.2., grave 345.

Kohler, Albert John Edward, Corporal, No. 7016376
Served in D Company and was killed by a gunshot wound on 7 June 1944 while at 'Wood Gazelle', Cambes, aged 24. He was the son of Albert Edward and Daisy Ethel Kohler of Bethnal Green, London; buried in La Delivrande War Cemetery, grave VII.K.5.

Lackey, John Campbell, Rifleman, No. 7015445
The son of Arthur and Sarah Lackey, and husband of Agnes, of Belfast, he died on 5 May 1940, aged 33. Buried in Belfast City Cemetery, Sec. J.1., grave 359.

Langford, Kenneth Leonard, Rifleman, No. 7015087
Born in Croydon, he died on 28 August 1940 and is buried in Pembroke Dock Military Cemetery, Sec. E., grave 12.

Laving, Leslie Frederick, Captain, No. 233304
Joined the Rifles in 1941. He was the second in command of the Anti-tank Platoon from its formation until Normandy. Prior to the crossing of the Escaut Canal, 18-19 September 1944, he was moved to Headquarters Company as 2i/c. Killed on Tuesday, 19 September 1944 by a gunshot wound to the side, he was 31 years old. The son of John and Ellen Laving and the husband of Janet Muriel Laving of Stevenage, Herts, he is buried in Leopoldsburg War Cemetery, grave IV.D.1.

Lazell, Edward Henry, Rifleman, No. 7017599
The son of Edward Walter and Ellen Lazell of Walthamstow, London, he died on 7 December 1941, aged 25. Buried in Chingford Mount Cemetery.

Ledger, Samuel Albert, Rifleman, No. 14714023
Born in Nottinghamshire, he was killed on 6 April 1945, aged 19. Buried in Rheinberg War Cemetery, grave 12.L.2.

Leen, Thomas John, Rifleman, No. 7020081
Born in Liverpool, he resided in Belfast. Died on 24 January 1941 in the United Kingdom. Buried in Millbrook RC Cemetery, Sec. A., row L., grave 36.

Leslie, Thomas, Sergeant, No. 7006851
The son of Thomas and Mary Ann Leslie (née Loughran) of Belfast, Northern Ireland, he died on 29 May 1940, aged 37. Buried in Woesten Churchyard, grave 5.

Lewis, James, Rifleman, No. 7011974
Born in County Down, resident in County Armagh, he was the son of John and Susan Lewis, and husband of Lily Hollander Lewis of Brixton, London. Died on 1 June 1940, he has no known grave and is commemorated on the Dunkirk Memorial, column 129.

Lewis, John Charles, Rifleman, No. 14437673
Killed on Friday, 1 December 1944, aged 19. The son of Thomas and Mary Jane Lewis of Sparkbrook, Birmingham, he is buried in Mierlo War Cemetery, grave III.F.13. His brother Samuel was also killed.

Lewis, William Henry, Lance Corporal, No. 5726309
Served in D Company and was fatally wounded by shrapnel on Sunday, 15 October 1944 at Overloon; he was 35 years old. The son of Alfred and

Louisa Walton Lewis of Bermondsey, London, he is buried in Overloon War Cemetery, grave IV.D.7.

Lillicrap, John Francis, Rifleman, No. 14206465
Served in the Anti-tank Platoon of Support Company and was killed on 9 June 1944 by a shrapnel wound to the heart while on the 'ridge' at Cambes; he was 21 years old. The foster son of Mr & Mrs J.A. Davis of Rock Ferry, Birkenhead, Liverpool, he is buried in La Delivrande War Cemetery, grave IX.G.7.

Lindsay, Hugh, Rifleman, No. 7012223
Born in County Antrim. Served in Headquarters Company, attached to the MT Platoon. He came ashore in Normandy on D plus 9 driving the Quartermaster's 3-ton lorry. He was killed on 13 July 1944 at La Delivrande. Buried in La Delivrande War Cemetery, grave VI.L.8.

Lockhart, James, Sergeant, No. 7009959
Died 26 March 1942. Buried in Belfast City Cemetery, Glenalina Ext. Sec.L., grave 307.

Lovatt, Roy Francis, Rifleman, No. 14757021
The son of William and Elenor Jane Lovatt, he was killed on 1 December 1944 and buried in Venray War Cemetery, grave 6.D.4.

Lynch, James Anthony, Colour Sergeant, No. 6978973
Born in Eire and resided in Liverpool; he was the son of James Edward and Mary Lynch, and husband of Phyllis Elizabeth Lynch of Belfast, N. Ireland. He was killed on 7 June 1945, aged 30. Buried in Reichswald Forest War Cemetery, grave 59.F.1.195.

Lyndon-Adams, Clifford, Lieutenant, No. 265000
Served in the Mortar Platoon of Support Company. He had joined the Battalion on 19 June, shortly after the fighting around Cambes Wood, becoming the Mortar Officer. Initially wounded on 20 June, he was in the process of being evacuated the following day when he was killed instantly by a direct hit from an enemy shell near Cazelle. The son of John and Katherine Lyndon-Adams and husband of Winifred, of Leamington Spa, Warwickshire, he is buried in La Delivrande War Cemetery, grave V.F.8; he was 26 years old.

Macarthy, John Papworth, Rifleman, No. 14655604
The son of John and Edna Violet Macarthy of Cambridge, he was killed on 9 June 1944, aged 19, and is buried in La Delivrande War Cemetery, grave IX.J.10.

Mallon, Rifleman
Served in D Company and was killed by shrapnel at Hill 60 on 9 July 1944. Listed in Sergeant Drumgoole's RAP Register; not listed on CWGC website as of 6 July 2005.

Martin, Edward Charles, Rifleman, No. 1475975
Killed in action on 26 April 1945, aged 20. He was the son of John Charles and Annie Elizabeth of Morden, Surrey. Buried in Becklingen War Cemetery, grave 4 F.1.B.

Martin, George Alexander, Rifleman, No. 7021483
Killed in action on Thursday, 20 July 1944, aged 21. The son of Henry and Margaret of Soldierstown, County Antrim, he is buried in Banneville-La-Campagne War Cemetery, grave 1.A.27.

Martin, Henry, Rifleman, No. 6985604
Served in A Company; was hit by shrapnel and killed on Friday, 9 June 1944 at Cambes. Buried at La Delivrande in collective grave IX.D.5-7; he was 20 years old.

Martin, Hugh, Lance Corporal, No. 7021559
Killed in action on Friday, 3 November 1944. Buried in Venray War Cemetery, grave 3.A.3; he was 21 years old. He was the son of Mr and Mrs H. Martin of Glenpark Street, Belfast; he had served for three years. A brother also served.

Martin, Hugh, Lance Sergeant, No. 7012185
Killed in action on Tuesday, 20 June 1944, aged 29. He was the husband of Violet Matilda of Leeds, Yorkshire; they had two children. He has no known grave and is commemorated on the Bayeux Memorial, panel 17, column 3. His brother Private Thomas Martin, aged 27, was killed in action while serving with the Royal Hamilton Light Infantry, having emigrated to Canada when he was 14 years old. Their parents resided at Matilda Street, Belfast.

Matthews, Ritchie Rea, Rifleman, No. 7013545
The son of Henry V. and Sarah Matthews of Belfast, N. Ireland, he died on 14 May 1940. He has no known grave and is commemorated on the Dunkirk Memorial, column 129.

May, Edward, Rifleman, No. 7014142
Born in York, he was the son of Ernest Walter and Sarah May of Kilmanahan, County Tipperary, Eire. He died on 29 May 1940, aged 30. Buried in Woesten churchyard, grave 1.

Maynard, Cyril, Rifleman, No. 701979
Killed on Friday, 9 June 1944 at Cambes, aged 30. The son of Alice Jane Maynard of Hackney, London, he is buried in La Delivrande War Cemetery, grave IX.J.9.

McAllister, George, Rifleman, No. 7009594
Served in D Company, he was killed by a gunshot wound on 7 June 1944 at 'Wood Gazelle', Cambes. Husband of Mary of Donegall Pass, Belfast and son of George and Elizabeth McAllister, Spruce Street, Belfast; his father had been killed in the First World War. Buried in La Delivrande War Cemetery, grave VII.G.1.

McAllister, Ronald, Rifleman, No. 7015463
D Company. Killed by a gunshot wound on 7 June 1944 at 'Wood Gazelle', Cambes. Husband of Mrs B. McAllister of 34 Strathroy Park, Belfast. Two brothers were also killed and two more severely wounded. His father was disabled in the First World War. Buried in Cambes-en-Plaine, row G 15.

McAlpine, Frederick, Rifleman, No. 7013683
The son of Mr and Mrs James McAlpine of Belfast, N. Ireland, resided in Armagh. Killed on 29 May 1940 and buried in Boezinge churchyard, grave 10.

McAnulty, Daniel Joseph, Lance Sergeant, No. 3241530
Born in Belfast, died on 26 November 1941, in the United Kingdom, buried in Milltown RC Cemetery, Sec. A. Row DF, grave 53.

McBride, James Adair, Lance Sergeant, No. 7012157
The son of Mr and Mrs J. McBride of 6 Lomond Street, Belfast, he was killed on Wednesday, 19 July 1944, aged 30, he had eleven years' service. Buried in Banneville-La-Campagne, grave I.A.26.

McCabe, James Sylvester, Rifleman, No. 14407007
Served in C Company and was killed on Wednesday, 19 July 1944; he was the son of William and Annie McCabe of Crumlin, Dublin, Eire and was 20 years old. Buried in Banneville-La-Campagne, grave I.B.29.

McCarten, George, Rifleman, No. 14820229
Born in Liverpool and killed on 31 May 1945, aged 18. Buried in Reichswald Forest War Cemetery, grave 59.E.3.

McCaul, James Charles, Corporal, No. 7011358
The son of James Charles and Mary McCaul of Ballyblack, Newtownards, County Down, N. Ireland, and husband of Gwendolyn

McCaul of Ash Vale, Surrey. He was killed on 19 June 1944 and is buried in Shorne (SS Peter & Paul) churchyard, SE of church.

McClean, Arthur James, Lance Corporal, No. 7016381
Killed on Monday, 8 April 1945, he was the son of William Francis and Harriet McClean of Nottinghamshire, and husband of Joan of Eltham, London. Buried in Hanover War Cemetery, grave 7.B.14.

McConnell, William John, Rifleman, No. 7020154
Born in County Down, he died on 4 December 1941; he has no known grave and is commemorated on the Brookwood Memorial, panel 14, column 3.

McCool, John Joseph, Rifleman, No. 14424619
Served in A Company, he suffered shrapnel wounds to the right ear and left ankle on 20 June 1944, at Cambes, and died on Thursday, 22 June 1944, aged 29. He was the son of Margaret and the stepson of Matthew McBride of Townparks, Raphoe, County Donegal. Before the War he had been employed by Messrs Honyford, Strabane. Buried in Ann's Hill Cemetery, Gosport, Hampshire, plot 189, grave 5. Given his place of burial it is possible that he was wounded in France and returned to hospital in England.

McCoy, William, Lance Corporal, No. 7017351
From Cahbrain Park, Whiteabbey, County Antrim, he was a Bren gunner in 16 Platoon of D Company. Killed on 26 April 1945, aged 23. Buried in Becklingen, grave 8.G.5.

McCracken, George Anthony, Rifleman, No. 7013828
D Company. He suffered shrapnel wounds to his left side on 20 June 1944, at Cambes and died the following day. His home was at 19 Ravensdale Street, Belfast. Two of his brothers also served. His wife and son resided in Plymouth. Buried in Bayeux War Cemetery, grave III.J.6.

McCready, James, Rifleman, No. 7023015
The son of James and Martha McCready of Belfast, N. Ireland, he died on 9 December 1945, aged 20. Buried in Carnmoney Cemetery, Sec. AF, grave 11.

McDowell, Robert, Rifleman, No. 7012084
Born in Belfast, he died on 29 May 1940, buried in Boezinge churchyard, grave 9.

McFarland, John, Rifleman, No. 25089
The husband of Anna Mina McFarland of Belfast, N. Ireland, he died on 25 March 1942 in the United Kingdom. Buried in Dundonald Cemetery, Sec. A.2., grave 241.

McFarlane, John, Rifleman, No. 7018909
Born in Eire, he died on 23 October 1941 and is buried in Holywood Cemetery, County Down, grave 1263.

McGennity, William H., Rifleman, No. 7015448
Born in Glasgow, he was the son of William H. and Isabella McGennity of Belfast. Husband of Bridget and father of Margaret, all three died on 16 April 1941, possibly as a result of the Belfast Blitz. Buried in Milltown RC Cemetery, Sec. B. row N.G.

McGlennon, Hugh Henry, Rifleman, No. 7012171, MM
Awarded the Military Medal for his actions as D Company runner on 9 June 1944. He was killed in action on Thursday, 26 April 1945. He was the son of Patrick and Margaret McGlennon of Kircubbin, County Down and is buried in Becklingen War Cemetery, grave 8.G.10. He was 30 years old.

McGrory, Patrick, Rifleman, No. 14424793
Born in Glasgow, he was resident in County Tyrone (possibly served in Support Company and wounded by shrapnel to the left leg on 6 August 1944 at Montisanger). Killed 26 April 1945; he was 20 years old. Buried in Becklingen War Cemetery, grave 8.G.2.

McIlvenny, James, WOII, No. 24502
Born in County Down, he died on 17 March 1941 and is buried in Belfast City Cemetery, Glenlina Extn. Sec. T., grave 407.

McKenna, Daniel, Rifleman, No. 7019244
Born in County Durham, he was the husband of Ivy McKenna of Harlesden, Middlesex. Died on 16 November 1940 and buried in Kensal Green RC Cemetery, Sec. G., grave 1083.

McKeown, John, Corporal, No. 25094
Born in County Down, he was the son of James and Mary McKeown and husband of Margaret McKeown of Belfast, N. Ireland. Died on 16 March 1941 and buried in Kilmore (Christ Church) Burial Ground.

McMichael, Daniel, 'Dan', Lance Sergeant, No. 7009901
(Possibly C Company, he was wounded by shrapnel to the buttock on 19 September 1944 at the crossing of the Escaut Canal.) Killed on Tuesday, 26 September 1944, he was the son of Alfred and Mary McMichael of 40

Louisa Street, Belfast. Buried in Leopoldsburg War Cemetery, grave V.C.2; he was 37 years old.

McMillen, Malcolm, Rifleman, No. 3196800
Born in Belfast, he died on 4 April 1945, aged 34. Buried in Reichswald Forest War Cemetery, grave 33.D.10.

McMillen, Richard, Rifleman, No. 7011809
The son of Samuel McMillen and stepson of Roseanna McMillen of Creagh, Belfast, N. Ireland, he died between 25 May and 4 June 1940. Buried in Bleuet Farm Cemetery, grave 1.AA.5.

McNeill, George, Rifleman, No. 7013035
Born in Belfast, he died on 28 May 1940, aged 20. Buried in Woesten churchyard, grave 2.

McQuillan, John, Rifleman, No. 7045462
Born in London. Killed on 28/29 March 1945, aged 30, he is buried in Reichswald Forest War Cemetery, grave 48.A.15.

McSperrin, Francis, Corporal, No. 7011222
Born in Belfast, he resided in County Armagh. Served in the Mortar Platoon of Support Company, he was a Mobile Fire Controller in Normandy. Killed on 19 July 1944, aged 33. Buried in Banneville-La-Campagne, grave 1.B.26.

McVeigh, Charles Joseph, Sergeant, No. 7013567
Served as the Battalion MT Sergeant and came ashore riding a motorcycle on D-Day from LCT (4) on Queen Red. Fatally wounded by shrapnel on 12 August 1944, aged 27. Buried in St Charles de Percy War Cemetery, grave VI.C.4.

McVeigh, James Thomas, Rifleman, No. 7017357
Born in Belfast, died on 11 March 1941, buried in Belfast City Cemetery, Glenlina Extn. Sec. S1., grave 202.

Merry, Kenneth Walter, Lance Corporal, No. 7022576
Died 9 June 1944, aged 21. Son of Henry Richard and Bessie Eliza Merry, of Walthamstow, Essex. Buried in La Delivrande War Cemetery, grave IX.D.9.

Michaelides, Michael, Rifleman, No. 7020577
Served in Headquarters Company and was mortally wounded by shrapnel at 'Farm Gazelle', Cambes on the night of 8/9 June 1944. Born in Cyprus, he was the son of Procopios and Agathoniki Michaelides, and husband of

Olive May of Walworth, London. Buried in La Delivrande War Cemetery, grave IX.D.8; he was 36 years old.

Middleton, George, Rifleman, No. 7011627
The son of John and Annie Middleton, and husband of Annie Middleton of Belfast, N. Ireland, he died on 29 May 1940, aged 28. He has no known grave and is commemorated on the Dunkirk Memorial, column 129.

Millar, Hugh Henry, Corporal, No. 7014297
D Company. Killed by a gunshot wound to the head on 7 June 1944 at 'Wood Gazelle', Cambes; he was 23 years old. The son of John and Isabella Millar of 9 Abetta Parade, Belfast, his two brothers also served in the Regiment (Robert and Thomas). Their father served with the Royal Irish Rifles in the First World War. Buried in La Delivrande War Cemetery, grave IX.D.8

Millar, William Thomas, Lance Corporal, No. 7011756
The son of William Thomas and Nancy Gertrude Millar of Stone, Buckinghamshire, and the nephew of Mrs E. Millar of 30 Hartley Street, Belfast, he was killed on 20 July 1944, aged 29. He had served in excess of thirteen years and his wife resided in England. Buried in Banneville War Cemetery, grave 1.A.28.

Milligan, James, Rifleman, No. 7019263
Served in B Company and was killed by a phosphorous bomb on Saturday, 8 July 1944 at Hill 60. The son of John and Ellen Milligan and husband of Emma of South Croydon, Surrey, he was 34 years old. Buried in Ranville War Cemetery, grave V.C.26.

Mills, Edward, Rifleman, No. 14380800
Served in B Company, he was admitted to the RAP with a sprain to the left foot as the result of an accident on 14 July 1944 at La Delivrande. Fatally wounded by shrapnel on Wednesday, 19 July 1944 at Troarn, he was 19 years old. The son of Thomas and Bertha Mills of Oldham, Lancashire, he is buried in St Charles de Percy War Cemetery, Calvados, grave 11.D.3.

Moffatt, Robert James, Rifleman, No. 7013481
The son of George W. and Daisy Jane Moffatt of Belfast, N. Ireland, he died on 28 May 1940 and is buried in Boezinge churchyard, grave 1.

Molloy, Valentine, Rifleman, No. 7019015
Born in County Armagh, died on 27 January 1942 and is buried in Donaghcloney old graveyard, grave 74.

Moore, John Henry, Corporal, No. 7011035
Born in Manchester, resident in County Tyrone, he died on 14 May 1940, aged 25. Buried in Leuven Communal Cemetery, row B, grave 10.

Moore, William Henry, Rifleman, No. 7020828
Killed in action on Saturday, 16 December 1944, aged 44 years. He was the son of John and Mary Moore and the husband of Kathleen Moore of Saunders Street, Belfast. Buried in Schoonselhof Cemetery, grave V.D.97, Antwerp, Belgium. Before the War he had worked for Messers McCaw, Stevenson & Orr Ltd, Castlereagh Road, Belfast.

Morgan, George, Rifleman, No. 7022454
Killed on Wednesday, 19 July 1944, aged 22. He was the son of Thomas Alfred and Kathleen Morgan of Euston, London. Commemorated on the Bayeux Memorial, panel 17, column 3.

Morgan, John J., Second Lieutenant, No. 315230
Born in County Navan, he was the son of Patrick F. and Anne Morgan of Liverpool. Seconded from the Royal Irish Fusiliers, he commanded 7 Platoon A Company from the end of August 1944. Killed in action by a gunshot to the head in the early hours of 19 September 1944 during the crossing of the Escaut Canal. Buried in Leopoldsburg War Cemetery, grave IV.D.2.

Morris, William Charles, Sergeant, No. 7011150
Served in D Company and was wounded by shrapnel in the right and left legs on 9 July 1944 at Hill 60, Normandy. Killed on Friday, 14 July 1944, aged 34. He was the son of William and Mary Morris of Belfast and the nephew of Margaret Carbery also of Belfast. Buried in Bayeux War Cemetery, grave III.H.16.

Morrison, Joseph, Rifleman, No. 7009709
Born in Eire, he was the son of Robert and Elizabeth, and husband of Kathleen Morrison of Derrygonnelly, County Fermanagh, N. Ireland. He died on 14 May 1940 and has no known grave; commemorated on the Dunkirk Memorial, column 129.

Mulcahy, Henry, Rifleman, No. 7010041
Born in County Armagh, he died on 5 November 1939 in France/Belgium, buried in Le Grand-Luce War Cemetery, row A.

Mullan, Robert James, Rifleman, No. 7021305
The eldest son of Mr and Mrs Samuel Mullan of Argyle Street, Belfast, he was killed in action in Normandy, aged 22. Buried in La Delivrande War

Cemetery, grave X.D.7. His father was twice wounded and taken prisoner in the First World War.

Mullen, John Thomas, Rifleman, No. 14778403
Killed on Thursday, 26 April 1945, aged 18. The son of James and Ellen Mullen of Gateshead, County Durham, he is buried in Becklingen War Cemetery, grave 8.G.3.

Mullen, Patrick, Rifleman, No. 704331
Served in A Company and was killed by a shrapnel wound to the head on 7 June 1944 at 'Farm Gazelle'. The son of Patrick and Mary Ann, and husband of Mary Ann Mullen of Roslea, County Fermanagh, N. Ireland, he was 33 years old. Buried in Hermanville War Cemetery, grave 2.I.7.

Murray, James, Rifleman, No. 7011091
Born in Belfast and resided in County Armagh. Killed in France on 29 May 1940 and buried in Boezinge churchyard, grave 7.

Nelson, Edward, Rifleman, No. 7012314
Born in County Antrim, the husband of Ellen Nelson of Gravesend, Kent; he died on 29 May 1940, aged 31. Buried in Hoogstade churchyard, grave 106.

Nesbitt, William, Lance Corporal, No. 7012895
Born in County Armagh, he was the son of Joseph and Jennie Nesbitt of Keady, County Armagh, N. Ireland. He died on 19 May 1940, aged 20, and is buried in Denderleeuw Communal Cemetery, grave 567.

Noble, William, Rifleman, No. 7015520
Killed on Thursday, 26 April 1945, aged 27. The son of George William and Edith of Belfast, he is buried in Becklingen War Cemetery, grave 10.D.9.

Norman, Ernest Frederick, Rifleman, No. 7015663
Served in the Carrier Platoon of Support Company. The son of Ernest and Bertha Norman of Bromley, Kent, he was killed on 30 November 1944; buried in Venray War Cemetery, grave 6.C.8; he was 28 years old.

Norman, Geoffrey Schuyler, Captain, No. 48899, MC
Born in Australia, he was the son of George Schuyler Cardew Norman and Ada Emily Norman. He died on 30 July 1941, aged 50. Golders Green Crematorium, panel 3.

Nugent, James, Rifleman, No. 14413635
The son of Thomas and Esther Nugent of Dublin, he died on 23 July 1943, aged 19, while on attachment to the 6th Battalion Royal Irish Fusiliers. Buried in Mount Jerome Cemetery, grave A. 88-61928037.

O'Beirne, Michael, Corporal, No. 7019276
Born in Eire and resided in London; he was the son of Peter J. and K. O'Beirne of Ballaghaderreen, County Roscommon, Eire. Killed in action on 9 July 1944 at Hill 60, aged 44. Buried in Ranville War Cemetery, grave IV.A.2.

O'Callaghan, Patrick Joseph, Corporal, No. 6975889
Born in London, he was resident in Eire prior to enlisting. Killed on Friday, 9 June 1944, he is buried in Hermanville War Cemetery, grave 1.H.15.

O'Connor, Percy Herbert, Rifleman, No. 7017833
The son of Eugene and Annie O'Connor of Millbank, London, he died on 3 March 1945, aged 31. Buried in Streatham Park Cemetery, square 14A, grave 19080.

O'Flynn, James Anthony Rourke, Captain, No. 109068
Died 3 May 1944, aged 31. Attached to 4th Prince of Wales' Own Gurkha Rifles. Son of Dennis and Harriett O'Flynn; husband of Teresa Carmen O'Flynn, of Carmarthen. Buried in Madras War Cemetery, Chennai, grave 6.A.16.

O'Hagan, Patrick, Lance Corporal, No. 7014265
Born in County Londonderry, he served in B Company and was wounded by shrapnel in the back on 19 July 1944 at Troarn. He died the next day and is buried in La Delivrande War Cemetery, grave III.J.8.

O'Halloran, John Patrick, Corporal, No. 7011733
The son of John and Bridget O'Halloran of Belfast, N. Ireland, he died some time between 28 May and 2 June 1940, aged 26. Commemorated on the Dunkirk Memorial, column 128.

O'Hare, Robert, Private, No. 7011777
Army Catering Corps attached to the Battalion. The son of Thomas and Bridget (née Kerr) O'Hare, of Belfast, N. Ireland, he was killed on 2 April 1945. Buried in Reichswald Forest War Cemetery, grave 48.D.2.

O'Reilly, Edward George, Corporal, No. 7018690, DCM
Born in London, resided in Brighton and was killed on 20 July 1944. (A Company, awarded the Distinguished Conduct Medal for his actions on 9 June 1944.) Buried in Ranville War Cemetery, grave IX.C.31.

Orr, Robert John Dillon, Lance Corporal, No. 7022204
The son of Mrs M. Orr of Empire Street, Belfast, he died of wounds on
19 July 1944. Buried in La Delivrande War Cemetery, grave VIII.A.6. His
father served in the First World War and was killed in the Second World
War while serving in the Royal Engineers in Northern Ireland.

Palmer, Ernest Leonard, Corporal, No. 6216113
Died 8 February 1945. Attached to Special Boat Squadron, SAS Regiment,
AAC. Son of Herbert Joseph and Grace Emma Palmer; husband of
Georgina V. Palmer, of Mitcham, Surrey. Buried in Taukkyan War
Cemetery, Burma, grave 3.F.16.

Parker, John Henderson, Rifleman, No. 7022745
Served in C Company and was wounded in the head by shrapnel on 9 June
1944, at Cambes. Evacuated to hospital in England, he died of his wounds
on 12 June 1944, aged 20. The son of William Charles and Ada Alice
Blanche Parker of Dublin, he is buried in Chapelizod C of I churchyard,
Dublin.

Parkin, Charles Rowland, Rifleman, No. 14655749
One of those selected to guard St Etienne Church, Caen, as reported in
the *Belfast Telegraph* of 11 July 1944. Killed in action on Wednesday, 19
July 1944, he was 19 years old. The son of John Charles and Margaret of
Little London, Spalding in Lincolnshire, he is buried in Banneville War
Cemetery, grave 1.A.22.

Patterson, John, Rifleman, No. 7020205
Served in C Company and was killed by shrapnel on Friday, 9 June 1944
at Cambes; he was 32 years old. Buried in Cambes-en-Plaine War
Cemetery, row C 16. He was the son of Mrs F. Patterson, Summerhill
Street, Belfast; his brother served in the RAF.

Patton, Richard George, Rifleman, No. 6979411
Born in County Armagh, he served in A Company and was mortally
wounded by shrapnel on 9 June 1944, at Cambes. Buried in Cambes-en-
Plaine War Cemetery, grave 7.B.4.

Payne, Ernest George, Corporal, No. 7019311
Killed on Friday, 9 June 1944, he was the son of William and Elizabeth
Payne of Southgate, Middlesex, and the husband of Grace; he was 31
years old. Buried in La Delivrande War Cemetery, grave VII.L.1.

Payne, Frederick, Lance Sergeant, No. 7017199
Served in B Company, he was killed by shellfire on Saturday, 7 July 1944
at Hill 60. The son of William and Elizabeth Payne of Southgate,

Middlesex, he is buried in La Delivrande War Cemetery, grave I.E.7 (may have been the brother of Payne, Ernest George).

Pearson, Edward Geoffrey, Second Lieutenant, No. 326352
The son of Edward and Beatrice Susan Pearson of Mitcham, Surrey, he was on attachment from the 9th Cameronians. Died on 3 December 1944, aged 26. Buried in Venray War Cemetery, grave 4.E.13.

Perkins, Gordon, Rifleman, No. 7046400
Killed on Friday, 30 March 1945, he was the son of Benjamin and Anna Perkins of Erdington, Birmingham. Buried in Reichswald Forest War Cemetery, grave 61.H.4.

Phillips, Robert, Rifleman, No. 7016338
Born in London, he was killed on Friday, 6 April 1945, aged 25. Buried in Rheinberg War Cemetery, grave 12.J.21.

Pickavance, James, Rifleman, No. 14735641
Born in St Helens. GSW to the chest at Overloon on 13 October 1944. Died 24 January 1945, aged 18, with No. 6 Commando. Buried in Nederweert War Cemetery, grave IV.E.6.

Plant, George, Rifleman, No. 7044475
Born in Coventry. Wounded by a gunshot to the left arm on 15 June 1944, while at Cambes. Received multiple shrapnel wounds at Troarn on 21 July, from which he died, aged 24. The son of Charles and Mary Plant of Exhall, Warwickshire and the husband of Betty Margaret, he is buried in La Delivrande War Cemetery, grave VIII.6.3.

Porterfield, George, Corporal, No. 1830237
Died 23 April 1946, aged 34. Son of Robert and Janet Porterfield. Commemorated on the Brookwood Memorial, panel 14, column 3.

Pratt, Victor George, 'Vic', Corporal, No. 7015875
Served in the Mortar Platoon of Support Company and was killed by shrapnel on Monday, 12 June 1944, at Cambes, aged 25. The son of George Albert and Edith Florence Pratt of West Norwood, London, he is buried in La Delivrande War Cemetery, grave VII.K.8.

Preist, Reginald Arthur, Rifleman, No. 5189229
Originally served with the Gloucestershire Regiment and was killed on Saturday, 24 March 1945, aged 31. He was the son of Thomas and Gertrude Preist of Bristol, and the nephew of Mr H.J. Pym, also of Bristol; he is buried in Groesbeek Canadian War Cemetery, grave VI.E.4.

Quinn, Charles, Rifleman, No. 7010989
Born in County Tyrone, he died on 29 May 1940, aged 30. Buried in Hoogstade Churchyard, grave 104.

Rapkins, Edgar Charles, Lieutenant, No. 293047
Lieutenant Rapkins joined the Battalion while it was stationed at Hawick. Appointed second in command of the Anti-tank Platoon at Troarn. He was killed by shrapnel wounds to the right and left leg and right arm at Overloon on Saturday, 14 October 1944, aged 30. The son of Charles and Olive Emma Rapkins, husband of Lilian Mary Rapkins of Alton, Hampshire, he is buried in Mierlo War Cemetery, Noord-Brabant, the Netherlands, grave VIII.E.6.

Reynolds, Frederick George, Rifleman, No. 14227586
Born in London. Served in D Company and was killed by shrapnel on Tuesday, 20 June 1944, at Cambes. Buried in Cambes-en-Plaine War Cemetery, row G 20.

Rice, William John, Rifleman, No. 7011646
Served in A Company and was killed by shrapnel on Friday, 9 June 1944, at Cambes. Husband of Mrs J. Rice, Arkwright Street, Belfast, he had served for thirteen years prior to his death. Buried in Cambes-en-Plaine War Cemetery, row G 6. His brother served in the Navy.

Richardson, Roy Joseph, Rifleman, No. 5187582
The son of Sidney and Mary Richardson, and the husband of Florence Irene of West Hartlepool, County Durham, he was 25 years old. Killed on Thursday, 29 June 1944 and buried in Hermanville War Cemetery, grave I.T.7.

Robinson, Arthur Douglas, Rifleman, No. 14714043
Born in Lincolnshire. Killed 1 December 1944, buried in Venray War Cemetery, grave 6.D.2.

Robinson, Joseph, Rifleman, No. 1772964
The son of Edward and Esther Robinson of West Kyd, County Durham. He was killed on 30 November 1944 and is buried in Venray War Cemetery, grave 6.C.13; he was 25.

Robinson, Ralf Hubert Reginald, Lieutenant, No. 130757
Died 8 June 1942, aged 24. Attached to 8th Battalion, Durham Light Infantry. Son of 2/Lt R.H. Robinson, and of Daisy G.M. Robinson, of Leigh-on-Sea, Essex. Buried in Knightsbridge War Cemetery, Acroma, grave 2.J.3.

Robinson, Samuel, Rifleman, No. 14428300
Served in A Company and suffered a mortal gunshot wound to the abdomen at Cambes on Sunday, 25 June 1944; died the following day; he was 18 years old. The son of Arthur and Elizabeth Robinson of Manchester, he is buried in La Delivrande War Cemetery, grave V.A.1.

Robinson, Thomas William, Rifleman, No. 11005766
From Paddington, London, he was killed on 30 November 1944, aged 32, and is buried in Venray War Cemetery, grave 6.D.3.

Robinson, William, Rifleman, No. 7013802
The son of William and Margaret Robinson of Lurgan, County Armagh and husband of Elizabeth, he died on 23 September 1943 in the United Kingdom. Buried in Lurgan (Shankill) Graveyard, grave 707.

Roche, Rupert Reginald Burke, Lieutenant, No. 304137
Died 21 June 1944, attached to the 6th Battalion, Royal Inniskilling Fusiliers. Buried in Orvieto War Cemetery, grave I.D.21.

Rogers, Ernest John, Corporal, No. 7017531
Served in Support Company and was killed by shrapnel on 8/9 June 1944 at Cambes Wood; he was 29 years old. The son of John and Ada Rogers, and the husband of Eileen of Forest Gate, Essex, he is buried in La Delivrande War Cemetery, grave X.D.5.

Rooney, Henry, Lance Sergeant, No. 7013785
Born in Belfast, he resided in Armagh. Served in D Company and was killed by a gunshot wound on 7 June 1944, aged 23, at 'Farm Gazelle'. Buried in La Delivrande War Cemetery, grave IX.D.10.

Rossiter, James, Rifleman, No. 6409584
Died 19 March 1945, aged 24. Son of Patrick and Brigid Rossiter, of Davidstown, County Wexford. His brother Michael Joseph also died on active service. Buried in Davidstown (St Aidan) Catholic churchyard, Wexford.

Rowley, Owen, Lance Corporal, No. 7021446
Served in D Company and was killed by a gunshot wound on Wednesday, 7 June 1944 at 'Farm Gazelle', aged 40. Born in Belfast, he was the son of Owen and Hannah Rowley of Sussex and is buried in Cambes-en-Plaine, row G 14.

Russell, William, Rifleman, No. 7022409
The son of Mr and Mrs William Russell, he died on 22 August 1944 and is buried in Dromara 1st Presbyterian Church, Dromara, County Down, grave 85.

Ruxton, Anthony Fane, Lieutenant, No. 95530, MC
Born in South Africa, he was the son of Charles Harcourt Vernon and Phyllis Maitland Ruxton (née Wood) of Waterrow, Somerset. He served with the Battalion in France in 1940 and was killed on 15 July 1943, while serving with the Commandos in Sicily. Buried in Syracuse War Cemetery, grave VII.D.13.

Ryan, Michael Kevin, 'Sticky', Rifleman, No. 6197005, MM
Awarded the Military Medal for his actions in France, 1940. Served in B Company as a runner, and was killed by shrapnel on Tuesday, 4 July 1944 at Cambes, aged 37. Buried in La Delivrande War Cemetery, Douvres, grave II.G.5. Born in Eire, he was the son of Timothy and Elizabeth Ryan of Tipperary, and the husband of Kathleen Marie of Weoley Castle, Birmingham.

Schofield, George Robert, Sergeant, No. 7011515
From Laleham, Middlesex, he served in 18 Platoon D Company and was killed on 1 November 1944 by a gunshot wound to the left side of the chest while at Venray. On the night of 31 October, Sergeant Schofield was returning to the company lines with a patrol. A pre-agreed signal was given, but somehow this was either not seen or recognized and the patrol was fired on. Sergeant Schofield was the only casualty. He is buried in Venray War Cemetery, grave 3.A.1; he was 32 years old.

Scott, James, Rifleman, No. 7013196
The son of Preston and Agnes Scott of Belfast, N. Ireland, he died on 29 May 1940 in France/Belgium, aged 26. Buried in Woesten churchyard, grave 8.

Scott, Richard, Rifleman, No. 7021372
Born in Belfast in 1922, he served in A Company and attended the RAP at Troarn on 21 July 1944 with 'sore feet'. He was killed by shrapnel on 14/15 October 1944, at Overloon. Buried in Overloon War Cemetery, grave 4.D.9.

Scott, William John, Rifleman, No. 7011203
Served in B Company and was fatally wounded by shrapnel on Friday, 9 June 1944; he is buried in Cambes-en-Plaine War Cemetery, row D 14.

Seabrook, John Robinson, Lieutenant, No. 284120
Born in Herefordshire, he was the son of Arthur John and Rosanna Kate, and husband of Margaret Eleanor Seabrook of West Hampstead, London. He died on 1 March 1945, aged 27, and is buried in Reichswald Forest War Cemetery, grave 48.B.13.

Sedgwick, John Henry, Rifleman, No. 24692
The son of William and Agnes Sedgwick, and husband of Margaret Sedgwick of Belfast, he died on 27 March 1942 in the United Kingdom, aged 51. Buried in Belfast City Cemetery, Glenlina Extn. Sec.T.1., grave 412.

Sewell, Nicholas John, Rifleman, No. 7019849
Served in D Company and was killed by a gunshot wound on 7 June 1944 at 'Farm Gazelle', aged 27. The son of Leonard and Ann Sewell of Tottenham, Middlesex, he is buried in La Delivrande War Cemetery, grave IX.J5-6, a joint grave.

Shaw, Albert Conn, Rifleman, No. 7014036
Born in Belfast. Killed on Friday, 13 April 1945, he was 22 years old. Buried in Becklingen War Cemetery, grave 4.H.4.

Shore, Robert, Rifleman, No. 14216344
Served in B Company and was fatally wounded on 9 June 1944, at Cambes. The son of Robert and Margaret Shore of Queenhill, Worcestershire, he is buried in La Delivrande War Cemetery, grave IX.J.5-6, a joint grave.

Simmonds, John Frederick, Rifleman, No. 5053293
Killed on Sunday, 9 June 1944, aged 24, he was the son of Harry and Sarah Simmonds and the husband of Iris Maud of Smethwick, Staffordshire. Buried in Ranville War Cemetery, grave V.C.9.

Slater, Walter, Rifleman, No. 3392759
Killed on Friday, 13 April 1945, he was 33 years old. The son of Mr and Mrs John Slater of Heywood, Lancashire, he is buried in Becklingen War Cemetery, grave 4.H.5.

Slavin, Henry, Rifleman, No. 7018428
Born in Belfast, died on 16 April 1941 and is buried in Belfast City Cemetery, Glenlina Extn. Sec. R1, grave 214.

Smith, Henry, Rifleman, No. 6982501
Served in Headquarters Company and was mortally wounded on Sunday, 9 July 1944 at Caen. The husband of Evelyn Smith of Wellingborough, Northamptonshire, he is buried in Ranville War Cemetery, grave V.C.23; he was 30 years old.

Smith, Herbert Corville, Rifleman, No. 14203182
Served in D Company and was killed by a gunshot wound on Wednesday, 7 June 1944 at 'Farm Gazelle'. The son of Tom and Eva Smith of Burnley, he was 20 years old. Buried in Cambes-en-Plaine War Cemetery, row J 10.

Smith, Lalor, Rifleman, No. 7011328
The son of Robert James and Agnes Smith of Belfast, and husband of Agnes Smith of Bessbrook, County Armagh, N. Ireland, he died on 28 May 1940 in France/Belgium. Buried in Dozinghem Military Cemetery, grave XVII.B.11.

Smith, Robert, Colour Sergeant, No. 24698
Born in County Down, he died on 14 June 1942 in the UK. Listed on the Army Roll of Honour, but not on the CWGC website as of 6 July 2005.

Smith, Samuel Edward, Lance Corporal, No. 7009692
Born in County Armagh, died on 29 May 1940, aged 34, in France/Belgium. Buried in Bleuet Farm Cemetery, grave 1.AA.4.

Smith, William Henry, Rifleman, No. 7013455
Served in D Company, he was killed by shrapnel on Tuesday, 20 June 1944, while at Cambes. He was the son of William Henry and Mary Smith and the husband of Mabel Beatrice of Hereford. Buried in Cambes-en-Plaine War Cemetery, row G 18.

Smyth, John Torbitt, Rifleman, No. 14411392
The son of William and Mary Smyth of County Antrim and husband of Gladys Rosie Smyth of Salisbury, he died on 25 August 1944. Buried in Bayeux War Cemetery, grave III.L.2.

Speers, John, Rifleman, No. 7601237
Born in Herefordshire, resided in Belfast, he was killed 13 April 1945, aged 21. Buried in Becklingen War Cemetery, grave 4.H.8.

Spence, Hugh, Sergeant, No. 24530
The husband of Rachel Spence of Belfast, he died on 31 March 1941, aged 50. Buried in Belfast City Cemetery, Sec.G.2., grave 349.

Starrett, Richard, Rifleman, No. 25132
Born in Barrow-in-Furness, he was the husband of Annie Starrett and died on 25 March 1943, aged 59. Buried in Dundonald Cemetery, Sec.B.1., grave 744.

Starrett, Samuel, Rifleman, No. 7013794
The son of Robert George and Annie Starrett of County Londonderry, and husband of Annie Starrett of Cullion, County Tyrone, he died on 2 March 1941. Buried in Glendermot C of I Churchyard, Sec.D, old ground.

Steadman, Henry Smith, Corporal, No. 5341308
Served in Support Company, he was killed on 19 September 1944, at the crossing of the Escaut Canal, by a shrapnel wound to the head. The son

of Henry and Lilian Steadman and the husband of Mary Alice of West Norwood, London, he is buried in Leopoldsburg War Cemetery, grave IV.D.3.

Stephens, James Patrick, Rifleman, No. 7012577
Born in Eire and resided in County Armagh; died on 27 January 1943 and is buried in Maidstone Cemetery, plot C.C.1., grave 13.

Stevens, Thomas George, Rifleman, No. 7017250
Served in D Company and was wounded by shrapnel in the back on 20 June 1944, at Cambes. He was killed on Thursday, 26 April 1945, aged 25. The son of Joseph and Florence Annie Stevens of Putney, London, he is buried in Becklingen War Cemetery, grave 4.G.1B.

Stevenson, James Ernest, Lance Sergeant, No. 7011810
Served in the Carrier Platoon of Support Company and suffered an accidental gunshot wound to the left foot on 27 June 1944, while at Cambes. Killed by shrapnel on Wednesday, 19 July 1944 at Troarn, aged 32. He was the son of Mr and Mrs Stevenson of Bapaume Avenue, Cregagh, Belfast, buried in Banneville War Cemetery, grave 1.A.30.

Stevenson, Robert James, Rifleman, No. 7019933
The son of Mr and Mrs Andrew Stevenson of Church Road, Carnmoney, County Antrim, he was listed as 'missing in action' in the *Belfast Telegraph*. He was killed in action on 7 June 1944 and has no known grave. Commemorated on the Bayeux Memorial, panel 17, column 3. Before the War he had worked for WA Ross & Sons, Mineral Water Manufacturers.

Stewart, Andrew Robert, Lance Sergeant, No. 7012091
Born in County Down. Served as a Lance Sergeant in the Intelligence Section. On D-Day he came ashore from a LCI (L) on Queen White. He was killed on Monday, 19 June 1944, aged 30. Buried in Hermanville War Cemetery, Calvados, France, grave 1.U.9.

Stewart, Arthur Lawrence, Corporal, No. 7010811
Served in the Carrier Platoon of Support Company and was killed by shrapnel on Monday, 24 July 1944 at Troarn, he was 34 years old. The son of Arthur and Laura I.A. Stewart, husband of Frances Elizabeth Stewart of Belfast, Northern Ireland, he is buried in Banneville-La-Campagne War Cemetery, Calvados, France, grave 1.B.25. Prior to the war he was employed by Alexandra Finishing Company Ltd, Cullingtree Street, Belfast. Two brothers also served, one in the RAF, the other in the Royal Navy. Their father was killed in action in 1914.

250

Stewart, Richard, Lance Corporal, No. 7020434
Killed on 30 November 1944, aged 28. He was the husband of Matilda Stewart of Ballycastle, County Antrim, Northern Ireland. Buried in Venray War Cemetery, Limburg, The Netherlands, grave VI.D.9; he was 28 years old.

Stewart, Robert McFerran, Rifleman, No. 6977397
The son of Hugh Boal and Ellen McFerran of Monkstown, County Antrim, he died on 12 May 1943, aged 30. Buried in Carnmoney Cemetery, Sec.S.S., grave 40.

Stock, Claude A. James, Rifleman, No. 7016593
Born in London, he was the son of William T. and Amy Hilda Stock.　　He was killed on 20 July 1944, aged 26. His wife, Sadie (née Kenneway) and two children resided at Springwell Street, Ballymena, County Antrim. Buried in Banneville-La-Campagne War Cemetery, grave 1.B.20.

Sunman, Richard, Rifleman, No. 14202691
Born in Hull, he was killed on 27 February 1945 and is buried in Reichswald Forest War Cemetery, grave 62.F.2.

Sutton, Patrick Gerald, Lance Corporal, No. 1628989
The son of James and Mary Sutton of Waterford, Eire, he was killed on 30 November 1944. Buried in Venray War Cemetery, grave 6.D.6; he was 26 years old.

Sweeny, Charles Raymond Patrick, Major, No. 74698, MC
Born in Limerick in 1917, he was educated at Hailebury and attended Sandhurst. Commissioned in the Regiment on 27 January 1938, awarded the MC while serving in Palestine. Served in A Company and was slightly wounded by shrapnel to the right leg on 24 July 1944 at Troarn; the wound did not require evacuation. Died 9 May 1945, buried in Becklingen War Cemetery, grave 2.F.2. Charles Sweeny was an ADC to Field Marshal Montgomery and one of his most trusted liaison officers. He was killed having returned senior German officers to their own lines following the signing of the surrender document.

Swindall, Horace, Lance Corporal, No. 14655361
Born in Burton-on-Trent. Taken to the RAP at Troarn on 19 July 1944 suffering from exhaustion. Killed in action on 13 April 1945 and buried in Becklingen War Cemetery, grave 4.H.3.

Talbot, Ronald Frederick, Rifleman, No. 912552
The son of Arthur and Mabel Talbot of Bournemouth and husband of Doris of Winton, Bournemouth, he died on 19 December 1943. Buried in Bournemouth North Cemetery, Sec.H.1. grave 13.

Tanner, Bernard Charles, Rifleman, No. 7022487
The son of John W. and Edith Tanner of Leicester, he was killed on 8 July 1944 and is buried in Ranville War Cemetery, grave V.C.12.

Taylor, Samuel S., Rifleman, No. 7011801
Born in Barnsley, resided in Nottinghamshire, died sometime between 29 May and 2 June 1940 in France/Belgium. He has no known grave and is commemorated on the Dunkirk Memorial, column 129.

Tebbutt, John Donovan, Rifleman, No. 14570786
The son of Henry Walter and Nora C. Tebbutt, he died on 28 June 1943, aged 18. Buried in Eltham Cemetery, Sec.H. grave 463.

Thompson, David, Rifleman, No. 7014034
The son of William and Elizabeth Thompson of Belfast, N. Ireland, he was killed on 29 May 1940, aged 22, and is buried in Boezinge churchyard, grave 12.

Thompson, Ernest Oscar, Rifleman, No. 7020212
The husband of Anna Thompson of Bangor, County Down, he died on 17 November 1943, aged 21, while attached to the 5th Battalion Royal Inniskilling Fusiliers. Buried in Bangor Cemetery, Sec.4.U., grave 25.

Thompson, Hugh Joseph, Rifleman, No. 7013406
The son of Johnny and Annie Thompson of Belfast and husband of E.L. Thompson of Belfast, he died on 3 June 1940, aged 20. Buried in Belfast City Cemetery, Glenlina Extn. Sec.A., grave 362.

Thompson, Kenneth, Rifleman, No. 14429341
Born in Belfast. Killed 7 April 1945, aged 19. Buried in Oldenzall Protestant Cemetery, grave 6.

Thompson, Thomas Foster, Rifleman, No. 7020888
The son of John and Sarah Thompson of Carnmoney, Belfast, he died on 8 January 1943, aged 22, while on attachment to the Pioneer Corps. Buried in Carnmoney C of I Churchyard, Sec.F.

Threlfall, Ronald, Rifleman, No. 14804107
The son of Wilfred and Elsie Threlfall of Morecambe, Lancashire. Killed on 6 April 1945 and buried in Sage War Cemetery, grave 6.B.11.

Todd, Raymond Sydney, Colour Sergeant, No. 7012226
Died 3 October 1942, aged 26. The son of Ralph and Sarah Anne Todd, of Loughbrickland; husband of Barbara Todd, of Sevenoaks, Kent. Buried in Glascar Presbyterian Churchyard, County Down, grave 41.

Toye, Frank, Rifleman, No. 25139
The son of John and Isabella Toye of Lisburn, County Antrim, he died on 29 December 1939 in the UK. Buried in Lisburn (Holy Trinity) RC Cemetery, Sec.4., grave 51.

Treanor, Patrick Joseph, Rifleman, No. 7014151
The son of James and Elizabeth Treanor of Newry, County Down, he died on 28 May 1940, aged 20. Buried in Woesten churchyard, grave 3.

Trolland, Jack, Corporal, No. 7013033
Born in County Antrim, he died between 27 May and 2 June 1940. He has no known grave and is commemorated on the Dunkirk Memorial, column 128.

Tuohy, Anthony, Rifleman, No. 14655365
The son of James and Mary Tuohy of Hull, he was killed on 17 October 1944 and is buried in Overloon War Cemetery, grave 4.D.14.

Turner, Ross Dickson, Rifleman, No. 14655365
The son of William and Bella Turner of Belfast, N. Ireland, he died between 29 May and 2 June 1940. He has no known grave and is commemorated on the Dunkirk Memorial, column 129.

Tweedy, Samuel, Rifleman, No. 14428101
The son of Samuel and Mary Tweedy of Belfast, N. Ireland, he was killed on 13 April 1945. Buried in Becklingen War Cemetery, grave 4.H.G.

Valentine, Henry J., Rifleman, No. 7016349
Born in London. Served in Headquarters Company as a stretcher-bearer and was killed in action by a shrapnel wound on 7 June 1944, aged 24. The son of Charles and Alice Amelia, and husband of Peggy Eileen Valentine of Holloway, London. Buried in La Delivrande War Cemetery, grave X.E.1.

Varnham, Joseph Charles Clifford, Rifleman, No. 5391622
The son of Joseph and Elizabeth May Varnham of Leicester, he resided in Birmingham. Killed on 9 June 1944 at Cambes. Buried in Cambes-en-Plaine War Cemetery, row G.17.

Vaughan, Denis, Rifleman, No. 14410586
The son of Jeremiah and Mary Vaughan of Spangle Hill, Cork, Eire, he resided in Belfast. Killed on 6 April 1945 and buried in Rheinberg War Cemetery, grave 12.I.24.

Wallace, James Thomas, Rifleman, No. 7013115
The son of William and Bertha E. Wallace of Belfast, N. Ireland, he died sometime between 29 May and 2 June 1940, aged 27. Buried in Marquise Communal Cemetery, plot 1, row D, grave 19.

Waller, John, Rifleman, No. 7019368
Born in London. He came ashore on D plus 17 attached to the MT Platoon and driving a 15cwt lorry loaded with small arms ammunition. Killed on 1 April 1945, aged 30, and buried in Reichswald Forest War Cemetery, grave 61.H.3.

Wallis, Frank Thomas George, Corporal, No. 7019327
The son of Thomas William and Florence Francis Wallis of Pinner, Middlesex, he served in Support Company. Fatally wounded by a gunshot on 19 July 1944 at Troarn, aged 29. Buried in Banneville-La-Campagne War Cemetery, grave 1.A.25.

Walsh, Stephen, Corporal, No. 6410418
The son of Stephen and Mary Walsh of Crumlin, Dublin City, Eire, he resided in Belfast. Served in B Company and was killed on 3 July 1944 at Cambes, aged 23. Buried in La Delivrande War Cemetery, grave II.G.2.

Walton, John Robert, Rifleman, No. 7020380
From Barnes, Surrey, he served in the Anti-tank Platoon of Support Company, and was killed on 3 November 1944. Buried in Venray War Cemetery, grave 3.A.10; he was 33 years old.

Watkin, Arthur Leonard Frank, Corporal, No. 7022463, MM
Born in Middlesex. Served in C Company and was killed 6 April 1945, aged 33. Buried in Rheinberg War Cemetery, grave 12.L.1. Received a Commendation Card.

Watson, John, Rifleman, No. 14217516
Died between 13 and 14 June 1944, aged 22. The son of Richard and Elizabeth Watson, of Dunmurry, Co. Antrim. Commemorated on the Bayeux Memorial, panel 17, column 3.

Watson, Norman Roland Victor, Captain, No. 121329
Born in Huntingdonshire, he was the son of Kenneth Elkins and Lily Winifred Watkins of Stratford. He joined the Battalion in June 1940. Originally a platoon commander in A Company, he later served as the

Battalion Intelligence Officer. Later still he was appointed second in command of C Company. On 30 June 1944, he was buried in his slit trench at Cambes Wood by a near miss from an enemy shell and died of his injuries. Buried in La Delivrande War Cemetery, grave VII.K.3.

Watters, Joseph, Rifleman, No. 7012390
The son of James and Mary Watters of County Antrim and the husband of Jean of Troon, Ayrshire, he died on 19 August 1942, while attached to No. 4 Commando. Commemorated on the Brookwood Memorial, panel 14, column 3.

Watts, Frederick George, Corporal, No. 10602995
Died 14 January 1945, aged 27. Buried in Imphal War Cemetery, India, grave 7.J.18.

Weir, William, Rifleman, No. 7013154
The son of Henry and Catherine Weir of Belfast, N. Ireland, he died on 29 May 1940, aged 26. Buried in Bleuet Farm Cemetery, grave 1.AA.6.

Wescott, Sydney E., Sergeant, No. 7007070
Born in Middlesex, died on 1 January 1941, buried in Blandford Cemetery, grave 60.

Wheatley, John Nicholson, Captain, No. 130394
Died 11 June 1944, aged 24. Attached to 8th Battalion, Durham Light Infantry. The son of Arthur and Evelyn Wheatley, of Reading, Berkshire. Buried in Jerusalem War Cemetery, Chouain, France, row A.13.

White, Henry George, Lance Corporal, No. 7019878
The son of Joseph John and Lucy Charlotte White, and husband of Sarah White of Bow, London, he served in A Company and was killed on 18 January 1945. Buried in Venray War Cemetery, grave 6.E.7; he was 25 years old.

White, Thomas, Rifleman, No. 4758984
The son of Charles and Jane White of Belturbet, County Cavan, he was killed on 6 April 1945 and is buried in Oldenzaal RC Cemetery, row 30, grave 2.

Whitehorn, Edmund James, Rifleman, No. 7016683
The husband of Emma Rose Whitehorn of Old Ford, London. Served in the MT Platoon as a fitter and was killed on 12 June 1944, aged 24; has no known grave. Commemorated on the Bayeux Memorial, panel 17, column 3.

Whiteley, Eric, Rifleman, No. 14655367
The son of Leonard and Mary Anne Whiteley of Killamarsh, Derbyshire, he served as a Rifleman and was killed on 1 December 1944. Buried in Venray War Cemetery, grave 6.C.11.

Whitely, Samuel, Lance Corporal, No. 6979048
The son of Mabel Whitely of Belfast, N. Ireland. Served in C Company and was wounded by a gunshot to the head on 19 July 1944 at Troarn. Died of wounds on 25 April 1945 and is buried in Becklingen War Cemetery, grave 10.G.13.

Wilkinson, Robert Stewart, Corporal, No. D/24552
Born in Belfast, died on 11 October 1940 and buried in Belfast City Cemetery, Sec. E., grave 287.

Williamson, George, Rifleman, No. 7022501
The son of George and Emily Williamson of Ballyclare, County Antrim, he served as a Rifleman and was killed on 30 November 1944. Buried in Venray War Cemetery, grave 6.C.5. His father died of wounds received in the First World War.

Williamson, James Campbell, Rifleman, No. 7018176
Served in D Company and was killed by a gunshot wound on 7 June 1944 at 'Farm Gazelle', Cambes. Husband of Mrs R. Williamson of 50 Harley Street, Belfast; his brother served in the RAF. Buried in La Delivrande War Cemetery, grave IX.J.7.

Williamson, Thomas Henry, Rifleman, No. 7019939
Served in C Company, he was killed in a landmine explosion on 4 August 1944 near 'Bocage'. Prior to enlistment he was employed by Messrs R. Stewart & Son of Lisburn; his home address was given as 8 Red Row, Sprucefield, Lisburn, County Antrim. Buried in Banneville-La-Campagne War Cemetery, grave XVI.C.28.

Wilson, Cecil, Rifleman, No. 14414731
The son of Samuel George and Hannah Jane Wilson of Lurgan, County Armagh. Wounded by shrapnel on 9 June 1944 at Cambes. Killed 24 July 1944 and buried in Hermanville War Cemetery, grave 2.G.15.

Wilson, Denis, Rifleman, No. 14552116
The son of Thomas and Annie Wilson of Northenden, Cheshire, he was killed on 9 June 1944 and is buried in La Delivrande War Cemetery, collective grave IX.D.5-7.

256

Winch, Hugh William, Rifleman, No. 7011832

Died 1 June 1940, aged 25. The son of William and Jessie Winch; husband of Lydia May Winch, of West Bromwich, Staffordshire. Commemorated on the Dunkirk Memorial, column 129.

Wolfe, Garrett, Rifleman, No. 6409448

Served in Headquarters Company, he was killed by shrapnel on Monday, 24 July 1944 at Troarn, aged 30. He was the son of Joseph and Catherine Wolfe; husband of Elizabeth Wolfe of York Road, County Dublin, Eire. Buried in Banneville-La-Campagne War Cemetery, Calvados, France, grave I.B.24.

Wright, Alexander, Rifleman, No. 7009511

Born in Belfast, resided in County Armagh; died between 28 May and 23 June 1940, aged 33. Buried in Le Clion-Sur-Mer Communal Cemetery, collective grave 4.

Wright, Derek, Rifleman, No. 14613429

Born in Liverpool. Killed on Wednesday, 26 July 1944 and buried in Hermanville War Cemetery, Calvados, France, grave 2.G.3. He was 19 years old.

Wylie, David, Rifleman, No. 7018832

Born in Londonderry, son of James Alexander and Sarah Ann Wylie. Died on 27 July 1942, aged 22. Buried Faughanvale Presbyterian Churchyard, grave 37.

Glossary

AVRE, Armoured Vehicle Royal Engineers.

Bailey Bridge, of British design, the Bailey Bridge is a temporary structure that, in only a matter of hours, can be erected to span a river and be strong enough to support the immense weight of a tank. The bridge can be broken down into assorted parts and carried in transport vehicles.

Battalion, an infantry unit containing 500–800 men, and commanded by a Lieutenant Colonel.

B Echelon, the battalion supply column in the field.

Bofors, Light anti-aircraft gun of 40mm calibre.

Bomb Happy, see Shell Shock.

Bren Carrier, see Universal Carrier.

Bren gun, a Light Machine Gun, an essential support weapon carried by every British and Canadian platoon.

Brigade, a formation of two or more Battalions acting together under the overall command of a Brigadier.

Brigade Group, a Brigade with attached support units; e.g. medical staff, engineers, and anti-tank gunners.

BSM, Battery Sergeant Major.

C-47 Skytrain, see Dakota.

CDL, Canal Defence Light.

CIGS, Chief of the Imperial General Staff.

CO, Commanding Officer.

Company, a subdivision of a Battalion, commanded by a Major and consisting of approximately 120 men. Parachute Battalions consisted of three rifle companies (normally designated A, B, and C) and an HQ and Support Company – the latter consisting of specialist groups such as Machine Gun and Mortar platoons. Airlanding companies, as with all other mainstream infantry, had an extra rifle company within their ranks. Also, whereas parachute companies had three platoons within these companies, other infantry units carried four.

Corps, a formation of two or more Divisions acting together as a self-contained unit under the overall command of a Lieutenant General. An Airborne Corps would consist of a number of Airborne Divisions, coupled with assigned Air Force Groups dedicated to their transport and resupply. Whereas a standard ground-based Corps would consist of a Division or more of tanks and other armoured vehicles, numerous infantry Divisions, additional transport vehicles, and supporting artillery.

Coup de main, French, literally translated as 'stroke of hand', but in a military context it refers to a sudden surprise attack. Or in the case of the bridges at Bénouville and Ranville, the seizure of an objective by a small group of lightly armed men who will hold it until the main force arrives on foot.

Crocodile, a version of the Churchill tank adapted to carry a flame-thrower.

CSM, Company Sergeant Major, the senior NCO in a Company.

Dakota, a transport aircraft used by the Allies for towing gliders, and dropping parachutists or supplies. Designed by the USA, under the name of the C-47 Skytrain, it was sold to the British under the name of the Dakota. It was the most efficient method of deploying parachutists that was available to the British, its competitors being converted bombers, which were not ideally suited to the task. A Dakota could also be used to tow a light glider, such as a Horsa or Waco, but not the larger Hamilcar.

D-Day, the term 'D-Day' has come to be accepted as the name of the Normandy landings through its constant association. However every single military operation has a D-Day, defined as the date upon which the operation is to take place. For Operation Overlord, D-Day was 6 June.

DD Tank, Duplex Drive Tank. An amphibious tank which, in Normandy, was used to swim ashore, under its own propulsion, with the first wave of infantry.

Division, a formation of two or more Brigades and assorted supporting units (e.g. artillery, engineers) acting together as one force under the command of a Major General, typically a Division would consist of 10,000 men.

Drop Zone, an area of land designated for the dropping of parachutists.

DUKW, an American designed 2.5 ton amphibious truck, used by the Allies.

Hamilcar, the largest of the British gliders, often used to carry the heaviest equipment (e.g. 17-pounder anti-tank guns, Universal Carriers, or the light Tetrarch tanks as used by the 6th Airborne Armoured Reconnaissance Regiment).

Horsa, the standard British glider, capable of carrying twenty-eight men, or heavy equipment such as Jeeps and 6-pounder anti-tank guns.

IO, Intelligence officer.

KIA, killed in action.

Landing Craft, there were several different types of Landing Craft used by the Allies in Normandy, each performing a different function. The assault infantry travelled in an LCA (Landing Craft: Assault), these were armoured against small-arms fire and carried four crew and thirty-five men, fewer than the larger but vulnerable, wooden-constructed LCIs (Landing Craft: Infantry), used as second-wave craft. Other variants of Landing Craft were LCTs (Landing Craft: Tank) and LCFs (Landing Craft: Flak).

Landing Ships, were much larger than the Landing Craft which carried out the assault, and they brought in large amounts of infantry and heavy equipment. Variants were LSI (Landing Ship: Infantry) and LST (Landing Ship: Tank).

Landing Zone, an area designated for the landing of gliders.

Lee-Enfield MkIV, the standard British infantry rifle.

LMG, light machine gun, in the British Army the Bren gun.

Mallard, the codename given to the airlift operation to bring the Second Lift of the 6th Airborne to Normandy on the evening of 6 June.

MG34, the German LMG.

MG42, successor to the MG34.

MMG, medium machine gun, in the British Army the .303 Vickers.

MO, Medical Officer.

NCO, Non-Commissioned Officer, such as warrant officers, sergeants or corporals.

'O' Group, Orders Group, a commander may order an 'O' Group to assemble his subordinate officers to give them their orders.

OP, Observation Post.

Overlord, the code name given to the invasion of Normandy on 6 June 1944 by the 21st Army Group and American allies.

PIAT, Projector Infantry Anti-Tank. A hand-held weapon that fires an armour-piercing projectile, most adept at dealing with lightly armoured vehicles.

Platoon, three platoons existed within a Parachute Company, four in an Airlanding or normal Infantry Battalion, and each was commanded by a Lieutenant. Platoons could consist of as many as 60 soldiers, though the glider-borne units were designed so that they could be transported in a single Horsa glider, and therefore consisted of 26 men. Parachute platoons were somewhat larger.

RA, Royal Artillery.

RAC, Royal Armoured Corps.

RAF, Royal Air Force.

RAMC, Royal Army Medical Corps.

RAOC, Royal Army Ordnance Corps.

RAP, Regimental Aid Post.

RASC, Royal Army Service Corps.

RE, Royal Engineers.

REME, Royal Electrical and Mechanical Engineers.

Roman Candle, a term used to describe a parachute that has failed to fully open. This condition would normally arise from a poorly packed chute that would cause the parachutist to plummet to his death.

RSM, Regimental Sergeant-Major, the most senior Warrant Officer in a battalion.

Sapper, a private of the Royal Engineers.

Self-Propelled (SP) Gun, a large artillery gun, mounted on its own vehicle like a tank, unlike the static artillery guns that were towed behind jeeps or lorries.

SHAEF, Supreme HQ Allied Expeditionary Force – the Headquarters of General Eisenhower, the Allied Supreme Commander.

Shell Shock, otherwise known as bomb happy, shell shock is a condition that arises from the fear and ceaseless noise of prolonged artillery barrages. Rendering such cases seemingly child-like or stricken into numbness, the condition can take many years to recover from, if at all.

Slit trench, the name given to a one-man trench that infantrymen dig with the shovels they carry. Providing the ground is soft, a trench can be quickly dug so that a single man can place his body as much beneath the level of earth as possible. Not only does this make the man a harder target during firefights, but it greatly reduces the chance of injury from artillery bombardment. Known as foxholes in the American and Canadian Armies.

SS, Schutz Staffeln, literally translated as Protection Detachments. The SS were separate to the Wehrmacht and were under the overall control of Himmler. The Waffen-SS was the elite of this Nazi corps.

Sten, Sub-machine Gun, usually carried by British officers and NCOs, not very reliable.

Stick, the collective term used to describe a group of parachutists in a single aircraft, as in 'a stick of paratroopers'.

Tonga, the code name given to the airlift on the first night of the 6th Airborne Division's landing.

Universal Carrier, a tracked and lightly armoured vehicle used by the British for, as its name implies, a number of duties from transport of men and supplies, to a weapons platform for mortars or mounting a Bren light machine gun.

USAAF, United States Army Air Force. Unlike the RAF, the American air forces during the War were not an independent service, but instead either fell under the jurisdiction of the Navy or Army.

Very Light, a cartridge fired from a flare pistol, providing light at night or a signal during daylight hours.

Waco, CG4A, the standard glider of the US Army. It was cheap and the design was easy to mass-produce, however it was not as robust as the British Horsa and was prone to structural failure.

Wehrmacht, German army forces, not including the SS.

WIA, wounded in action.

Bibliography

Barber, Neil, *The Day The Devils Dropped In*, Pen & Sword, 2003
Carruthers & Trew, *The Normandy Battles*, Cassell, 2000
Collier, Richard, *Sands of Dunkirk*, Collins, 1961
Corbally, M.J.P.M., *The Royal Ulster Rifles, 1793–1960*, N. Ireland, 1960
Delaforce, Patrick, *Monty's Ironsides*, London, 1995
Divine, D., *The Nine Days of Dunkirk*, Faber & Faber, 1957
Dungan, Myles, *Distant Drums*, Appletree Press, 1993
Graves, C., *History of the Royal Ulster Rifles, Vol. III; 1919–1948*, Belfast, 1950
Grimal, Pierre, *Classical Mythology*, Penguin Books, 1990
Harclerode, P., *Go To It*, The Illustrated History of the 6th Airborne Division, London, 1990
Jewell, Brian, *Over The Rhine*, Spellmount, 1985
Lorentin, E., *Gateway To Victory*, Guide Books, undated
Mace, Paul, *Forrard*, The Story of the East Riding Yeomanry, undated
Reynolds, Michael, *Steel Inferno, II SS Panzer Corps in Normandy*, Spellmount, 1997
Rymen, Carl, *Het Oude Land van Loon*, 1995
Tout, Ken, *Tanks Advance*, Grafton, 1989
Truesdale, David, *Brotherhood of the Cauldron*, Redcoat Publishing, 2002
Tute, Costello, Hughes, *D-Day*, Pan Books, 1974
Weeks, John, *Assault From the Sky*, Canada, 1978
Whiting, Charles, *Bounce The Rhine*, London, 1985
Wilmot, Chester, *The Struggle for Europe*, London, 1954
Blackthorn (Journal of the Royal Irish Rangers, various issues)
Quis Separabit (Regimental magazine of the Royal Ulster Rifles, various issues)

UNPUBLISHED SOURCES

England, John, letters
Hyde, John, letters
Lieutenant Colonel C.S. Durtell, OBE, written account
Pegg, Harry, letters
S/Sergeant Harry Howard, Glider Pilot Regiment, written account

RUR Recruit Book, 1931–1939

Armagh Gazette, War years
Belfast Telegraph, War years
Newtownards Chronicle, War years

War Diary 1st Battalion RUR, RUR Museum, Belfast
War Diary 2nd Battalion RUR, RUR Museum, Belfast
War Diary East Riding Yeomanry, PRO WO171/862

Index

Addenkirk Bridge 27
Albania 64
Aldworth, John Richard St Leger, Major
37, 38
Alexander, CG 'Charlie', Captain 10, 52,
60, 96, 97, 99
Alost 14
Altenlingen 94
Allen, Charles, L/Sergeant 128,
Allenbostel 178
Allman, Captain 27
Allwood, Ronald, Rifleman 99
Anderson, Lieut-Colonel 130
Anderson, Bill, Major 174
Anderson, Fred 69
Anisy 41, 42
Anguerny 37
Anzio 127
Archdale, Micky, Lieutenant 118, 123,
124, 126, 127, 128, 131, 132, 133,
135, 136
Archer, John Phillip, Lieutenant 153, 154
Ardennes 149, 152, 175, 179
Arnhem 66, 67, 73, 148
Arras 26
Ash, Rifleman 39,
Ashton, Philip John, Captain 12
Aubne, John Young, Rifleman 83
Ave-et-Auffe 151
Avery, Rifleman 62

Badajoz 5
Bailey Bridge 68, 89, 95, 171, 174
Baker, William, Sergeant 118
Baker, Thomas Joseph, Corporal 41
Bande 155
Banton, Harold John, Rifleman 82
Barker, E G, Lieutenant 70
Barnekow 178
Barrien 100, 101

Barry, Denis Michael Gavin, Captain 95,
96, 99
Barry, Patrick Edmund, L/Corporal 127
Baudains, William H 'Billy', Major 10, 22,
56, 58, 68, 76, 85, 86, 90, 92, 93
Bayeux 3
Beattie, Rifleman 80
Beck, Rifleman 49, 91
Becker, Alfred, Major 125
Beggs, CSM 117
Belgium 3, 13, 14, 31, 67, 85, 149, 155,
156
Bell, L/Corporal 156
Benerville 34
Bennett, Lieutenant 136, 141
Bennett, William, Rifleman 95
Benson, Major 21
Berville –sur-Mer 147
Betty, M, Lieutenant 71, 72
Bevan, S, Captain 88, 92
Bieville 63
Biggs, Corporal 76
Bingham, Stanley Henry 46
Birchall, 'Bertie', Rifleman 160, 166
Bird, Alan Curtis Dicky, Major 60, 74, 75,
81, 83, 101, 108
Blackburn 132
Blakehill Farm 119
Blasheim 174
Blitterswijk 78, 79, 81, 83
Bocholt 92, 94
Boesinghe 22, 23
Bois de Bavent 138
Bomber Command 119, 171
Bonass, L/Sergeant 54, 88, 105
Bonneville 145, 146
Borkel 73
Bossuyt 20
Boulogne 20
Boustead, John Derek Athling 'Geezil',
Lieutenant 127

Boyce, Richard 'Fenian Dick', Colour Sergeant 118, 126
Boyd, Eric, Corporal 10
Boyes Anti-Tank Rifle 9, 17, 22, 26
Bradley, George, L/Corporal 53
Brady, L/Corporal 39
Brankin, Rifleman 84
Bray-Dunes 26, 28
Bredin, Lieutenant 22, 28
Bremen 100, 102, 103, 108
Bren Gun 9, 15, 16, 24, 26, 28, 31, 35, 39, 40, 45, 57, 59, 72, 75, 82, 84, 86, 88, 90, 93, 94, 96, 102, 108, 129, 143, 144, 160, 162, 165, 166, 167, 168
Breville 134, 135
Brickworks 58, 59
Brieville 50
Brinkum 102, 108
Broadwell 117, 119, 122
Brown, Trooper 61
Brown, Gordon, Major 119
Brown, Corporal 60,
Browne, Jimmy, Captain 128
Brownlow-Rea, Captain 177
Brunswick 175
Brunton, Corporal 117
Brussels 17, 18
Bryan, Lieutenant 135
Bryans, 'Shots', Rifleman 118
Bryant, Lieutenant 163
Buer 173
Buffalo 101, 102, 103, 104, 106, 107, 108
Bulford 114, 119, 148, 149
Bulscamp 24, 25
Burges, Brian Ravensdale, Lieutenant 53, 61
Burke, Lieutenant 135, 144, 147, 173
Burrows, Stanley, Rifleman 35, 48, 49, 65, 113

Cabourg 140, 141
Cadden, RQMS 15,
Caen 3, 31, 50, 52, 53, 56, 57, 64, 67, 84, 127, 136
Café De La Poste 155
Calais 20, 150
Calar 91
Calix 53
Calvados 147
Cambes 36, 37, 39, 42, 44, 46, 51, 64, 99, 106
Cameron Highlanders 59, 133
Campbell, L/Corporal 39
Campbell, Lieutenant 130

Campbell, James Moorland, Major
Campbell, Jim, Lieutenant 47, 48, 54, 81, 108,
Campbell, Captain 109
Campbell, Lieutenant Colonel 112, 114
Canloan 148, 150, 172
Capell, Herbert, Rifleman 82
Carroll, Corporal 83
Carruthers, Rifleman 100
Carson, R.J.H. 'Hank', Lieutenant Colonel 114, 115, 116, 137, 140, 141, 142, 143, 144, 145, 146, 147, 149, 154, 164, 168
Cazelle 48, 63
Chambers, Thomas, L/Corporal 119, 133
Champion 154
Chapman, William John 'Jack', Lieutenant 118, 119, 130, 133
Charles, A, Rifleman 59, 63
Charleroi 150
Cherbourg 11
Cheshire Regiment 29
Chilton Foliat 115
Chlorine gas 14
Ciergnon 151
Class V Raft 68
Clayton, Rifleman 76
Cleve 89
Cochrane, Sergeant 75, 93, 94
Cochrane, Rifleman 156
Coesfeld 170, 171
Cohen, Rifleman 118
Coldstream Guards 94
Colleville Sur Orne 139
Colombelle 51, 127, 129, 132
Cologne 89, 158
Commandos 10, 115,
Conboy, Rifleman 64
Conneville 140
Connolly, Alexander, L/Corporal 118
Connolly, John, Rifleman 38,
Coombes, Frank, Rifleman 177
Cooper, John Lieutenant 43
Cope, Rifleman 43
Corbett, Thomas, Sergeant 62
Cordner, Rifleman 117
Cotter, Robert, Sergeant 119, 133
Cours de Janville 58
Courtrai-Bossuyt Canal 20
Courtrai-Coyghem Road 21
Coyle, John, Sergeant 117, 126
Coyle, Joseph, Rifleman 16
Cramer, James, Sergeant 118
Crangle, Hugh, Rifleman 49

Cranston, Lieutenant 136, 137
Crawford, Rifleman 76
Creaney, Sergeant 62
Crockett, Robin, Major 172, 178, 179
Crocodile 95, 96, 99
Croft, Harry, Captain 117,152
Crowe, Jim, Corporal 23
Cullen, Rifleman 64, 129
Cully, Tommy, Rifleman 148
Cummins, M L, Major 98, 99, 107
Cunningham, Redmond, Major 33
Cunningham, J.C. 36
Curle, Gunner 62
Curran, D P R, Lieutenant 75
Cuyk 74

Dakota 122, 160
Dalton, L/Corporal 106
Daniels, Sergeant 155
Davis, Captain 25
Davies, 'Trotsky', Lieutenant Col 64
Davis, Lieutenant 16, 19
Dawson, Rifleman 179
DD Sherman 169
DD Tank 18
de Longueuil, J C Stuart G, Major 17, 24, 44, 56, 70, 73, 75
Dean, Lieutenant 126
Deauville 144, 145
Degrelle, Leon 155
Delmenhorst 100, 108,
Dempster, Edward, Corporal 136
Descanneville 140
Devine, Edward, L/Corporal 26
Devlin, 'Paddy', Rifleman 160, 166, 167
Devons 124, 138, 140, 141, 144, 147, 156, 161, 162, 164, 167, 169, 172, 174, 176
Dick, James, Rifleman 82
Dicken, Frank, Colour Sergeant 99
Dickinson, Captain 27
Diepholz 99
Dinant 149, 150, 151
Diserens, Robert Charles, Lieutenant 45
Distinguished Conduct Medal 47, 63
Dives 143
Doherty, Corporal 178
Donnelly, Rifleman 61
Donnelly Captain 129
Donnelly, Ken, Major 151, 165
Dooley, Tim, Lieutenant 148
Dowling, Michael Joseph 'Mike', Lieutenant 119
Drilsma, Maurice, Rifleman 177

Drumgoole, James, CSM 39, 46, 181
Drummond, John 84, 95
Drummond, John, Major 116, 125, 130, 139, 149, 151
Drummond Lieut-Col 85, 86, 92, 99, 100, 109
Duhault, Maurice C, Captain 148
Dunkirk 3, 20, 21, 29, 31, 33, 35, 111, 116, 117
Dunlop, 'Duffy' 124
Durtnell, Charles, Major 29, 30
Dwyer, Sergeant 117
Dyball, A.J. 'Tony', Major 118, 125, 129, 150, 159, 162, 163, 171, 173

Eagle, Rifleman 136
Edwards, Corporal 129
Eifel 158
Eglise de St. Etienne 57, 59, 62,
Eglise de St. Pierre 56
Egypt 5, 13, 114, 116, 117, 118
Elbe 178
Elbe-Traue Canal 178
Ellis, Bandsman 23
Ellis, Reginald 'Reg', Lieutenant 131, 161, 174
England, Lieutenant 156,
Erskine, Kenneth, Rifleman 76
Escaut Canal 67
Escoville-Troarn Road 59, 60

Fairey, Rifleman 39
Fairman, Lieutenant 97
Falconer, Lance Bombardier 39
Farrell, L/Corporal 69
Feeney, Charles, Rifleman 126, 135, 137, 146
Fife and Forfar Yeomanry 73
Firefly 37, 51, 97
Firth, Lieutenant 68
Fitz-Donlea, Basil G, 111
Fitzgeorge, Corporal 100
Flack, Gordon P, Lieutenant 34, 44
Fleming, Samuel, RSM 31, 45, 47, 62, 65
Fleur 65
Flying Fortress 136
Focke Wulf 190 132
Fogt, Maurice Peter, Lieutenant 132, 156
Forrieres-St-Martin 152, 153, 154
Foster, Rifleman 65
Franceville Plage 141

Gaffikin, Captain 65, 68, 70, 71, 75, 83
Gale, John James, 82

Gale, Richard 'Windy' Major General 115, 140, 177
Gallipoli 6
Gammon Bombs 126
Gann, Frederick, Captain 151
Garrett, Sergeant 155
Garrett, Lieutenant 16
Garstin, Lieutenant 14, 22, 28
Gates, Gunner 39
Genovese, 'Tony', Corporal 81
Gibbs, George, L/Corporal 160
Gillate, Flight Sergeant 160
Gilliland, John 'Doggy', Corporal 137
Glass, Samuel, Rifleman 117
Glatigny 145
Glider Pilot Regiment 160, 163, 167, 168
Glinchy, Stephen, Rifleman 57, 59
Glover, L/Corporal 98
Goch 89, 90
Gold Beach 36
Gooding, L/Corporal 35,
Gordon, R.W. 'Bobby', Major 136
Gordon, Robert W, Lieutenant 22, 28, 34
Gordon, Alexander, Colonel 4,
Gort, General 21
Gough Barracks 9, 116, 117
Gourley, William, Rifleman 95
Granville 63
Gravelines 21
Gray, Captain 65, 76, 106
Green, Harry, Lieutenant 38
Green, Billy, Rifleman 62, 73
Green, Rifleman 69
Green Howards 22
Grenadier Guards 66, 170, 172, 173, 175, 176
Gresse 178
Griffith, G, RSM 116, 128
Grimshaw, Nicholas O'D, Captain 21
Grissam, David, Rifleman 173
Grossdeutschland Brandenburger Training Regiment 94
Grote Barrier 73
Guards Brigade 14,
Guderian, Heinz, General 20
Guezenhock 21,
Gunning, Henry 'Harry', Rifleman 118, 127

Hacqueville 66
Haguemont 151
Halifax bomber 50
Hall, Robert Stewart 'Ronnie', Lieutenant 45

Hamburg 178
Hamilton, William, Rifleman 16
Hamminkeln 159, 164, 167, 168
Hammersley, Sergeant 80
Hancock, Lieutenant 81, 85, 87, 88, 108
Hanstedt 176
Hankey, Thomas, Rifleman 127
Hanover 172,
Hardy, William, Sergeant 134,
Harpstedt 100
Harris, Captain 102, 103, 104, 108
Harris, I.C. Major 32, 36, 39, 44, 46, 52, 58, 60, 62, 64, 67, 68, 69, 70, 72, 75, 79, 83, 84,
Harris, Leslie Charles, Lieutenant 92, 97, 100,
Havenne 151,
Hawkins Grenade 117, 168
Hayes, Rifleman 45, 94
Headland, Peter, Corporal 177
Helling 79,
Henderson, Sergeant 22,
Henniker, Captain 25
Henry, Corporal 127, 131
Highland Division 92, 101, 108, 133
Hill, Rifleman 124
Hill 30 147
Hill 60 51, 54, 64
Hitlerjugend Division 42,
Hilter Youth 91, 99, 100, 101,
HMS Arethusa 125
HMS Campbelltown 32
HMS Danae 42
HMS Esk 29,
HMS Icarus 31
HMS Kent 111
HMS Ramillies 34
HMS Warspite 34
Hodgkinson, Sergeant 64,
Hoeken 86, 87, 88
Hoey, Robert 'Bob', Rifleman 137
Hogan, Lieutenant 85, 86,
Holland 13, 85, 156, 156, 157
Holman, Sergeant 122,
Holt, Corporal 101, 107
Hong Kong 114, 116, 117, 118,
Horsa 114, 120, 122, 123, 160, 161, 163, 164, 167
Horst 78
Hotspur 114
Houlgate 34,
Hourigan, Padre 116
Howard, Harry, Sergeant 122,
Huddy, Rifleman 136

Hursey, James, Rifleman 38
Hussey, Colonel 39,
Hutchinson, James, Rifleman 132, 141
Hyde, John, Major 31, 34, 35, 45, 49, 52, 53, 55, 58, 59, 65, 66
Hynds, Major 118, 124, 130, 147, 147

Ijssel 159, 162,
Ilfracombe 114
India 5, 6, 10, 11, 22, 111, 112, 114, 116, 117, 118, 148
Ingham, John, Rifleman 95
Inniskilling Dragoons 15
Inverary 31
Ironsides 33, 63, 102
Irvine, L/Corporal 133,
Irwin, Rifleman 84

Jarman, Richard, Rifleman 142
Jefferson, Alan, Lieutenant 155
Jefferson, Corporal 126, 127
Johncock, Cecil, Rifleman 173
Johnston, Rifleman 65, 75, 144
Johnston, Major 135, 137, 145
Johnston, John, Padre 116
Johnston, 'Curley', Rifleman 135
Jones, Gunner 62

Kane, David, Rifleman 99
Kane, Thomas, L/Corporal 38
Kattenturm 102, 103, 106, 107
Keogh, Rifleman 135
Keys, Thomas, Rifleman 62
Kindersley, Brigadier 115, 140
King's Own Scottish Borderers 14, 26, 27, 39, 46, 51, 58, 64, 68
Kinsella, Lieutenant 136,
Kiwi Barracks 119
Knox, Fergus 'Ghandi', Lieutenant Col 13, 14, 16, 17, 19, 20, 22, 23, 24, 26, 27, 36
Kohler, Albert, Corporal 38
Krefeld 89

L'Escaut 18, 20,
La Gallonerie 64,
La Panne 26, 27
La Poterie 145,
Lacy, L/Corporal 45
Laird, Fred, Lieutenant 164
Laird, Lieutenant 145, 161
Lambourne, L/Corporal 106, 108
Lancaster bomber 50,
Laving, Leslie, Captain 70, 73

LCI 34, 35, 47
Lebisey Wood 50
Le Cateau 19
Le Petit Homme 141
Le Plein 140, 143
Les Andelys-sur-Seine 66
Les Panoramas 142
Leende 73
Lehmke 176
Lengerich 172
Lewis, John, Rifleman 83
Lezennes 12, 67
Liberator Bomber 168
Liddle, 'Paddie', Major 160, 161, 162, 164, 175
Lieu Ste. Laurent 143, 144
Lille 12, 21, 60
Lincolnshire Regiment 63
Lindsay, Martin, Lieut Colonel 119
Lingen 94, 95, 99
Lion-sur-Mer 36
Lithuanian 134
Lomm 86
London Irish Rifles 7, 118, 181
Longueval Woods 124, 125, 126, 129, 134, 140
Lorie, Rufus H, 115
Loughran, Rifleman 105
Louvain 10, 14, 15, 16, 17, 67, 89
Lovat, Lord 123,
Lucy, John, L/Corporal 160
Luftwaffe 13, 14, 60, 101, 117
Lutton, CSM 70,
Lyndon-Adams, Clifford, Lieutenant 48
Lyttle, Robert 'Bobby', Lieutenant 59, 63

Maas MDS 156
    Dressing Station 135, 138, 168
Maginnis, Lieutenant 138,
Maidment, C.M., Lieutenant 168
Malcolm, Alan Ronald, Lieutenant 124, 133, 135, 139, 148, 156
Manneville le Raoult 146, 147
Maritime Artillery Regiment 10
Market Garden, operation 66, 67, 157
Martin, Corporal 22,
Martin, George, Rifleman 62
Martin, Robert, Captain 142, 154
Matthews, Ritchie Rea, Rifleman 15
McAleavy, Sergeant 105
McAlpine, Jackie, Sergeant 137
McCartney, 'Punter', Rifleman 30, 31
McCayna, George, Corporal 126, 137
McConkey, Rifleman 151

McConnell, William 'Billy', Corporal 117
McConville, Sergeant 17
McCoy, L/Corporal 108
McCrainor, J, Lieutenant 99, 107
McCrea, Charles, Rifleman 160, 166
McCrory, Joe 'Bash On', Sergeant 163
McCullough, Corporal 58
McCully, Sergeant 117
McCutcheon, Sergeant 36, 64, 148, 168
McGlennon, Rifleman 108
McGrath, Rifleman 35
McGrath, Daniel, Lieutenant 145
McGrory, Patrick, Rifleman 64
McIlroy, Rifleman 130
McMillan, Jack, Corporal 57
McNally, Rifleman 59, 64
McQuillan, John, Rifleman 93,
ME 109, fighter 132
Meerlo 78, 79
Mellon, Rifleman 105
Merville Battery 2, 119
Meuse 74, 79, 82, 84, 85, 88, 89, 150
Meyerstein, Rifleman 101
Michaelides, Rifleman 41
Middlesex Regiment 19, 23, 42, 43
Military Cross 10, 11, 12, 22, 23, 33, 47,
    63, 91, 99, 111, 147, 177
Military Medal 10, 12, 22, 63, 73, 94,
    108, 137, 146, 148, 163
Milliken, Lieutenant 129, 135,
Milliken, Captain 153, 156
Mills, Lieutenant 173
Milne, L/Corporal 139
Mona's Queen 11
Montgomery, James 'Jim', Captain 37, 38,
    47
Montgomery, Field Marshall 3, 12, 13, 14,
    17, 18, 20, 22, 31, 84, 137, 157, 158,
    158
Monty's Moonlight 70
Mons 6, 67
Moordyke 100, 101
Moore, Rifleman 40
Moore, John, Corporal 15,
Morgan, Lieutenant 72, 73, 125, 126, 127,
    137
Mullins, L/Corporal 127
Mullins, Patrick, Rifleman 128
Monroe, Lieutenant 136
Murphy, 'Spud' 126
Murphy, Edward, Major 79, 80
Murray O'Hara, Colin, Lieutenant 139,
    143, 145, 165, 172

Nassogne 154
Nebelwefer 177
Neil, Padre 21
Nelson, Rifleman 64
Nesbitt, William, Corporal 19
Netheravon 113, 114, 148
Nicholson, Major 86
Normandy 2, 3, 10, 33, 35, 36, , 37, 38,
    42, 47, 48, 49, 50, 66, 78, 85, 108,
    113, 115, 118, 119, 120, 122, 125,
    129, 131, 132, 136, 140, 141, 142,
    146, 147, 148, 153, 166, 175, 179
North West Frontier 22, 111, 116, 137
Northamptonshire Yeomanry 51, 52,

O'Beirne, Michael, Corporal 53
O'Callaghan, L/Sergeant 39
O'Connor, Colour Sergeant 117
O'Connor, Timothy, Rifleman 135
O'Connor, General 67, 73
O'Halloran, Rifleman 39
O'Hara, Lieutenant 156
O'Neill, Lieutenant 70,
Oppenheim 158,
O'Reilly, Charles, Corporal 47
Orne 57, 63, 125, 127, 139
Orr, ADG, Colonel 36,
Osnabruck 173
Ostend 149
Otway, Terence, Major 2, 119
Otway, Captain 112
Oudenarde 14, 19
Overloon 74, 77
Overlord, operation 1,
Oxfordshire and Buckinghamshire Light
    Infantry 111, 115

Palmer, Lieutenant 54
Pancott, Sergeant 64,
Panzerfaust 37, 65, 72, 76, 81, 82, 101,
    104, 105, 106, 107, 174
Panzerschreck 72, 174
Parennes 11,
Parkin, Charles Rowland 57, 62,
Payne, Edward, Rifleman 128
Peel, Sergeant 72
Pegg, Harry, Sergeant 118, 124, 127, 128,
    133, 134, 139 .
Periers-sur-le-Dan 36,
Perona-Wright, Captain 69
Petershagen 174
Petit Brogel 67
PIAT 65, 66, 76, 82, 126, 163, 164, 171
Picture Post 156